The Romance of the Western Bower

西 厢 记

Wang Shifu

王实甫（元）

Adapted by Zhang Xuejing

张雪静 改编

刘幼生 审订

New World Press

新 世 界 出 版 社

First Edition 2000

Translated by Kuang Peihua and Liu Jun
Edited by Zhang Minjie
Book Design by Li Hui

ISBN 7-80005-552-3

Published by
NEW WORLD PRESS
24 Baiwanzhuang Road, Beijing 100037, China

Distributed by
NEW WORLD PRESS
24 Baiwanzhuang Road, Beijing 100037, China
Tel: 0086-10-68994118
Fax: 0086-10-68326679

Printed in the People's Republic of China

张生

崔莺莺

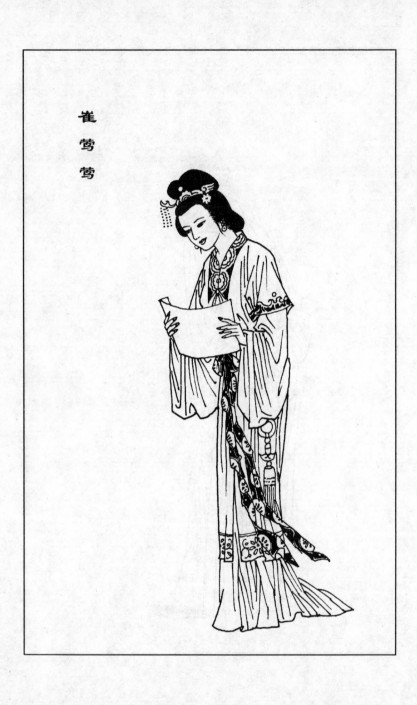

红娘

老夫人

FOREWORD

The love story of Oriole and Zhang Junrui has been loved both by scholars and ordinary people for hundreds of years. *The Story of Oriole* written by Yuan Zhen of the Tang Dynasty (618-907) defined the story's basic framework, but it has a tragic ending inasmuch as Zhang Junrui finally abandons Oriole. In the Song Dynasty (960-1179), there appeared a version in the colloquial language (as opposed to the classical language of the earlier versions), and *The Story of Oriole* by Qin Guan and Mao Pang, which is composed in the *Daqu* style, that is, the narrative parts are written in prose and the lyrical parts are written in verse, as well as *Shangdiao Dielianhua*, with the same theme, by Zhao Delin. In the Jin Dynasty (1115-1234), two *zaju* dramas titled *Rose* and *The Chastisement of Rose*, respectively, were created. In the same period, *The Western Bower Zhugongdiao* written by Dong Jieyuan (later known as Dong's *Western Bower*) became the most influential version of the story. In the Yuan Dynasty (1279-1368), Wang Shifu wrote a *zaju* drama titled *The Romance of the Western Bower*, including 21 scenes which fall into five acts. This work is the most important lyrical drama in the history of Chinese classical theater, with its brilliant anti-feudal theme, excellent artistic techniques, classical style, and beautiful and resourceful language. Like a beautiful and eye-catching flower, it has attracted readers and tugged at their heart-strings for years.

However, the version by Wang Shifu is a story that can only be read by well-educated readers, and is not very suitable for performance. There are no records of the play being performed during the Yuanzhen and Dade reign periods (1295-1307) of the Yuan Dynasty, when *zaju* dramas were thriving, and it was not until the Ming Dynasty (1368-1644) that the version by Wang Shifu was spoken highly of by men of letters, and became fashionable for a time. Since the Ming Dynasty, there have been more than 30 varieties of scripts of this love story, proving how great the artistic charm of the story is.

To make this excellent classical opera better known, especially among younger readers, we have adapted it into a novel in the vernacular, while striving to be faithful to the original. As novels and operas are different kinds of artistic forms in terms of performance and literary technique, we have edited the original and added chapter headings in accordance with the development of the plot.

We are conscious of the fact that this version does not reflect the true charm and artistry of the original, and would be grateful for readers' suggestions for improvement.

前　言

　　千百年来被文人墨客和普通百姓广泛传诵的崔莺莺和张君瑞的爱情故事，来源是很久远的。最早在唐代，有元稹所撰传奇《莺莺传》，已经确定了这个故事的基本框架，但其结尾是悲剧性的，张生对崔莺莺始乱终弃。其后，宋代时有话本《莺莺传》及大曲《莺莺传》，还有秦观和毛滂创作的两种供转踏使用的韵散相间的崔张故事，赵德麟的〔商调蝶恋花〕鼓子词等。递及金代又产生了两种院本杂剧《红娘子》和《拷梅香》，以及对后来影响最大的董解元的《西厢记诸宫调》（后世习称"董西厢"）。直到元代王实甫创作的共五本二十一折的《西厢记》（后世习称"王西厢"）问世后，崔张故事才算基本定型。"王西厢"后出而居上，以其反封建的光辉主题思想，精美圆熟的艺术技巧，优美典雅的独特风格，隽拔机智的文学语言而著称于世，成为中国古典戏曲史上的不朽名著。它如同一朵鲜艳夺目的奇葩，吸引着历代的读者，拨动着人们的心弦。

　　可是，"王西厢"本属"案头之曲"，适于阅读而并不适合演出。并且，它的阅读范围也只限于那些文化水平较高、文学修养较深的读者。在元代杂剧最兴盛的元贞和大德时期（1295—1307），有关"王西厢"的演出不见于史料记载。直到明代，"王西厢"才大为文人赏识，一时风靡。从明清两代至今，有关的改编演出本有近三十种之多，由此也可看到"王西厢"所具有的艺术魅力。但是，对于广大读者来说，直接阅读原作仍有一定困难。

　　为了普及优秀的古典戏曲代表作品，帮助广大青年读者深入了解、阅读古典戏曲名著，我们在忠实于原作的基础上，将其改编为适合当代读者阅读的白话小说形式，献给大家。由于小说和戏曲是两种不同的艺术形式，表演艺术和文学艺术在客观上存在着距离，在改编过程中，我们对原作有所增删，章节的题目也是根据情节自拟的。这种忠实于原作的改编工作，我们也在尝试之中，希望得到广大读者的喜爱和支持，那将使我们感到莫大的欢欣。

　　由于改编者水平有限，时间也不够充裕，本书中一定还有许多不尽如人意的地方，能否准确传神地表达出原作的艺术水准和神韵，我们也没有把握。殷切希望能够得到诸位方家和广大读者的批评指正。

BRIEF INTRODUCTION

On his way to the capital to sit for the civil service examination, Zhang Junrui, a gifted scholar of the Tang Dynasty, arrives in Mid-River Prefecture. He pays a visit to the Salvation Monastery, where he meets and falls in love with Oriole, daughter of late Prime Minister Cui. Madame Cui and her daughter are escorting the coffin of the prime minister to his ancestral burial ground Boling, and are resting for a while at the monastery.

Master Zhang's attempts to approach Oriole are interrupted by a bandit named Sun the Flying Tiger, who surrounds the monastery with his rebel band of 5,000. Sun has heard of the legendary beauty of Oriole, and demands that she be handed over to him as his wife, otherwise he will sack the monastery. In desperation, Madame Cui promises to give her daughter's hand to whoever can lift the siege. Zhang writes a letter to his sworn brother Du Que, known as the White Horse General. Du Que comes immediately to the rescue, routs the bandits and captures their leader. But now that the crisis has passed, Madame Cui begins to regret her rash promise. In her husband's lifetime, Oriole had been engaged to be married to her worthless cousin Zheng Heng, and Madame Cui thinks that it would be the height of impropriety to break the engagement to give her daughter to a poor scholar like Zhang. Oriole's maid, Rose, acts as the secret go-between for the young lovers, and Madame Cui finally reluctantly agrees to allow Zhang to marry Oriole, but only on condition that he first comes top in the examination, and returns as the No. 1 Scholar. Zhang and Oriole have a tearful parting at the Pavilion of Parting. Zhang wins the highest honor in the examination and is made prefect of Mid-River Prefecture. But when he returns in triumph he finds that Zheng Heng has claimed his bride, having tricked Madame Cui into believing that Zhang has married the daughter of Minister Wei in the capital and only intends to make Oriole his concubine. Once again, the White Horse General comes to uphold justice. Zheng Heng's lie is exposed, whereupon he kills himself. Zhang and Oriole are married on the spot, with her mother's blessing.

内容简介

　　唐代才子张君瑞赴京赶考,游历河中府,随喜普救寺,巧遇扶柩寄寓寺中的相国千金崔莺莺,一时惊为天人,顿生爱慕之心。为了接近莺莺,张生巧借西厢,道场附斋,却无缘亲近。恰在此时,原河桥守将孙飞虎率乱军兵围普救寺,欲抢莺莺做压寨夫人。张生得老夫人佛殿许婚,写信请义兄白马将军杜确解围。书至兵来,贼兵退却。不料,老夫人宴前赖婚。红娘出于不愤,为崔张传书递简,促成其好事。事情泄露后,老夫人拷打红娘,红娘据理力争,老夫人只得将莺莺许与张生,但又以崔家三代不招白衣女婿为由,逼张生赴京赶考夺魁,实为明许暗赖。张生与莺莺长亭洒泪而别。张生终于考中状元归来,不料老夫人之侄郑恒谎言离间,老夫人信以为实,将莺莺复许郑恒。亏得白马将军做主,张生当面将其谎言戳穿,一对有情人历尽曲折艰辛之后,终成眷属。

Contents
目　次

CHAPTER ONE

Enchantment at the Hall of Buddha

During the reign of Emperor Dezong of the Tang Dynasty (618-907), a scholar named Zhang Gong and with the literary style Junrui, lived in Luoyang. Zhang Junrui was born into a family which had produced officials for generations. His father was the president of the Ministry of Rites. As the only son of the family, Junrui was regarded by his father as the apple of his eye. His father personally instructed the boy whenever he had time to spare from his duties, and engaged famous teachers to reside in his mansion and give Zhang Junrui lessons. It was his cherished wish that his son would become well enough versed in both polite letters and martial arts to be fit to attend the emperor himself, and bring honor to the Zhang family. Junrui was a bright boy. At the age of seven he began his studies, and proved so intelligent and adept that he could recite a passage of his books by heart having read it no more than once. As time went by, he acquired a good command of *The Four Books* (namely, *The Great Learning, The Doctrine of the Mean, The Analects of Confucius* and *The Mencius*) and *The Five Classics* (namely, *The Book of Songs, The Book of History, The Book of Changes, The Book of Rites* and *The Spring and Autumn Annals*), as well as of the four accomplishments of Chinese poetry, music, chess, and calligraphy and painting. In addition, he was as handsome as Song Yu and Pan An (two ancient Chinese Adonises), and had an outstanding poise and manner. However, when he was 17, his father, distressed by the corruption at court, died of apoplexy. One year later, his grieving mother passed away too. From then on, Zhang Junrui had only a small legacy to live on. He dismissed all his family servants, keeping only one young boy as his page, with whom he left home to travel, visit friends and seek out teachers. To broaden his knowledge and widen his horizons, Junrui was determined to "travel 10,000 miles" and "read 10,000 books."

In the spring of the 17th year of the Zhenyuan reign period, Emperor Dezong issued a decree, announcing that the civil service examination

第一章
佛殿惊艳

　　话说大唐德宗皇帝在位年间,中州洛阳有个书生,姓张名珙,表字君瑞,出身于世代书香的官宦人家。其父官拜礼部尚书,膝下只有一个儿子,视如掌上明珠,常于公事闲暇之余,亲自为儿子启蒙课业,又请名师宿儒于府中坐馆,一心想让儿子"学成文武艺,货与帝王家",以光大门楣。这张君瑞天资聪颖,七岁从学,便能吟诗答对,过目成诵。及长,凡四书五经,诸子百家,诗词歌赋,琴棋书画,拆白道字,顶针续麻,件件俱能,样样精通。他不仅满腹绵绣,文章盖世,而且生得面如宋玉,貌比潘安,风流倜傥,卓尔不群。只可惜十七岁时,父亲因与朝中奸佞势不两立,负气而亡。一年后,母亲也因哀伤过度,驾鹤西去。自此家道中落,所幸祖上尚有一些薄产,可供勉强度日。张生将家仆遣散,只留小厮琴童一人与己为伴。自此书剑飘零,四处游学。投师访友,以增学问;游山玩水,开阔眼界。正所谓"行万里路,读万卷书",倒也颐然自乐。

　　转眼到了贞元十七年之春,德宗降诏,朝廷明年开科取士录用贤才。举子们闻讯纷纷向京师汇聚。一来是就近温习功课,准备考试;二来是寻机走些门路,将自己的得意文章诗作送到名家或大臣的府上,请他们鉴赏推荐,即当时盛行的"温卷"之风。

would be held in the following year at the capital to recruit people of talent for official positions. At the news, scholars all over the country lost no time making preparations for the journey to the capital, where they could study for the examination and present their essays to influential persons, hoping to be recommended for the emperor's attention.

Confident that he would easily pass the examination and make his name resound throughout the country, Zhang Junrui packed his belongings and set off with his page boy for the capital.

On the way, the sun shone and spring breezes blew. Letting his horse plod along at its own pace and his thoughts flow wherever they would, Zhang felt as if he were soaring like a swallow. One day, he saw before him by a fork in the road a boundary marker with the words Pujin Pass written on it. Startled, he suddenly thought of his old classmate Du Que.

His former classmate and good friend, Du Que had similar tastes and interests with him. They were inseparable, and finally became sworn brothers. Du Que was fascinated by *The Art of War*, written by the master strategist Sun Zi of the Warring States Period (475-221 BC), and later gave up the pen for the sword. Coming first on the list in the imperial military examination, Du was appointed General of the Western Front, commanding an army 100,000 strong stationed at the Pujin Pass. Zhang, who had not met Du Que for quite a few years, thought to himself that this was a good opportunity to renew their acquaintance and at the same time enjoy the scenery of the pass.

Soon Zhang found himself in Pujin. The Pujin Ferry faced Xiayangjin, across the Yellow River. Standing on the bank of the roaring river, he felt a poem well up inside him:

Of the tortuous, turbulent Yellow River,
Where is the most perilous part?
Surely it's there.
The River girds two Eastern States
And keeps two Western States apart
And bars the Northern Gates.
White-crested waves surge up high
Like autumn clouds in the boundless sky.
The floating bridge, boats joined by ropes of bamboo.
Looks like a crouching dragon blue.
From west to east its waves through nine states go;

张生自恃经纶满腹，文章盖世，也忙着拾掇书剑琴囊，带着琴童前去应试，以图一跃龙门，扬名天下。

一路上，阳光和煦，春风送暖，张生信马由缰，只觉身轻如燕，情思流动。这日正在控辔缓驰之际，就见前面岔路口上立着一块界碑，上书"蒲津关"三个大字。张生不由一怔，猛然想起旧时同窗好友杜确杜君实来。

杜确与张生同乡，自幼与张生同窗读书，二人意气相投，遂义结金兰，成为八拜之交。杜确爱习孙子兵法、太公阴符，后投笔从戎，练就了一身武艺，先中了武举人，接着高中武状元，官拜征西大元帅，统兵十万，镇守蒲关。二人已有数年未曾谋面，张生想，自己此番路过，不妨与杜兄会上一面，一来西窗剪烛，把臂话旧；二来盘桓游玩，饱览风光。

不觉已来到蒲津。这蒲津渡本是个交通要道，与关中夏阳津相对，中间隔着一条九曲黄河。那黄河水至此奔腾咆哮，飞浪拍空，一条竹缆铁索桥，颤悠悠似苍龙横卧波涛之上，连通秦晋。面对着这浩淼宽阔、波涛汹涌、一泻千里的黄河，张生心潮澎湃，诗兴大发，朗声吟道：

"九曲风涛何处显？则除是此地偏。这河带齐梁，分秦晋，隘幽燕。雪浪拍长空，天际秋去卷；竹索缆浮桥，水上苍龙偃。东西溃九州，南北串百川。只疑是银河落九天；渊泉云外悬，入东洋不离此径穿。滋洛阳千种花，润梁园万顷田，也曾泛浮槎到日月边。"

吟罢，不禁暗想道，自家萤窗雪案，刮垢磨光，学成满腹经纶，

From north to south a hundred streams into it flow.
The river, like the Milky Way, falls from the sky;
Beyond the clouds its source hangs high.
It runs its course unchanged to the Eastern Sea.
It makes a thousand Luoyang flowers dance with glee.
And waters ten thousand acres in the Eastern land.
Skyward I'd sail till sun and moon are near at hand.

Zhang then fell to musing: "In spite of having studied unceasingly for years, and having acquired a deep knowledge of literature, I'm still a wanderer and do not know when I can achieve my goals. Lofty talent cannot be confined to lowly posts, and a noble character cannot fulfil his ambition in troubled times. O Yellow River, you run directly to the Eastern Sea. Do you know what the future holds for me?" So thinking, he could not help shedding tears.

My precious sword lies hidden by the autumn streams;
My sorrow-laden saddle's bursting at the seams.

Suddenly Zhang heard the din of horses and carriages. Looking around, he saw a throng of people all jostling each other. Unawares, he had reached Puzhou City. The city lay on the bank of the Yellow River, facing Shaanxi Province and separated from Henan Province in the south by Mount Zhongtiao. Legend has it that Puzhou was the capital of a kingdom in remote antiquity. During the Warring States Period it was under the jurisdiction of the State of Wei, and was called Puban. In the Tang Dynasty it was the capital of Hezhong Prefecture. The ancient stone streets were lined with shops, tea houses, taverns, restaurants and inns. Though the city was not as prosperous as the metropolis, it was the hub of traffic bound for the eastern and western states, and on a post road leading to the capital. The city was bustling with people.

Zhang's first thought was to find an inn where he could stay for the night. Suddenly he caught sight of a signboard inscribed with three Chinese characters: "No.1 Scholar Inn." The innkeeper, who was standing in front of the door, seeing a handsome young man with a dignified bearing mounted on a horse and followed by a page, thought that he must surely be from an aristocratic family, and so he hurried over to catch hold of the horse's reins. "Please come in, Master!" he cried. "If you are going to the

如今二十有三,尚在湖海飘零,不知何日方能得遂大志!才高难入俗人眼,时乖不遂男儿愿。黄河水呵,你径奔东海而去,可知我张珙的胸怀?思着想着,竟落下两滴泪来。正是:

> 万金宝剑藏秋水,满马春愁压绣鞍!

　　不知过了多久,只听得车马声喧,人来人往,热闹起来。原来不知不觉已来到蒲州城中。这蒲州城位于黄河之滨,隔河与陕西相望,南隔中条山与河南接壤。相传古时虞舜在此立都,到了战国时,韩、赵、魏三家分晋,归属魏国,名叫蒲坂。原是一座古城,经历了改朝换代的沧桑之变,依旧保存着它的古朴风貌。唐代河中府便在此安衙。但见青石砌就的街道两旁,商号店铺、茶坊酒肆、秦楼楚馆、旅舍客栈,鳞次栉比,虽比不上通都大邑灯红酒绿、纸醉金迷的繁华,但由于是秦晋商旅往来要道,也是通往京城的驿道,也有一种繁盛都市人烟辐辏、接踵摩肩、熙熙攘攘的景象。
　　张生在马上左顾右盼,欲找一家店舍安歇。正行间,就见前面一家客店的门面颇为气派,黑亮的招牌上写着"状元坊"三个金漆大字。站在门口揽客的店小二见来客端坐马上,丰姿俊逸,气宇轩昂,后有琴童肩挑书箱琴囊伺候,料想这定是一位世家公子,上等客人,连忙陪着笑脸,点头哈腰快步来到客人跟前,扯过马缰,殷勤招呼道:"这位公子,里面请!敝店叫状元坊,您老若是前往京城应试,图个吉利,定能蟾宫折桂,独占鳌头,考上状元;若是游山玩水,踏青览胜,俺店里有上等客房,屋舍敞亮,衾枕洁净,包您满意。"

capital to take the examination, you should put up at our No.1 Scholar Inn. It is an auspicious place. I guarantee you'll be a successful candidate if you stay with us. You can have the best room in the house — with immaculate and comfortable bedding, and a superb view."

Zhang was pleased to hear this, and thought that indeed the No.1 Scholar Inn was an auspicious name for a hostelry. So he decided to put up at the inn. "We'll stay here," he told the page. Dismounting, he said to the innkeeper: "Very well, give me your best room, and unsaddle my horse and feed it with fine forage."

The innkeeper called out, "We have an honored guest. Take the horse to the stables, and prepare some tea."

An attendant appeared, took the horse's reins from the page and led the horse to the yard at the back of the inn.

Following the innkeeper, Zhang was shown to the best room in the inn. It had white walls, bright windows and clean furniture. There were some tasteful paintings and works of calligraphy hung on the walls. Zhang was satisfied with the room, and ordered his page to unpack their things.

Soon afterwards, the innkeeper brought in a basin of clean water for Zhang to wash with, and prepared tea personally for the guest. Sipping the delicious and refreshing tea, Zhang immediately felt relaxed. He then began to question the innkeeper about the local attractions. "Are there any famous mountains, scenic spots, historical sites or ancient temples here?" he inquired.

"The most famous attraction around here is the Salvation Monastery to the east of the city," the innkeeper answered. "You really should pay a visit to it, sir. It was erected by the imperial order of Her Majesty Empress Wu Zetian. It has magnificent buildings. Visitors come from all over to see it. It is really the only thing worth seeing in the city. In addition, the abbot of the monastery is a learned man. You may discuss sutras and the classics with him."

This piqued Zhang's fancy, and, giving his page orders to prepare lunch, he said that he was going to see the monastery and would be back before long.

Leaving the bustling streets of the city behind, he came to the main road leading out of the eastern gate. In the full bloom of spring, the road was lined with green grass, tall trees, red peach blossoms and white plum flowers. In the distance, tree-covered mountains could be seen, with

张生见小二招呼殷勤,话说得顺耳,也觉着这"状元坊"正好切合自己赴考夺魁的吉利口彩,便决定下榻于此。回头对琴童说道:"咱们就住在这里。"说着甩蹬离鞍下马,对小二颔首道:"好,那就住你店中的头等客房。先把马儿牵去遛遛,再喂些精料。"

小二向里边喊道:"来贵客了,速速泡茶牵马。"

话音未落,里面已走出一个打杂的伙计,接过琴童手里的缰绳,将马牵往后院。小二将张生带到了一套两间的上等客房。张生一看见房内粉壁洁白,挂着几轴字画,窗明几净,布置不俗,心中十分满意。琴童见主人中意,便安放书箧琴囊等物。

不多时小二送来净面水,待张生洗漱后,又沏上一壶香茗,随即为张生斟了一碗茶道:"请相公品茶。"

张生接过茶碗抿了一口,觉得清香润喉,便点头赞道:"好茶,好茶。"说着放下茶碗又道:"小二哥,此间可有什么闲散去处?名山胜境、福地古寺皆可。"

小二道:"要说俺这里最有名的,莫过城东的普救寺了。"

张生道:"普救寺?小二哥可说得详细些。"

小二清了清嗓子,眉飞色舞地说道:"想是公子初次到俺河东,说起这普救寺可不同寻常寺庙,它乃是国朝则天娘娘的香火院,气派非常了得,气势宏伟,殿阁庄严。南来北往,三教九流,但凡途经此地的,无不去观光随喜。也只有那里,可供公子游玩。寺里方丈是个博学之士、得道高僧,正好与公子谈经论典。"

张生听到有这等佛国圣地,又是武后敕造,心里煞是高兴,恨不得立刻就去游玩,便吩咐琴童道:"你好生料理晌午饭,俺到那普救寺走一趟便回来。"

tumbling streams, swallows feeding their young, and other birds chirping merrily. Viewing the scenery along the road was just like appreciating a beautiful landscape painting. Zhang felt relaxed and happy. Before long, he saw a grand monastery with lofty buildings shrouded in trees on the slope of the mountain ahead of him. "That must be the Salvation Monastery," he thought to himself. Walking closer, Zhang found that the monastery, shaded by thick stands of tall pine and cypress trees, had red walls and was roofed with green tiles; its main buildings and pavilions were scattered here and there in picturesque disorder. In front of the monastery, there was a flat, open space big enough to hold 10,000 people. The whole setting seemed to him to be ideal for a place of worship and meditation.

Looking up at the cluster of buildings from the foot of the mountain, Zhang saw a flight of 108 steps leading to the gate of the monastery. In the middle of the gate there was a horizontal board inscribed with six elegant characters, announcing "The Salvation Monastery, constructed by imperial decree," and above them there was a line of smaller characters, reading "Built in the second year of the Chuigong reign of the Tang Dynasty." Zhang plodded up along the steps. At the gate he saw an acolyte of about 16 years old coming out of the monastery. Seeing Zhang, the monk pressed his palms together and chanted, "Amida Buddha! May I ask where you are from, sir?"

Zhang was pleased at this gentle greeting. He replied, "I come from Luoyang. Having heard that your renowned monastery has a quiet and elegant environment and beautiful scenery, and moreover that the abbot is a learned man, I have come to worship Buddha and pay my respects to the abbot. May I ask if the reverend gentleman is in?"

"I am afraid that my master left the monastery this morning to conduct a religious ceremony. I am Fa Cong, a disciple of Abbot Fa Ben. Since my master is absent, perhaps I may keep you company. May I invite you to have tea in the hall?"

"Since the abbot is out, I will not trouble you to offer me tea," Zhang replied. "But may I prevail upon you to show me around the monastery?"

"With pleasure, sir." So saying, Fa Cong led Zhang into the monastery grounds. While Zhang is being shown around the Hall of Buddha, the Bell Tower, the Pagoda Courtyard, the Arhats Hall, the kitchen, the monks' living quarters, etc. Let us recount the details of the connection of the monastery with the late Prime Minister Cui Jue.

　　琴童素知主人性情,忙应道:"是。"

　　张生当下出店,直往普救寺而去。走出热闹的街市,边走边问,来到了东门外的官道上。时值仲春,草长林翠,桃红李白,水绿山青,鸣鸠呼妇,乳燕携雏,落红缤纷,飞絮蒙空,漫步途中,恍若置身画间,真正心旷神怡,赏心悦目。走了一程,远远见前面山垣上有一座建造宏伟的寺院,琉璃殿相近青霄,舍利塔直侵云汉。想必那就是普救寺了。但见寺外翠柏森森青掩日,苍松郁郁绿遮天。红墙碧瓦,楼阁重叠,错落有致。山门前一块平地开阔平整,能容万人,想是为百姓赶庙会开辟的场所。整座寺院盘踞山顶,果真气势不凡。

　　张生来到了山门前一百零八级台阶下仰头观看,宏伟的山门正中高悬一块蓝底金边的匾额,上书"敕建普救禅寺"六个烫金大字,上首一行小字:"大唐垂拱二年修。"张生拾级而上,刚到山门,顶头碰上一个十六七岁的小和尚从寺里出来。小和尚一见张生,忙双手合十,口诵佛号道:"阿弥陀佛,敢问施主从何方来?"

　　张生见这小和尚眉清目秀,聪明伶俐,礼数周全,心下喜欢,便还礼道:"小生自洛阳到此,适闻宝刹幽雅清爽,风景优美,方丈佛法宏深,学贯古今,故慕名而来。一则瞻仰浮图,礼佛祈佑;二则拜谒长老,聆听法教。敢问小师父,长老可在?"

　　小和尚道:"不巧得很,俺师父一早赴斋去了。贫僧法聪,是寺中住持法本长老的座下弟子。既然施主远路而来,师父外出,小僧理当奉陪。请先生到方丈处拜茶。"

　　张生听说住持不在寺中,便道:"既然长老不在,就不必讨扰吃茶了,敢烦小师父相引在下于寺内瞻仰一番,也就心满意足了。"

11

The Salvation Monastery was a temple dedicated to the merit and virtue of Empress Wu Zetian. When he was in charge of the monastery's renovation, Prime Minister Cui contributed funds to have a courtyard built adjacent to the western wing for himself to live in after his retirement. Wearing straw shoes and leaning on a bamboo cane, he would worship Buddha every day and take good care of himself, so as to fulfil his allotted life span. But he had unexpectedly died of illness three years previously, in the capital; now that the three-year period of mourning was about to end, his wife, Madame Cui, his daughter, Oriole, his adopted son, Merry Boy, and their maids and servants, a total of a dozen people, were on their way to take his coffin to his family graveyard at Boling, his hometown. However, as the prefect of Mid-River Prefecture had just passed away, Puzhou City was in great disorder, and it was not safe for Madame Cui and her party to continue. Madame Cui decided to put her husband's coffin temporarily at the Salvation Monastery. Then she wrote a letter to her nephew Zheng Heng, to whom Oriole had been betrothed, to ask him to come right away and take charge of matters. Madame Cui was a capable lady, especially good at handling family affairs. She was very strict with her daughter, seeing to her education and keeping her as much as possible in seclusion.

That very afternoon of Zhang's visit to the monastery, Madame Cui had just woken up to the sound of her daughter singing sadly, accompanying herself on the *qin* (a seven-stringed zither):

> Here we are, east of Puzhou City, when spring is late,
> Shut up in a lonely temple with a barred door and gate.
> The flowing stream is red with fallen blooms,
> Laden with gloom,
> I bear a silent grudge against the eastern breeze,
> Blowing down flowers from the trees.

Upon hearing this, Madame Cui felt a pang in her heart. She raised her head, looked out of the window, and saw that the spring scenery was very attractive. Believing that her daughter must be very lonely all by herself in her room, she called to Rose, Oriole's maid: "Rose, it is such a warm and sunny day, and the spring scenery is charming. There is no one in the front courtyard or in the Hall of Buddha now. Why don't you take your

　　法聪道:"请先生随小僧来。"说着引张生进了山门。取了钥匙,开了佛殿、钟楼、塔院、罗汉堂、香积厨等,引着张生依次到各处游览。

　　这里暂不说张生如何在法聪的引导下畅游普救寺,且说这寺里正住着几位已故宰相崔珏的家眷。这普救寺本是为则天娘娘修造的功德院,后来崔相国记名剃度,主持重修,并出资于寺院西厢新建了别院,打算日后避位去官,芒鞋竹杖,参禅礼佛,颐养天年。不期三年前老相国染疾亡故。如今三年丧期将满,老夫人郑氏带女儿莺莺、儿子欢郎以及丫环婆子小厮院子一行二三十人,扶枢回博陵老家安葬。途经此地,不意河中节度使身故,蒲州军乱,路上不太平,好在普救寺座落在驿道旁边,又有老相国亲修别院,正可闲居避乱,暂作栖所。老夫人又修书到京城唤娘家侄儿、未来女婿郑恒前来陪灵,待路上太平了,好回博陵下葬。崔老夫人一向处事温恭,治家有方,是是非非,人莫敢犯,特别是对女儿莺莺,更加管教严厉,生怕女儿有些闪失。

　　这天午后,老夫人午睡刚醒,忽听得一阵哀婉凄切的琴声响起,随着就听到女儿悠悠吟唱道:

　　人值残春蒲郡东,门掩重关萧寺中。花落水流红,闲愁万种,无语怨东风。

　　老夫人听罢,看着窗外春景明丽,想到女儿独居深闺,也着实是寂寞可怜,未免心疼,思虑再三,终于唤过丫头红娘,吩咐道:"红娘,今天风和日丽,景色宜人,趁着此时游客已空,佛殿上无人烧香,你和小姐出去散散心,随喜一回,也免得终日守在闺中,闷伤了身子。"

young mistress to divert yourselves there for a while. I'm afraid she will be bored staying in the room all day long."

Rose was a girl of about 15. She had been attending Oriole since they had both been children, and the two girls were as close as sisters. In the previous few days, as Madame Cui had prevented them from going out, neither of them had dared set foot outside their quarters. So, upon hearing Madame Cui's suggestion, Rose responded with delight. She ran to Oriole's room right away. There she chattered to her young mistress: "Miss! Get ready to go out right now! Your mother has given permission. We can go to the Hall of Buddha."

Oriole feigned indifference. "Oh, is that all?" she said. "I thought it must be something important. But if you are so keen to go, let's go." Oriole tidied herself up, and the pair headed for the Hall of Buddha.

Now let us return to Zhang. In the company of Fa Cong, he had visited the Hall of Buddha, the quarters of the monks, the bell tower and the monks' cells. He had climbed the pagoda, traversed all the passages, counted the Arhats, worshipped Buddha and bowed to saints and sages. In high spirits, he walked out of the courtyard where the pagoda was located, and came to another spacious courtyard at the end of the western wing of the monastery. There he espied a horizontal board bearing the words "Pear Blossom Yard." The two-leaf door in the shape of a crescent moon was slightly open. Zhang pushed open the door and tried to step in. But he was pulled back by Fa Cong. Turning round, he asked in surprise: "Why do you stop me?"

Fa Cong lowered his voice, and said, "I'm sorry, sir, but you shouldn't go in there...."

"Why not?" Zhang asked sharply.

"Sir, it is the residence of the family of His Excellency the late Prime Minister Cui."

"Why do they live in a monastery?"

Fa Cong looked around, and seeing that no one was near, said, "When our monastery became dilapidated, Prime Minister Cui had it rebuilt, and constructed this courtyard residence adjacent to the western wing for himself. He planned to live here after his retirement to worship Buddha, study the scriptures and spend his remaining years in tranquility. Unfortunately, His Excellency died before he was able to enjoy the use of the residence. Now his widow, together with her daughter and adopted son, is taking the late prime minister's coffin to

红娘是个十五六岁的丫头,生性活泼,自幼伏侍小姐,与莺莺情同姐妹。这些天来由于老夫人拘束得紧,不敢出门一步。今日见老夫人破禁,真是喜上眉梢,应了一声"谨依严命",一路小跑到绣阁给小姐报信。才一进门,便对春山含怨、秋水凝愁的莺莺说道:"姐姐,姐姐,快收拾一下,老夫人让咱们到佛殿散心呢。"

莺莺神色不动,嗔道:"就这点子事,也值得你大惊小怪的,如今你是大姑娘了,凡事都该稳当些才是。"话虽这么说,可脸上也漾起一缕春风。

红娘头一歪,嘴一噘道:"知道了。姐姐,快快走吧,难得夫人开恩。"莺莺略微打扮,便随红娘踏出院门,朝前面佛殿走去。

再说张生此时由法聪陪着随喜了上方佛殿,遍游了下方僧院,观了法堂,上了钟楼,游了僧房,登了宝塔,览了经阁,将回廊绕遍。数了罗汉,参了菩萨,拜了圣贤,这会子正兴致勃勃从塔院走出,来到寺院北首西厢尽处,见有一座方方正正的小院,垂花门上一块泥金匾上写着"梨花院"三个字,两扇月牙门微合,张生抬腿便要推门往里走,却被身后的法聪一把拖住,急回头惊问:"这是做甚?"

法聪轻声说道:"施主莫恼,此处可进不得……"

不待法聪把话说完,张生便道:"为何进不得?"

"施主有所不知,这院里现住着已故崔老相国的家眷。"

"这相国宝眷,如何住到你们这和尚寺院里来了?"

法聪看左右无人,这才说道:"敝寺本是则天娘娘的香火院,后来荒废倾圮了,是崔老相国重新修建起来的,并在这西厢下又修了这座宅子,本欲告老还乡时在此处修身养性,礼佛参禅,颐养天年。可惜天不假年,他老人家还没来得及享用,就撒手西归。崔

his hometown, Boling, to have it buried there. It so happens that the officials have lost control of this region, and Sun the Flying Tiger, a bandit chief, is rampaging everywhere at the head of 5,000 men. Madame Cui is afraid that they will run into the bandits if they travel any further for the time being, so they have put up at the monastery to await the end of the emergency."

The young man nodded his understanding, and said, "Oh, I see." On his way back past the Hall of Buddha, Zhang suddenly got a whiff of exquisite perfume. He turned his head to see where the delightful scent was coming from, and was immediately rooted to the spot: An incredibly beautiful girl was coming out of the hall. Her eyebrows were arched like crescent moons, slanting upward towards her cloud-like hair. Her lips were cherry-red, and her teeth as white as jade. Dressed in a flimsy silk robe, she held a rose in her hand. She looked like an angel from Heaven to Zhang, who thought to himself: "I have seen thousands of beauties as I traveled here and there, but I have never seen such a charming face. This is surely no monastery inhabited by dreary monks, but some paradise where lovers engage in dalliance. Who would have thought that I would meet an angel here? This beauty must have seen me. But instead of hastening away she lingers and caresses that flower. Perhaps she is not unimpressed by my appearance." Zhang's eyes were dazzled, and his soul seemed to soar up into the sky.

The girl called her maid hesitantly, like an oriole warbling in a flower garden: "Rose, Rose!"

"I'm coming, young mistress! It's really a fine building!" So saying, Rose ran out from the hall.

Oriole knitted her brows and sighed. She then recited two lines of verse:

"The monks are gone; empty their rooms,
The steps are covered with red fallen blooms."

Zhang was impressed by the girl's ready turn of phrase. Just then, Rose noticed the young man standing there staring at her mistress as if transfixed to the spot. She said to Oriole: "Miss, there is a stranger over there. Let's go back." So saying, she pulled Oriole by the sleeve, urging her to leave.

Oriole blushed. She lowered her head and walked slowly back

老夫人携儿带女,扶枢欲回祖籍博陵安葬,不料丁文雅失政,孙飞虎引五千乱军在这一带烧杀奸淫。老夫人怕有个闪失,是以暂寓此院,待路上太平了再走。"

张生听罢,点头道:"原来如此。"只得缩步回身。途经大佛殿院时,不意被一股扑鼻而来的如兰似麝的香气所吸引,驻足四望,猛然间双睛一亮,呆立在当地。原来眼前正有一位千娇百媚的妙龄女子,袅袅婷婷仙子凌波般从殿中走出来。只见她眉弯新月,眼横秋水,鼻倚琼瑶,口含新荔,粉面含春,似笑还嗔,葱指纤纤,捻一枝玫瑰,通身缟素,裙裾飘飘,真正俏丽似三春之桃,清洁若九秋之菊。张生心想:"自家走南闯北也曾见过无数佳丽,可像眼前这位娇娘,却是头一遭遇见,这里定然不是六根清净的青灯古寺,而是有情人成双结对的兜率天宫,但愿不会变成让人痛苦的三十三层离恨天。啊呀,想不到张珙我在寺中遇到了神仙!那女子定然也看到小生了,可是她不躲不藏,依旧垂着香肩,笑捻花枝,想是对小生我也有些意思。"张生痴呆呆、意悬悬,只觉得眼花缭乱,魂灵儿飞在了半天。

此时就听那女子莺啼鹂啭地唤道:"红娘,红娘!"

"哎,姐姐,我来了,这大殿果真好耍得很。"应声从大殿又出来一个蛛首蛾眉的俏丫头。

那女子蛾眉微蹙,轻叹一声道:"唉,红娘,你看这:寂寂僧房人不到,满阶苔衬落花红。"

这两句诗,听得张生如醉如痴,心里直叫:"我死也,我死也。"

又听得那叫红娘的丫头接言道:"姐姐锦心绣口,吟得好诗。"正说着,一眼瞅见痴痴呆呆直盯着这边的张生,便警觉地对那女子说道:"姐姐,那边有人,咱们回去吧。"说着搀着那女子便走。

towards her quarters. When she arrived at the threshold, she turned and cast an amorous glance at the young scholar before vanishing inside, which sent Zhang into transports of delight. He rubbed his eyes, and asked Fa Cong: "Was that the Goddess of Mercy that appeared just now?"

Fa Cong smiled and said, "Sir, the very idea! She is the daughter of the late Prime Minister Cui. The Goddess of Mercy indeed!"

Zhang sighed, "I never thought there could be such a beauty on this earth. She is the most charming girl I have ever seen. And she has such exquisitely tiny bound feet!"

Fa Cong could not hold back a guffaw: "She was standing over there, and she was wearing a full-length gown; how could you see her feet?"

Zhang took Fa Cong by the hand, and led him to where the girl had been standing. Pointing to her footprints on the petal-strewn path, he said, "Look, there you can see how delicate her feet must be. Her glance showed the feelings in her heart, and the tiny footprints also convey her love."

Fa Cong opened his eyes wide, and examined the path carefully. But he had to confess that he saw nothing.

"Ah, well, if you could see such things you would not be a monk," Zhang teased him.

Remembering how Oriole and Rose had walked into the Pear Blossom Yard with their ornaments tinkling, like two fairy maidens returning to paradise, he ran towards the yard, hoping to catch another sight of them. But he found that the red doors were already closed. Looking about him, Zhang saw that the poplars and willows seemed to be weeping, the birds were uttering mournful chirps, the gate was shut at the yard where pear trees bloomed and the whitewashed walls seemed as high as the azure sky. Zhang bemoaned his lot: "Why does Heaven not help me? How can I endure my tedious life? Young mistress, the musk and lily fragrance you spread still lingers. I am undone by your bewitching glance, and I am at a loss what to do this long day. The willow branches wave in the east breeze, and gossamer threads retain the petals of the peach trees. Your lotus face has disappeared behind the beaded screen. Is this the residence of the former Prime Minister Cui or the Temple of the Goddess of the Southern Sea?"

Seeing Zhang standing in front of the Pear Blossom Yard as if in a trance, Fa Cong tried to take him away: "Sir, please don't make trouble. This way please."

那女子一时双颊飞红,低垂粉颈,袅袅婷婷一步挪不了半尺,及至转弯时,缓缓回眸,秋波一转,送来万种风情,与张生火辣辣的目光碰了个正着。张生顿时麻了全身,风魔了一般,揉揉眼睛喃喃道:"小师父,适才怎么观音现身了?"

法聪嘻嘻笑道:"施主休要胡说,这是崔相国家的千金小姐,小名唤作莺莺,哪里是什么观音?"

张生幽幽叹道:"世间竟有这等女子,岂非天香国色乎?休说那模样,光是那一对小脚儿,也值百镒之金。"

法聪失笑道:"偌远地,又系着长裙儿,施主怎知她脚儿小?"

张生拉着法聪走出殿门,指着阶下道:"法聪小师父,你且仔细看了,若不是这落红满地柔软芳径,怎能显出这步香凌尘的浅浅鞋印。咱且休提她眼角处与我留情,只这莲印脚踪已将她的心事传递过来。"法聪睁大眼睛看了半晌,也没看到什么,摸着靛青的光头不解地说道:"俺却没看出来。"

张生戏道:"你若能看出来,便不做六根清净的和尚了。"他见莺莺小姐和红娘一路环佩叮咚,神仙归洞天般进了梨花院,抬腿便追。可等他追到跟前,那两扇朱漆大门早已得铁紧。环顾四周,只见杨柳轻烟,鸟雀喧鸣,门掩着梨花深院,粉墙高似青天,张生暗暗叫苦:"老天呀,我好生恨你,怎不与人行个方便,好叫人难消遣,怎生留恋。小姐呵,我被你引逗得意马心猿,东风摇曳垂杨线,游丝牵惹桃花片,想是珠帘里掩映着你芙蓉面。人说你是河中府宰相家,我说是南海水月观音现。"

法聪跟过来,见张生立在梨花院前痴呆呆半晌不动,便上前劝道:"施主休惹事,这边请。"

Zhang had lost all interest in sightseeing. He muttered, "I will give up everything for this charming girl. I'm not going to the capital to take the civil service examination."

"Are you crazy?" Fa Cong exclaimed. "How can you give up your official career?"

Zhang thought to himself: "Lovesickness has penetrated to the marrow of my bones. How could I resist her bewitching glance when she was about to part from my sight? Even if I were made of iron or stone, I could never forget her in my heart. Rank and wealth and fame mean nothing to me now. Suddenly, this monastery has been converted into a fairyland." After a long pause, he hit upon an idea. He made a deep bow to Fa Cong, and said, "I want you to do me a favor."

"Just tell me what I can do for you," Fa Cong said.

"As you know, I'm going to the capital to take the civil service examination. So I should make good use of my time to review the classics. However, the inn where I am staying is so crowded and noisy that I cannot concentrate on my studies. Your monastery is a quiet place, with plenty of empty rooms. Could you please ask your master if I can rent a room here so that I can spend my time reviewing my lessons? Please say some good words for me. I'll come back tomorrow to receive your reply."

Fa Cong showed signs of reluctance. "This is no easy matter. You see, our monastery has never rented out rooms before."

But, seeing that Zhang was determined to move into the monastery, Fa Cong finally agreed to see what he could do. Thereupon, Zhang returned to the inn.

In the meantime, Abbot Fa Ben had been overseeing a religious ceremony in a nearby village, and did not return to the monastery until nightfall. As soon as he had crossed the threshold, Fa Cong reported to him Zhang's visit to the monastery, and told him that the young scholar wanted to rent a room at the temple. He described Zhang in glowing terms, hinting that a little favor done now for a person from an undoubtedly excellent family and obviously with an illustrious official career ahead of him would be a wise investment for the future.

Fa Ben nodded in agreement, and said: "Oh yes, I have heard of Zhang Junrui. He is a gifted scholar. It's a pity I failed to meet him today. Fa Cong, keep watch at the gate tomorrow, and let me know the minute he arrives."

"Certainly, sir," the acolyte replied. Walking out of the room, Fa

张生此时游兴全无，自言自语道："十年不识君王面，始信婵娟解误人。小生便不去京师应举也罢。"

法聪道："秀才发疯也，如何便放弃了功名？"

张生心内忖道："小生这相思病是害上了，她临去时秋波一转，休道是小生，便是铁石人也会意惹情牵，我又在乎什么区区功名？只可惜玉人不见，这座梵王宫，我直疑是个武陵源。"停了半晌，突然灵机一动，对法聪深深一拜，说道："小生尚有一事相求，不知小师父能否应允？"

法聪道："但说无妨。"

"小生此番进京赴闱，本应珍惜光阴，温习经史，无奈旅邸冗杂，实在是难以静心苦读。宝刹清静，甚惬我意。敢烦小师父对长老说知，可有僧房借与小生半间，以供早晚温习经史。房金依例拜纳。请小师父一定替小生在长老面前美言几句，小生明日便来。"

法聪面呈难色道："此事可不大好办。本寺从未有过出租僧房的先例。"

张生佯怒道："若不肯周全，我便要埋怨杀你个法聪和尚。"

法聪见张生立意要来，只得答应。张生这才出寺回城。

却说法本长老出去赴斋，月上中天才回到寺中，法聪便将张生游寺以及要借僧房温习经史一事禀过，连带叙述了张生风度翩翩蕴藉潇洒之态，并道："依徒弟看来，张君瑞当是一位世家公子，饱学秀才，他日定能高中得官，留他住在咱寺，日后也好做个靠山。"

法本听了点头道："噢，这个张君瑞，倒也听说过，他乃当今才子，可惜来而未遇，明日你到山门外候着，来时速报与我知道。"

法聪应了一声："是。"走出外面，边走边嘀咕道："那风魔秀才

Cong thought to himself: "The silly young fellow will surely come tomorrow. The 'Goddess of Mercy' who lives here has captured his soul even before he dies."

There was little sleep night at the No.1 Scholar Inn that night for Zhang. No matter whether his eyes were open or closed, the divine beauty of Oriole was before them all the time. The glance that she had given him showed the feelings in her heart, he was convinced. He decided that fate had stepped in and brought them together. Finally, day dawned, and brought an end to his tossing and turning. He washed and dressed as hastily as if the inn were on fire, and set out alone for the Salvation Monastery. Long before he got there he saw Fa Cong standing in front of the temple gate, craning his neck and looking down the path. Zhang quickened his pace, reached the gate, and bowed to Fa Cong: "Good morning!" he said.

Fa Cong bowed in return. "Good morning, sir," he said. My master is waiting for you. Please wait while I go and inform him. The abbot will come to welcome you in person."

Zhang protested, "But I cannot trouble the abbot to lower himself to come out to greet such a worthless person as myself."

Nevertheless, Fa Cong insisted that it was the wish of the abbot himself, and without more ado he fetched his master.

At the sight of Zhang, Fa Ben pressed his palms together before his chest, and said, "Amida Buddha! Please come in and take a seat, sir. Yesterday I was not at home, and failed to welcome you. I hope you will forgive me."

Zhang found Fa Ben to be an elderly monk with snow-white hair. Yet his face still maintained the vibrancy of youth. He had an air of profound sanctity about him, and his voice was strong and clear. In fact, he looked as serene as Buddha himself. Zhang was filled with a deep sense of awe. He bowed to the abbot, saying "I have long heard your renowned name, and wished to come and hear you preach. I am sorry to have missed you yesterday. But now that I have met you at last, I am truly happy."

Following this exchange of greetings, they entered the abbot's room, and took seats. Fa Cong presented each of them with a cup of tea, and then stood behind the abbot.

The abbot started the conversation by saying, "Sir, you are a famous scholar from the City of Luoyang. What brings you here to Mid-River Prefecture?"

22

菩萨都不须问，明日肯定会来的，咱这里的活观音早把他的魂儿牵去了。"

再说张生从寺中回到状元坊，一夜颠来倒去地睡不着觉，睁眼闭眼皆是那个观音般的莺莺小姐，总觉得她那临去一瞥，似有顾盼自家之意，这就是缘份。思来想去，一定要向长老借一间僧房，一则早晚温习经史，二则倘遇那小姐出来，也能饱看一会儿。好不容易等到天亮，匆匆梳洗了，便吩咐琴童在房里候着，自己一人又往普救寺来。远远就见小和尚法聪在山门外企踵引颈，朝官道上张望。张生紧走几步，来到近前拱手一揖道："小师父早。"

法聪连忙还礼道："施主早，师父特让小僧出来迎接。施主在此少待，小僧通报师父去，他老人家要亲自来迎接你哩。"

张生道："小生何德何能，敢劳长老法驾。"

法聪道："施主少待，我即去通报。"说罢转身往里面去了。

不多时，法本长老携法聪从里面出来，一见张生便双手合十，朗声道："阿弥陀佛！请先生方丈内叙话。昨日老僧不在，有失迎迓，望先生恕罪。"

张生见这老和尚慈眉善目，鹤发童颜，气宇轩昂，活脱脱是僧伽再生，玄奘重现，不由心生敬意，上前来一拱到地还礼道："小生久闻老方丈清誉，欲来座下听讲。今日来的实在唐突，还请方丈原谅才是。"

两人互相谦让着进入方丈，分宾主落座后，法聪送上香茗，就侍立于长老身后。

法本微微欠身说道："先生名满洛阳，来到河中，不知有何贵干？"

Zhang replied, "Since my parents died, I have been living the life of a wanderer. In the course of my travels I heard of the magnificence of the Salvation Monastery and of the lofty scholarship of its abbot. As I was passing through here on my way to the capital to take the civil service examination, I thought I would take this opportunity to pay you a visit."

Fa Ben said, "You have a dignified and imposing appearance. I suppose your late father bequeathed a great deal of property to you?"

Zhang shook his head. "My late father enjoyed great renown as the president of the Ministry of Rites. During his life he was just and upright, but, alas, after his death he left no legacy. I have come here hoping to hear you preach, but I am afraid that, as a homeless vagabond, I have not the means to show my proper respects to you. A poor scholar's gift is as light as a scrap of paper." So saying, he took an ounce of silver out of his sleeve, and said, "I can only offer this ounce of silver for the upkeep of the monastery. Would you kindly accept it?"

"You are my guest, sir; such a thing would be unthinkable," Fa Ben protested. This superficial banter went on backwards and forwards for some time. Knowing that if his gift was not accepted, he could proceed with the next stage of his plan, Zhang shot an appealing glance at Fa Cong.

The acolyte understood well what was on Zhang's mind, and he thought: "Why are you so anxious, Zhang? Silver does not entice us monks. We don't care about your money." Fa Cong avoided Zhang's eyes.

Fa Ben too knew exactly what was behind the young man's generosity, as Fa Cong had told him what he wanted. Confronted with the abbot's intransigence, Zhang blushed, and finally blurted out, "To tell you the truth, reverend sir, I want to request a favor from you."

The abbot burst out laughing, and said, "A favor? Well, don't be shy; let me know what it is."

"I am a stranger here, without any relatives or friends," Zhang said. "At the moment I am living in a crowded inn. It is noisy from morning to night, and I am unable to study there. I wish to rent a room here, so that I can not only concentrate on studying but also benefit from your teaching. As for the rent, I will pay whatever you wish."

The abbot said, "It is true that there are plenty of spare rooms in our monastery, but most of them are old and bare. I am afraid that they are not suitable for you, sir. If you like, you may share my room."

Zhang groaned inwardly. To get out of this situation, he said, "Thank you very much for your kindness, reverend sir. I would be happy to share

张生道:"小生自双亲故后,琴剑飘零,游学四方。久闻河中普救寺殿宇巍峨,长老乃有道高僧,今日幸而路过此地,特来拜谒。"

法本道:"老衲观相公风度翩翩,想是老相公余荫尚在。"

张生摇头道:"先严虽官拜礼部尚书,位尊名高,然平生正直无邪,可谓是风清月朗,清介寒素。小生无意求官,有心听长老讲经。此次是特地来拜谒长老,奈路途奔驰,无以相馈,这有一锭银子,奉与寺中公用,略表寸心,万望笑纳。"

法本推辞道:"先生客中,何必如此?"

张生道:"这银两也难买柴薪,不够斋粮,不成敬意,也就是能备些茶汤。"说着不住地向法聪使眼色,口中喃喃道:"这一锭银子不为厚礼,还望长老笑纳才是。"

法聪明白张生之意,心想你个酸秀才,着哪门子急,什么都不成便先拿出银子来,倒好像俺出家人图着你什么?所以垂着眼帘,对张生的暗示不理不睬。

法本长老阅历颇深,见张生初见便赠送银两,就知他有求于己,便道:"想先生必有所请,何不直言?"

张生面红过耳,嗫嚅道:"实不相瞒,小生的确有事相求。"

长老哈哈一笑道:"先生但讲无妨。"

张生道:"小生客居异乡,并无亲友投奔,目下暂居在招商客寓,整日里人来车往,噪杂烦嚣,早晚难以温习经史,因此欲借寺内一间僧室,晨昏听讲。房费按月任意多少。"

长老道:"敝寺房屋倒也颇有几间,但大都简陋不堪,有屈先生,于心不安。若果真想来住,不如与老僧同居一室,先生以为如何?"

张生一听心中暗暗叫苦,口中忙道:"长老一片盛情,小生心

a room with you and learn from your esteemed teaching. But it is my habit to recite the classics at night; I am afraid I would disturb you. It would be far better, I think, if I lived by myself."

Fa Ben was impressed by this line of reasoning, and finally consented, "You may choose whichever room you wish."

Inwardly rejoicing, Zhang explained that a room on the sequestered side of the monastery would be most suitable for his study purposes; in fact the nearer the western bower the better, he added, as if an after-thought had just struck him. Nodding, Fa Ben said, "It is quiet there, an ideal place for you to read books. I'll have the room cleaned, and then you may move in. May I ask how much luggage you have?"

"One load. I also have a page boy."

"When do you wish to move in?"

Zhang, who couldn't wait to move in, jumped up and said, "Today." As he was about to take a hasty leave of the abbot and the acolyte, a girl appeared in the doorway. Zhang was surprised to find that it was the maid of the vision of loveliness he had seen the previous day. Thereupon, he sat down again.

Clad in a mourning dress of pure white, Rose wore her hair in two coils, in one of which was stuck a purple silk flower. She had thin eyebrows and clever eyes, like a bird's. She stole a look at Zhang, but her eyes revealed not a hint of her thoughts.

Zhang heaved an inward sigh, and thought to himself: "What a nimble girl! If I could put my head on your young mistress' pillow, I would not trouble you to make the bed for us. I would ask your mistress and her mother to set you free. I would even write a guarantee for you myself. Though you are young, your manner shows not the slightest trace of coquetry. You have the graces of a girl who has grown up in a rich and influential family."

Rose approached the abbot slowly, and made a deep bow. She said, "Ten thousand blessings, Reverend Abbot! My mistress has ordered me to inquire when it will suit you to perform the funeral service for my late master."

The abbot put his palms together before his chest and said, "Amida Buddha! The offerings and other preparations are all ready for the service in the Hall of Merits and Virtues. The 15th is the day Buddha will receive the offerings and I shall perform the funeral service for your late master."

"May I go with you to the hall to view the preparations before I

领了，能和长老同住，得以朝夕相处，实属幸事，无奈小生素好夜读，恐有扰长老清梦，于心难安，还是另住的好。"

法本觉得此话在理，心中赞道："是个懂道理的秀才！"便点头道："也好，那就任凭先生择一处房间吧。"

张生高兴得两眼放光，道："就是那个塔院后的西厢，方才最称我的心愿。"

法本点头道："那里果然清静，是个读书的好去处。就依先生。待老僧命人将西轩打扫停当，先生便来住下。请问先生可有多少行李？""一肩行李，一个伴读僮儿。""不知先生何日屈驾小寺？"

张生巴不得现在就住进去，忙说："就是今日吧。"说罢就打算起身告辞。正在这时，从外面进来一个人，张生只觉眼前一亮，这不是昨日那活观音莺莺小姐身边叫红娘的丫环么？便把已经抬起的屁股又重新落在椅子上。只见红娘身着缟素，头挽丫角双髻，鬓插一支紫色绢花，两弯细眉，一双会说话的大眼睛忽闪忽闪，进得门来，便用眼角余光将张生扫了一遍。张生暗叹道："真是个好丫头啊！小生若共你个多情的小姐同鸳帐，怎舍得让你叠被铺床，我定会替你央求小姐，央求老夫人，给你写个从良的状子，还你个自由身。看她年纪虽小，举止端详，全没半点儿轻狂相，不愧是大户人家调教出来的。"

红娘款款来到长老面前，敛衽深施一礼道："长老万福！红娘奉我家老夫人之命，特地前来问长老几时与我家老相公做法事？"

长老见红娘问讯，连忙合掌念佛道："阿弥陀佛，请回禀老夫人，就说斋供、道场都已准备停当，本月十五日，是个黄道吉日，便可以与老相公做好事。"

红娘道："如此，便与长老同去佛殿看了，也好回老夫人的话。"

report to Madame Cui?"

"Certainly you may." The abbot then turned to Zhang and said, "Would you mind waiting here for a little while? I will soon be back." So saying, the abbot stood up.

Zhang realized that he must become well acquainted with Rose and make a good impression on her if he was to gain access to her mistress. So he decided to waste no time, and said to Fa Ben: "Abbot, why do you leave me alone here? Please let me go with you."

The abbot replied, "There is no need to trouble yourself about monastery matters, young sir. I assure you, you will find this business of no interest to you at all."

This dismayed Zhang, but suddenly an idea came to him. "What I mean, Reverend Sir, is that you must be more discreet."

Fa Ben stopped and looked back. "What do you mean, Master Zhang?" he asked.

The young man feigned surprise. "How can such a large family have no male servant, and have to send a maid as a messenger?"

"Madame Cui insists that there be not a single male servant in her household," the abbot replied. "Then don't you think Madame Cui or the young mistress should have come to inquire about the date of the ceremony in person?"

Zhang pursued, "An old saying goes: Don't pull on your shoe in a melon patch, and don't adjust your cap under a plum tree. Aren't you afraid that you might arouse suspicion by going into an empty hall with a pretty young girl?"

Abbot Fa Ben was stung by this remark. "How dare you say such a thing?" he cried. "As a monk, I have long been free from all human desires and passions. I do not need to avoid suspicion."

"Please don't be angry, Abbot," Zhang said. "You misunderstand me. But I cannot help reminding you that gossip is a fearful thing."

"That is preposterous!" the abbot snorted. "However, just to put your mind at rest, I suppose you had better come with us."

"It would be my pleasure to go with you," Zhang said, with a solemn countenance but gleeful inside. He hurried to follow the abbot. "It would be more seemly, I think, to allow the maid to precede us by a few paces," he suggested.

Fa Ben nodded his agreement, saying, "Spoken like a true gentleman! You are a worthy disciple of Confucius."

长老点头道："好。"转过头对张生道："先生请稍坐,老僧同小娘子看一遭便回来,失陪了。"说罢起身要走。张生心里好生不快,想道："你老和尚陪了红娘一走了之,把我干摆在此,有何意思?"就说道："长老,为何推却小生,便同行一遭,又有何妨?"

长老见张生面呈不悦之色,知其误会了自己,便说道："先生休要见怪,老僧想此事与先生无关,故不敢有劳清神。"

张生心说："这出家人真不与人作美?红娘是莺莺小姐的贴身丫环,我要亲近小姐,岂能少得了她?"只是长老的话已说明,可如何是好?也是急中生智,他冲着法本说："长老,可要小心谨慎噢!"

法本听得张生话中有话,便停步回头问道："先生此话怎讲?"

张生故作惊奇道："偌大的一个相府,怎么偏生就没一个儿郎,却支使个梅香来传话论事?"

法本道："老夫人一向治家严肃,内外并无一个男子出入,不叫梅香出来,难道要老夫人和小姐亲自来说?"

"古人云:'瓜田不纳履,李下不整冠。'长老与那俏丫头孤男寡女,就不怕有瓜田李下之嫌吗?"

法本长老心生不快,道："先生,老僧偌大年纪,况六根清净,焉能做出什么有伤风化之事?又避什么瓜田李下之嫌?"

"长老莫气,您误会了,小生实则担心人言可畏呀!"

"这是什么话?幸亏那红娘没听见,若听了去,多少尴尬,岂不是要惹出口舌来?"长老说罢要走,转念一想,不如让这秀才一同去,省得他疑三疑四的,便道："既然如此,就有劳先生一同走走如何?"

张生心说："老和尚,我就等你这句话呢。"当下应道："小生理当奉陪。"他紧跟长老,见红娘已走出门外十几步了,便说道："请

Both Fa Ben and Zhang followed Rose to the Hall of Merits and Virtues. Located at the northeastern corner of the monastery, behind the Hall of Buddha, the Hall of Merits and Virtues was also known as the Beamless Hall, because it had been constructed without the use of beams. Above the door of the hall there was a horizontal signboard painted blue and inscribed with the three golden characters: Hall of Merits and Virtues. An antithetical couplet hung on both sides of the door, reading, "This hall abounds in merits and virtues, and the Salvation Monastery saves all monks who come to it." It had been written by Ouyang Xun, a famous calligrapher of the Tang Dynasty. The three of them inspected the hall, finding everything in readiness for the funeral service, including yellow curtains, cloth flags, bells, wooden fishes (percussion instruments made out of hollow wooden blocks and used by Buddhist priests to beat the rhythm when chanting scriptures), mourning articles, paper horses and money, incense burners and candles. Fa Ben said to Rose: "The offerings are ready, and all the other preparations have been made for the service. I request that Madame Cui and your young mistress come on the 15th day of this month to offer incense."

At this, Zhang interrupted: "May I ask why you need to offer incense?"

Fa Ben replied, "It is to express the filial piety of the young mistress towards her late father, ahead of the funeral service, as the mourning period is about to come to an end."

Zhang was intrigued at this news. "So the young mistress will come here on that day!" he mused. "That will be a good opportunity for me to meet her. I must not let this opportunity slip from my grasp." So thinking, he suddenly hit upon an idea. He burst into tears, and sobbed, "I'm so ashamed!" "What's the matter, young sir?" cried Fa Ben, in consternation.

His voice choking with tears, Zhang said, "You have reminded me of what an undutiful son I am. I have neglected to burn incense in honor of my deceased parents ever since I started my wanderings. How I wish to repay them for their boundless kindness, just like the young lady!"

Upon hearing this, Fa Ben was filled with a feeling of deep veneration, impressed with how well educated, dutiful and filled with a sense of propriety he was. "Master Zhang," he urged gently, "I beg of you to restrain your grief. Please do not be too sad."

Zhang wiped his eyes and said, "Will you be kind enough to allow me to subscribe something so that I may be included in the service, for

那小娘子先行一步,俺靠后些。"

　　长老点头道:"是一个有道理的秀才,不枉为圣人之徒。"

　　法本长老和张生一前一后出了方丈,跟着红娘来到功德堂。这功德堂在大殿后面的东北角,设计精巧,不用屋梁,所以叫无梁殿,也叫无量殿,取功德无量之义。殿门上方是一块蓝底金字匾额,上书"功德堂"三个大字,门口两旁挂一副对联,是:"功德堂功德无量,普救寺普救众僧。"皆出自当代大书法家欧阳询之手。进殿中看了一遭,只见黄幔布幡,钟磬木鱼,疏文表章,香烛纸马……一应佛事法物,样样俱全。法本长老对红娘道:"这斋供道场都已准备就绪,到时请老夫人小姐前来拈香。"不待红娘启齿,张生一旁插言道:"小生冒昧问一声,为何要做道场拈香?"

　　法本道:"这是崔相国小姐至孝,一则为报父母养育之恩,二则是老相爷弃世孝满除服的日子,所以要做一坛道场法事。"

　　也是说者无心,听者有意,张生听罢心花怒放,小姐亲自来拈香,真乃天赐良机,须设法与她见上一面,机不可失,时不再来。眼珠一转,计上心来,一时间长嘘短叹,潜然泪下,说声:"惭愧啊,惭愧!"便失声痛哭起来,把个法本长老与红娘都弄得莫名其妙。长老忙问道:"先生,为何如此伤心?"

　　张生抽噎道:"哀哀父母,生我劬劳,欲报深恩,昊天罔极。想那相府小姐乃一女子也,尚然有报答父母之心,小生湖海飘零数年,并不曾有一陌纸钱焚化相报,岂不枉为七尺男儿!是以伤心。"

　　法本听了不禁肃然起敬,这秀才知书达理,也是个至孝之人,心中不觉同情,就劝道:"先生节哀,也不必过于伤心!"

　　张生抹了把泪道:"请长老慈悲为本,方便为门,设法与小生

the salvation of the souls of my deceased parents?"

The abbot replied, "Since your purpose is to fulfil your filial duty, I must of course consent."

Zhang, delighted to hear this, said, "I only have five thousand cash on me. I don't know if it is enough."

"It is enough, if your desire is sincere," the abbot said. Then he called to Fa Cong: "Arrange to include Master Zhang in the service."

"Yes, Master," Fa Cong answered.

Zhang bowed to the abbot, and said, "Thank you very much for everything you've done for me. But I'm not sure if Madame Cui and the young mistress will agree to my request. If they do not, it will be difficult for me to fulfil my filial duty."

"Do not worry about that, Master Zhang," Fa Ben said. "I will persuade Madame Cui of the rectitude of your intentions. But both Madame Cui and her daughter are reasonable people; I don't believe that they will object."

Zhang saluted the abbot again: "I'll never forget your kindness," he said, glancing at Rose, who betrayed not a hint of what she was thinking.

"Well now," said Fa Ben. "Everything is arranged. Would you like to come to my room for a cup of tea?"

They left the Hall of Merits and Virtues, Rose walking in front, followed by the abbot. Zhang fell behind so that he could have a word with Fa Cong. "Will the young lady be present at the service?" he whispered to the acolyte.

"How could she be absent from a service being held specially for her father?" Fa Cong answered carelessly.

Zhang felt as though a load had been taken off his mind. "Then that was five thousand cash well spent," he thought to himself with satisfaction.

The next step in his plan, he decided, was to worm himself into the confidence of Rose. He made an excuse not to go to the abbot's room to drink tea, but lingered outside until Rose should come out.

Saying good-bye to the abbot, Rose set off back to the Cui family quarters. As she was walking along, with her head bent modestly, who should suddenly appear in front of her but the young scholar who had cried so sadly in the Hall of Merits and Virtues! Although she was somewhat displeased to be so accosted, Rose had no choice but to return the young man's greeting: "Ten thousand blessings on you, sir."

Rose's reserved manner was not lost on Zhang. Although he

带一份斋,追荐俺那亡化的双亲。"

长老道:"先生如此孝心,老僧理应方便。"

张生心中欢喜,忙道:"小生备钱五千,不知够不够一份斋礼?"

长老道:"钱不在多,心诚则灵,足矣,足矣。"转身对殿门外的法聪道:"法聪,与这位张先生带一份斋。"法聪应道:"遵命。"

张生忙向法本长老施礼道:"多谢长老费心安排道场! 只是长老虽然答应,不知老夫人和小姐同意否? 如若不允,也是枉然,我仍是难以尽人子之心。"

长老道:"先生放心,便是夫人知道也无妨,自有老僧为先生说情。想老夫人和小姐通情达礼,谅无不允之理,先生放宽心便是。"

张生又施礼道:"长老恩情,小生没齿难忘!"说着偷眼看了看红娘,红娘却不动声色。长老道:"正事已毕,二位施主请到方丈用茶。"一行人陆续走出功德堂,红娘走在头里,长老随后。张生有意放慢脚步,与法聪同行,悄声问道:"崔府做道场那天,小姐一定来么?"

法聪随口答道:"专为报答她父母设的道场,她如何不来?"

张生一听心中一块石头落了地,暗道:"小生这五千文大钱是用对地方了。"又想,那红娘到了方丈,大概快出来了,不妨等她一会儿,也好和她说上几句话,便故意放慢了脚步。

红娘道过谢,出了方丈,低着头往回走,猛闻一声:"小娘子拜揖。"把她着实吓了一跳。她瞪大眼睛一看,竟是适才同到佛堂的那个哭天抹泪闹着要附斋的秀才,正冲着自己做揖。心中虽有些恼火,但碍着情面,不好发作,便不很情愿地敛衽还礼道:"先生万福!"

张生见红娘表情淡淡的,不愿搭理自己,也觉得没趣,便明知故问道:"小娘子莫非是相国小姐的侍妾么?"

knew the answer, he asked, "Are you the personal maid of Miss Oriole?"

Rose replied in an icy manner: "I am, sir. Why do you ask?"

Zhang was at a loss what to say. But, afraid that he would miss his chance if Rose left right away, he forced himself to ask, "May.... May I tell you something?"

Rose scoffed at him: "What a strange person you are! An old saying goes, 'Like arrows, words must not be freely spread. Once they are heard, they cannot be unsaid.' So, if you have anything to say, please say it with decorum."

Zhang felt ill at ease in the presence of this self-assured girl. After hesitating a short while, he spoke evasively: "I am Zhang Gong, styled Junrui, a native of Luoyang. I was born on the 17th day of the first moon. I am 23 years old, not yet married...."

Rose found the young scholar both annoying and amusing. She gave him a supercilious look, and said, "Why do you entrust me, a stranger, with such deep secrets?"

Regardless of the consequences, Zhang plunged ahead: "I have another question to ask you. Does your young mistress sometimes go out of doors?"

Rose was taken aback at this. She thought to herself: "This young gentleman must be up to no good, asking about my mistress." She replied in a haughty manner: "You are an educated gentleman. So you should know that the revered sage Mencius said, 'Is it not the rule that males and females shall not allow their hands to touch in giving or receiving anything?' The ancients said, 'Speak not a word and make not a movement contrary to propriety.' Cold as ice and frost, my mistress rules her family strictly. Even a servant boy dare not enter the western bower unbidden, and my young mistress is seldom allowed to leave her room in case she is seen even by the monks. Now you, who are no way connected with the family, come asking impertinent questions. You really must recover your sense of propriety." With that, Rose stalked away, leaving the young man very discomfited.

Zhang stood there, his knitted eyebrows showing his grief and gloom. He mused, "Rose said that her mistress is as cold as ice and frost, and no one, unless summoned, dare enter her room. Oriole, if you stand in awe of your stern mother, perhaps you will never give me so much as another glance before you depart. Even if I never see you again, I will never be

红娘心中不悦,没好气地说道:"我便是,又何劳先生动问?"

张生一时尴尬万分,又怕红娘走开,错过机会,只好硬着头皮道:"小生有句话……不知……不知当讲不当讲?"

红娘面沉似水,语带讥诮地说道:"你这个人好生奇怪,常言道:'言出如箭,不可乱发,一入人耳,有力难拔。'你思量当讲则讲,不当讲就免开尊口,何必再问?"

张生越发局促不安,支吾半晌,方不知所云地说道:"小生姓张名珙,字君瑞,本贯西洛人也,年方二十三岁,正月十七日子时建生,并不曾娶妻……"红娘听到这里,觉着又好气又好笑,白了他一眼道:"哎,你我素昧平生,谁问你来着?"

张生不管不顾,又道:"敢问姐姐,你家小姐经常出来么?"

红娘心想这个穷酸,怎么问起我家小姐来了?定是不怀好意。不由怒从心头起,陡然变色道:"先生可是读圣贤书的君子,孟夫子曰:'男女授受不亲,礼也。'古人云:'非礼勿视,非礼勿听,非礼勿动。'俺老夫人治家严谨,有冰霜之操。内无应门五尺之童,年至十二三者,未奉传唤,也不敢擅入中堂。前些日子,俺小姐潜出闺房,被夫人窥见,当即召到庭下训斥,小姐当时就认了错。老夫人对亲生女儿尚且如此,何况对我们下人?今天也是合该你走运,碰上了妾身,尚可以容恕,倘若碰上我家老夫人,决不能与你善罢甘休。"说罢鼻子"哼"了一声,转身就走。

张生被红娘劈头盖脸地一顿训斥奚落,心里痛苦之状难以描述。说什么老夫人有冰霜之操,不召唤,谁敢进入中堂?好我的小姐哩,你既是惧怕老母威严,就不该临去时回头秋波那一转。此时要想丢开手,你叫小生我如何丢得下?我张生今生若得不到你这

able to stop yearning for you. Your image is so deeply engraved on my heart. If we could be joined like twin lilies in this life I would hold you for ever in my warm embrace and set you in my heart! The Amorous Hill is far away in the celestial sphere, but the place of our meeting seems even farther away. What Rose said makes me feel you're too high to reach. Would you dare to defy your stern mother, and confess the feelings in your heart to me, your forlorn lover? Are you not aflame with love when you see the butterflies flying in pairs? Could I but hold you in my embrace, I would steal your fragrance like a bee steals the pollen from the flowers. I cannot banish from my mind your lightly penciled brows and thinly powdered face, your jade-white neck and lily-like feet, your crimson sleeves and exquisitely tapered fingers...."

Waking from his reverie, Zhang recollected where he was, and decided to go and say goodbye to the abbot. He found Fa Ben waiting for him. Asked about the arrangements for Zhang's lodgings in the monastery, the abbot explained, "There is a room adjoining the western bower. It is delightful and quite suitable for you. It has already been cleaned. You may move in at your earliest convenience, sir."

"You have been very kind, abbot. I will return to the inn forthwith and bring my luggage here."

"There will be a meal ready for you when you return," the abbot said.

Zhang took his leave. On his way back to the inn, he pondered, "After I move to this quiet monastery, I will have only vegetables to eat, and no wine will be available. How will I be able to while away the lonely hours? Even if I attain my goal, there will still be many lonely nights to be endured before that happens. I'll be alone in a room deep in the heart of a courtyard, with only a flimsy mat and a single oil lamp throwing fitful shadows on old books for company. Sleepless at night, I'll toss from left to right. How many times will I sigh and groan, and beat the pillow all alone, pining for Oriole?

美娇娘，定是前世里烧了断头香，有朝一日我得到了你，定会将你手掌里擎护，心坎儿里温存，眼皮上供养。此刻，我这身躯虽立在寺院回廊，魂灵儿已在你那儿。因此上，你还怕什么威严拘束的亲娘？那老夫人也太过虑，小生也不妄自空想，我与莺莺郎才女貌很相当，她有德言工貌，小生有恭俭温良。千万不要眉儿浅淡思张敞，春色飘零忆阮郎，到那时可就来不及了。一想起她眉儿浅描脸儿淡妆，粉香腻玉搓就的颈项，翠裙下微露的小小金莲，袖口伸出的笋尖细指……不由人不动心，不由人不思量，小姐啊，你抛撒下半天风韵，小生我拾得万种思量。

张生独自在回廊神思飘荡，猛然间方想起应该向长老告辞了，赶紧走进方丈。长老已经等候了一会儿，见张生进来，问道："先生哪里去了？"

张生哪敢如实回答，只好撒谎道："小生更衣去来，敢问长老，房舍之事怎么样了？"

"就依先生之意，在塔院侧边西厢有一间小房，十分安静，甚是潇洒，正适合先生居住。现已收拾好了，先生随时可以搬来。"

"多谢长老，小生即刻回店中搬行李去。"

长老道："既然如此，老僧准备下斋饭，先生一定要来。"

张生告辞出来，心想若在店中，到好消遣，搬到寺里，禅堂清静，僧房寂寞，茹素戒酒，终朝枯坐，让我怎生捱这凄凉？纵然酬得今生之志，可用什么来消磨这萧寺长夜？到那时，院宇深，枕簟凉，一灯孤影摇，睡不着辗转反侧如翻掌，少说也得有一万声长吁短叹，五千遍捣枕捶床！我那娇羞花解语、温柔玉生香的小姐呵，你我相逢，此时记不真你那娇模样，我只能在今夜里手抵着腮儿慢慢想了。

CHAPTER TWO

An Exchange of Verses

Ever since she had seen Zhang at the Buddha Hall the day before, Oriole had been in a trance, as if her soul had left her body. In her mind's eye, the handsome and graceful young scholar was ever-present. Whenever she remembered that her father had betrothed her to Zheng Heng, her ugly, ignorant and incompetent cousin, she would groan: "How wonderful it would be if my cousin were like that handsome young scholar!" Suddenly she thought of Rose, and wondered what was keeping her so long on the simple errand she had been sent to perform. She made up her mind to scold the little truant as soon as she got back.

At this moment, Rose entered the room, beaming. Oriole put on a grave expression and asked, "Rose, what about the funeral service? Why did it take you such a long time to find out?"

"I have just told my mistress about it, and now I want to tell you. The 15th day of this month is the date on which the service will be held, and the abbot requests that you and your mother burn incense on that date." So saying, Rose laughed again.

Oriole gave Rose a supercilious look and said, "What are you laughing at?"

Rose burst into louder laughter.

Oriole, puzzled and somewhat annoyed, said, "Rose, have you taken leave of your senses? You're behaving most improperly!"

Rose became serious. "Miss, I have something amusing to tell you. The young scholar we saw the other day was today sitting in the abbot's room."

On hearing this, Oriole blushed, and with feigned indifference asked, "Why do you think that that is so amusing?"

"But let me tell you more, Miss," Rose said, with a smile. "When the abbot took me to the Hall of Merits and Virtues, the young scholar followed us. After we went back to the abbot's room, the young man

第二章
隔墙和诗

　　却说相国小姐崔莺莺自昨日佛殿里偶遇张生后，便有些神思恍惚，魂不守舍起来。眼前总是浮动着那仪容俊雅、举止潇洒的书生身影。只是……父亲生前实不该将自家许与那形态猥琐、不学无术的表兄郑恒。如若郑恒也像那书生该有多好！又想，这半天了，不见红娘的影子，娘叫她去问长老何时做法事，这小贱人怎么还不回来？准是又游佛殿，数罗汉，乐而忘返。也不管别人急不急，真真该打！

　　正在胡思乱想之际，就见红娘"吃吃"笑着进来，莺莺脸儿往下一沉道："红娘，使你问长老几时做法事？如何这时候才回来？"

　　红娘忍笑答道："恰才回了老夫人话，正待回姐姐的话，这月十五日，请老夫人、姐姐拈香。"说罢又"吃吃"地笑了起来。

　　莺莺白了红娘一眼："死妮子，有什么好笑的？真真不成体统。"

　　红娘止住笑道："姐姐，你不知。我对你说一件好笑的事。咱昨日在寺里见的那秀才，今日也在长老方丈里。"

　　莺莺听了，芳心不禁一动，脸上泛起红晕，可口中却淡淡地说道："在又怎样？有什么好笑的？"

　　红娘笑道："姐姐听我说么，长老带着红娘去看斋堂，那秀才也

41

waited for me outside. When I left the abbot's room he stopped me, and said, 'I am Zhang Gong, styled Junrui, a native of Luoyang. Born on the 17th day of the first moon, I am 23 years old and not yet married.' I said nothing. Then he asked me: 'Are you the personal maid of Miss Oriole? Does your young mistress often go out of doors?' I, of course, berated him for his impertinence. Young mistress, I don't know what on earth he was thinking about. I never imagined there could be such a foolish young fellow!"

Oriole joined in Rose's merriment, but in spite of her mocking tone, she was secretly impressed by Zhang's forwardness. She abruptly checked herself, and put on a serious expression. "There's no need to mention this to my mother, Rose. I hope you understand," she said.

Rose assured her that she did.

Afraid that Rose would start to guess what was on her mind, Oriole looked out of the window and suggested, "It's a fine day today, and that means a bright moon tonight. Arrange the incense table, and we shall go to the garden to offer incense to Heaven later."

Meanwhile, Zhang finished his preparations for moving into the monastery together with his page. A small room near the western bower had been made ready for him by Fa Cong. Though somewhat small, it had been charmingly furnished. Under the green screen window stood a purple sandalwood desk, on which there were the four treasures of the study (writing brush, ink stick, ink slab and paper). Beside the desk, there was a tea table, on which sat a potted landscape, with a miniature pine tree growing from a curious white stone. In a small niche in one wall was a white jade statue of the Buddha Avalokitesvara. Flanking the niche, there was an antithetical couplet, which read, "Avalokitesvara is free from trammels in the purple bamboo grove; and Tathagata sits on the White Lotus Altar." In front of the statue there was a gilded incense burner, with wisps of smoke and the fragrance of joss sticks coming from it. A traditional Chinese painting titled Crossing the River on a Reed, painted by the famous painter Wu Daozi hung on one of the white walls, together with an antithetical couplet written by the famous calligrapher Yan Zhenqing: "An elegant room need not be large; and fragrant flowers need not be many." Zhang pushed open the green screen window, and found himself gazing out onto a small courtyard with green grass, two weeping willows and a clump of peach trees. In one corner of the wall, there was a rockery made of stones brought all the way from Lake Taihu. The young man was

跟着去看,在回方丈时,那秀才却在门外等着,看到红娘出来,便深深唱个诺道:'小生姓张名珙,字君瑞,本贯西洛人也,年二十三岁,正月十七日子时建生,并不曾娶妻!小娘子莫非莺莺小姐的侍妾么?小姐常出来么?'这可是他个秀才该问的?被红娘好一顿抢白。姐姐,不知他个穷酸想甚么哩,世上竟有这等傻瓜!"

莺莺听罢不觉由衷地笑了起来,心中暗道:"好一个多情多义的秀才!"随即叮咛红娘道:"这事休对夫人说起。"

红娘看了看小姐,眼睛一转,点点头道:"姐姐放心就是。"

莺莺怕红娘瞧破心事,转头向窗外望了望,道:"今日天气晴朗,晚间月色必定佳妙,早些安排香案,咱们到花园内烧香拜月去。"

再说张生受了红娘一番奚落后,仍壮志不改,当下返回城里退了客房,收拾行李,带着琴童搬到普救寺中,住在近着西厢的"容膝山房"。此房恰如其名,不过一丈方圆,仅可容膝。然布置得雅趣横生,绿纱窗下放一张紫檀书案,上陈文房四宝,旁边紫檀小茶几上摆着一盆清供,玲珑剔透的清虚石上布满绿苔,上面长着棵小小的苍虬古朴的五针松。小佛龛里供着一尊白玉鱼篮观音,佛龛两旁有一副对联:"紫竹林中观自在,白莲坛上现如来。"佛前小巧精美的镏金香炉里青烟袅袅,香气氤氲。白粉墙上挂一幅立轴,乃当代大画家吴道子画的达摩禅师《一苇渡江图》,两旁配一副颜真卿写的对联:"室雅何须大,花香不在多。"推开绿纱窗,栏杆外是个小庭院,院内绿草茸茸,栽着两棵垂杨柳,四五棵碧桃花,近墙角有一堆太湖石叠就的假山。张生为这室内外的幽雅氛围所陶醉,连连对着为自己收拾安排房舍的法聪和尚致谢道:"多谢小和尚了,请受小生一拜!此屋陈设幽雅,布置得宜,和尚可谓大手笔。"

charmed by the scenes both indoors and outdoors. He expressed his gratitude to Fa Cong, and complimented him on his fine taste.

The acolyte demurred, but was delighted with the compliment all the same. He knew full well, of course, why Zhang had moved into the temple, but he assuaged his conscience by reminding himself that his duty to Buddha was to help others. He said to Zhang: "Sir, let me tell you something. Miss Oriole goes into her garden to offer incense to Heaven and pray to the moon almost every night."

The young scholar was excited when he heard this, and asked, "Where is the garden?"

"On the other side of your own garden wall, sir." So saying, Fa Cong took his leave.

Zhang ate his supper absent-mindedly. Then he sent his page to bed. He sat up until the moonlight shone on the eastern wall and he judged that all the monks must have gone to sleep. Zhang walked on tiptoe out of his room, and furtively climbed up the rockery in the corner of the wall. Peeping over the top of the wall into the other garden, he saw that it was full of spring flowers.

Meanwhile, there was not a speck of cloud in the jade-like sky, in which the Milky Way sparkled like diamonds. The silver moon sailed on high, shedding its light on the enchanting scene.

Just as he was wondering if and how he should approach Oriole on this night, Zhang heard the creaking of the garden gate, and caught a whiff of fragrance borne on the wind. Still on tiptoe, he fixed his eyes intently on the gate. Rose entered the garden, holding a green lantern and followed by Oriole. "Ah, she is more charming and graceful than ever tonight," thought Zhang. "She is like a fairy who has fled from the Heavenly Palace." With her hair tied up in a bun, Oriole wore a light green jacket buttoned down the front and a white silk scarf. Below the jacket, she wore a silk skirt. She looked like the Fairy Queen standing in front of the crimson door of the imperial temple or Lady Chang'e in the moon, worthy of the praise of a great poet. Zhang's soul was ensnared at that instant.

Oriole told Rose to place the incense table near the fantastic Taihu Rock. Rose did as she was bidden. "Young mistress, everything is ready for you to light the incense," she said.

Oriole placed three sticks of incense in the incense burner, one by one, and, with a bow, started to pray to the moon: "As I burn the first stick of incense, I pray that my deceased father may soon ascend to Heaven.

　　法聪听了张生的称赞,觉得耳内和顺,心里舒坦。对张生颇有好感,也知张生为何借住寺中,虽说自家是跳出三界外,不在五行中的出家人,但"君子成人之美","佛有好生之德",当助秀才一臂之力。便对张生道:"先生,小僧告诉你一件事,那莺莺小姐几乎天天晚上都要到花园里烧香拜月。"

　　张生一听,心中激动,问道:"花园在哪儿?"

　　"这里和花园只有一墙之隔。"说罢法聪告辞了。

　　张生魂不守舍地吃罢晚饭,先打发琴童歇息了,待到初更已起,月上东墙,两廊的和尚们都睡熟了,便蹑手蹑脚出了房门,来在太湖石畔墙角儿边,悄悄爬上假山,坐在一块石墩上,抬头刚好探出墙头,隔墙花园里的一切景象便尽收眼底。他敛声屏气,眼睛一眨不眨地注视着,单等心上人儿出来,好饱看一番。

　　此时张生置身春霭飘香的庭院之中,只见玉宇无尘,银河泻影,皓月横空,花阴满庭,只觉神清气爽。猛然间听得"吱呀"一声,就见隔壁花园中角门儿缓缓开启,他忙站立起来,踮起脚尖,定睛观看,只见门开处,一盏碧纱灯先从里面伸了出来,紧接是红娘,随后便是自家朝思暮想的小姐莺莺。只见她一头乌云松松挽就一个堕马髻,上身穿淡湖绿对襟衫儿,白凌抹胸,下系一条淡湖绿百褶湘裙,裙裾垂地,款款行来。似湘陵妃子,斜倚舜庙朱扉;如月殿嫦娥,微现蟾宫素影。张生觉得魂儿都被她勾走了。

　　莺莺对红娘说:"红娘,去把香桌搬出来,放在那边靠近太湖石处。"红娘手脚利落地照小姐的吩咐安排好香桌,说道:"小姐,快来烧香吧。"莺莺移到香桌前说声:"红娘取香过来。"

　　这边隔墙偷看的张生忙将耳朵支楞起来,要听小姐祷告些什

As I burn the second, I pray for longevity for my dear mother. As I burn the third...."

Noticing her young mistress hesitate, Rose said, "You're always silent when it comes to the third one. Let me pray for you. I pray that my young mistress may marry a man whose literary talents are second to none, and who is talented and good-looking, gallant and gentle, and who will also be kind to me, Rose."

Oriole was overcome with shyness. "Don't talk nonsense, Rose," she said. Then she raised her head, bowed to the moon again, and stood up slowly. Leaning on the balustrade, Oriole heaved a deep sigh as she pondered what was in her heart.

Zhang, having observed all this, thought to himself: "She burned the third stick of incense praying that she could meet her ideal husband. This scene has inspired me to compose a poem. And he recited:

> The moonlight dissolves the night,
> Spring's lonely in flowers' shade.
> I bask in the moonbeams bright
> Wondering, where is the lunar maid?

Oriole and Rose were startled to hear these murmured lines. "Someone is chanting a poem over by the corner of the wall!" Oriole exclaimed.

Rose said, "It sounds like the voice of that foolish young scholar, who is 23 years old and still unmarried."

Oriole felt a surge of excitement running through her. She thought, "I have been thinking of him, and now he has been brought near, to recite an affectionate poem for me!" She could not help saying: "What a pure and fresh poem! I will compose one to match it."

And, without further hesitation, she recited as follows:

> In a lonely room at night,
> Spring and youth wither and fade,
> You who croon with such delight,
> Pity the sighing maid!

Zhang was surprised and overjoyed. He thought, "Not only has she captivated me with her beauty; now I discover that she is intelligent and

么。莺莺接过红娘递来的三炷香，依次插在香炉上，轻声对月祈祷：
"这头一炷香，愿逝去的先人早升天界！这第二炷香，愿堂中老母身
安无事，健康长寿！这第三炷香么……"红娘见小姐欲语还羞，便在
一旁说道："这一炷香我替姐姐祷告：愿俺姐姐早寻一个才貌双全、
称心如意、知冷知热的姐夫，也拉扯红娘一把。"莺莺听了娇羞不
胜，长叹了一声。正是：心中无限伤心事，尽在深深两拜中。

　　张生在墙头将莺莺的一举一动、一言一行，全都看了个清清楚
楚，听了个明明白白。小姐的第三炷香果然是为了终身大事，她那
一声长叹给这更深人静、月光如水的良宵平添了一丝凄凉，怎不令人
为之动情。我张君瑞虽不及司马相如，但观小姐倒颇有卓文君之
意。不妨吟诵一绝，权作投石问路，看她有何反应。略作沉思，便脱口
吟道："月色溶溶夜，花阴寂寂春。如何临皓魄，不见月中人？"

　　沉思中的莺莺和立在一旁的红娘被这吟诗声惊得同时叫了
一声"呀！"莺莺道："有人在外边墙角吟诗。"

　　红娘说："啊呀，这声音好生耳熟，对了，对了，好像就是那个
二十三岁不曾娶妻的傻角。"

　　莺莺听了，不禁芳心一动，自家正在思念于他，却不想他近在咫
尺。适才所吟诗句抑扬顿挫，掷地有声，且情意绵绵，不由轻声赞道：
"好清新的诗句呀！"随即复自语道："我何不依韵也做一首？"红娘心
中好笑，早知小姐之意，便戏谑道："你两个是好做一首。"

　　莺莺听了，不加思索地吟道："兰闺久寂寞，无事度芳春。料得
行吟者，应怜长叹人。"

　　张生听了欣喜万分，原以为莺莺只是身材窈窕，脸蛋俊俏，哪
曾想她聪明绝顶，唱和诗句如此之快！且一字字、一声声都在倾诉

accomplished too! She matched my verse perfectly and effortlessly. Each word revealed what her heart is feeling. Her words and rhymes were soft, clear and apt."

Thereupon, completely under the spell of the moonlight and infatuation with the beautiful and talented Oriole, Zhang stood up, ready to climb over the wall into the garden. As he did so, he looked straight into the face of Oriole, who was gazing at that part of the wall.

Oriole startled when she saw him.

Rose saw him, too. "Miss, there's someone looking over the wall," she whispered urgently. "We ought to go back indoors, or else the mistress will be displeased."

Oriole reluctantly followed Rose out of the garden. But as she did so, she could not help glancing back, giving Zhang a look that was full of tender feelings. The young man stood where he was, mute and stupefied at this turn of events, and it was only when the garden gate clicked shut that he came to his senses. Uttering a sigh, Zhang heaved a deep sigh, as if awakening from a dream, and gazed around him. It was the dead of night. Cold dew glistened on the green moss, the bright moonlight filtered through the shadows cast by the flowers and a soft breeze blew, making the dark trees shiver. The Dipper hung crookedly in the heavens.

Zhang came down from the rockery, and shuffled back to his room in low spirits. With only a flickering oil lamp for company, Zhang lay sleepless. Gusts of chilly wind filtered through the shutters, tearing the paper which covered the windows.

As he tossed and turned, he longed for the day when, amid flowers and beneath a willow tree, behind a mist-like curtain or surrounded by a cloud-like screen, he and Oriole would swear an oath as everlasting as the mountains and seas. Then at the dead of night they would enjoy their fill of love. And the future would unfurl, shining before them. These thoughts cheered him up, and he blessed his good fortune.

Truly, his situation was like this:

"Feigning leisure, I seek lore
From the abbot's learned store.
But my verses are addressed
To the bower in the west."

着衷情,诗句清新,音律轻盈,吟唱得珠圆玉润,煞是动听。她若是和小生能隔墙唱和至天明,该有多好?何不趁机撞将过去,看她说些什么?想到此,张生猛地从假山上站立起来,就要跨墙进园。月光下与正朝这边张望的莺莺小姐打了个照面。莺莺虽然知道张生就在墙那边,但突然见到张生从墙头上探身而起,还是被吓了一跳,可她惊诧刹那,便含情脉脉,秋波盈盈,望着张生。

红娘猛然见墙头长出了半个人来,也吓了一跳,定睛一看,果真就是那个穷酸,急忙道:"姐姐,墙上有人,咱们快回家去吧。"说罢,拉着莺莺就走。莺莺虽未说话,心里却直怨不做美的红娘太薄情,出于无奈,只好随了红娘,就在转身的刹那,又情不自禁地回过头来深情地看了张生一眼。这一回眸,张生哪里把持得住,一时如石雕泥塑般呆立在那里,及至角门"呀"地关了,这才如梦方醒地长叹道:"小姐,你去了呵,可哪里发付小生!"无奈,角门关闭,心上那"长叹人"已去,空撇下碧澄澄苍苔露冷,明皎皎花筛月影。

张生跌跌撞撞从假山上下来,无精打采地回到房中,独自对着一盏碧荧荧的矮油灯,愈感到衾单枕孤,凄凉难耐。

张生在床上翻来倒去,怨不能,恨不能,坐不安,睡不宁。又想着有朝一日柳遮花映中,雾障云屏里,待到夜阑人静时,自家与莺莺海誓山盟,两下情浓,那才是真正的风流嘉庆,美满恩情,画堂春生,锦片儿似的前程……张生想着想着,越想越美,看来这一天的好事从今天开始就算定局了,那首诗就是最好的凭证。小生再不必在梦中寻找意中人了,就去那碧桃花树下等着便是了。正是:

闲寻方丈高僧语,闷对西厢皓月吟。

CHAPTER THREE

Uproar at the Funeral Service

On the 15th day of the second moon, the Hall of Merits and Virtues was all set for the funeral service for the late Prime Minister Cui to begin. Banners waved to and fro, and clouds of incense smoke formed a dense canopy overhead. The sacred drums and bronze cymbals sounded like thunder, bells pealed, and the steady chanting of the monks reverberated through the air.

Abbot Fa Ben, who had been moved by Zhang's filial plea a few days before and agreed that he be allowed to offer incense to intercede for his deceased parents during the service, had had second thoughts. Afraid that Madame Cui would be unhappy about the arrangement, he planned to let Zhang burn incense first to avoid him meeting Madame Cui and her daughter. So he sent Fa Cong first thing in the morning to summon the young man to the hall. The latter, who had long been ready, lost no time following the acolyte. On the way, he was looking forward to feasting his eyes on the object of his infatuation.

Fa Ben greeted him at the door of the Hall of Merits and Virtues: "Amitabha! Good morning, sir!"

"Good morning, abbot!" Zhang replied, bowing low.

Fa Ben led Zhang to a table set up for him to sacrifice to his deceased parents, and invited him to burn incense.

Zhang picked three sticks of incense from the table, lit them with a burning candle, dropped to his knees, and prayed silently: "In burning the first stick of incense, I pray that those who are alive enjoy long life and happiness. In burning the second stick of incense, I pray that those who have passed away be happy in Paradise. In burning the third stick of incense, I pray that Rose will hasten my suit and Madame Cui may be kept long in the dark about my coming trysts with her daughter. Oh Buddha, show me your favor." Then he made three kowtows in great earnest before getting up.

第三章
道场闹斋

　　话说二月十五这天，功德堂里设定道场，正中央是一座荐亡台，台上供奉着崔相国的木主神位，神位前摆着各色供果，香炉烛台。在不远处还设有一座荐亡台，便是张生花五千文大钱为其父母附的一份斋。整个佛堂中幡影飘摇，香烟缭绕。法鼓金铎，似二月春雷鸣殿角；钟声佛号，如半天风雨洒松梢。

　　法本长老那日里为张生孝心所感，答应为他附一份斋，可是过后总觉得不妥，怕老夫人怪罪，便想让张生赶在老夫人小姐拈香前先举办法事，以免双方碰面。于是便让法聪去请张生。张生早已收拾停当，见法聪来请，忙随他往功德堂来。

　　法本长老见张生到了，双手合十，说道："阿弥陀佛！先生早！"
　　张生拱手一揖："长老早！"
　　法本长老忙将张生领到他父母的荐亡台前，道："先生请拈香。"
　　张生遵命从案桌上拈起三支香，就烛火点燃后，双手捧着跪在父母神位前，默默祷告："第一炷香，惟愿在世的亲人寿比南山；第二炷香，祝愿亡化的先人早升仙界，皈依三宝；这第三炷香么，保佑小生我与那莺莺小姐早些成就了幽期密约！"祝祷完毕，他虔虔诚诚地叩了三个头，方才起身。

Seeing that Zhang had finished his offering, Fa Ben came up to him, and said, "If Madame Cui asks you, please tell her that you are a relation of mine."

Zhang knew by this that Fa Ben was somewhat afraid of the imperious Madame Cui. But he was grateful to the abbot, and promised him to do as he asked.

At this moment, there was heard the clatter of jade pendants and a medley of footsteps. An elegant and dignified old lady entered the hall, surrounded by a group of female servants. It was Madame Cui. Then came a middle-aged female servant with a boy of about seven or eight years old, who were followed by Oriole and Rose.

Fa Fen hurried to greet Madame Cui: "It was remiss of me not to come out to greet you, Madame Cui. I hope you'll pardon me," he gushed obsequiously.

Madame Cui gave him a curt nod of recognition, and said, "You don't have to stand on ceremony, Abbot." She raised her head, and caught sight of her husband's tablet on the table. Immediately, tears welled up in her eyes, and she tottered over to the table, lit the candle, went down on her knees, and made a deep kowtow. As she did so she reminisced: "When my husband was alive, we had hundreds of attendants, sumptuous banquets were served, and the courtyard was as crowded as a market place every day. In the capital my husband ended his life, leaving his fatherless children and widow. Now I have for company only a few faithful servants, visitors are few and far between, and I and my children have no one to rely on. My late husband's coffin has a long way to go before it reaches its final resting place. Though I have written a letter to my nephew Zheng Heng, to whom my daughter is betrothed, up to now not a single word has been heard from him. I planned to depend on Zheng Heng in my remaining years. But no one knows where he is."

These gloomy thoughts made her burst into tears. Finally, after being comforted by some of her servant girls, she recovered sufficiently to order her young son to burn incense for his deceased father. The child, known as Merry Boy, did so, with the help of his nursemaid.

Then came Oriole's turn. Before she reached the table, tears were cascading down her cheeks. She lit three sticks of incense and planted them in the incense burner. Then she fell to her knees, and made several kowtows, sobbing.

Zhang, standing at the back of the hall, had his eyes fixed on Oriole

　　法本长老见张生拈香已罢,说道:"先生,呆会儿老夫人出来,见了这个附斋恐怕要问,你便说是老僧的亲戚好了。"

　　张生知法本惧怕相国夫人之威,又要成全自家之孝,不得已方想出此策,心中十分感激,点头道:"小生明白,多谢长老成全。"

　　此时,就听堂外一阵环佩叮咚、弓鞋杂沓之声,众人抬眼望去,就见众丫环婆子拥着一个雍容华贵的老夫人走进堂来,想必就是相国夫人了。后面跟着一个三十来岁的婆子,领着一个七八岁的男童。最后是红娘扶着小姐进来。

　　法本长老见老夫人走来,忙紧走几步迎了上去:"老夫人驾到,老衲未及远迎,请夫人恕罪!"

　　老夫人微微一颔首道:"长老不必多礼。"说着,一眼望见堂中老相爷的荐亡台,一阵哀伤涌上心间,眼中已蓄满了泪,颤巍巍地来到台前,点燃香烛,双膝跪下,深深一拜,不觉已泪湿襟袖。想当年相爷在世之日,僮仆如云,一呼百诺,门生故吏,夤缘奔走,门庭若市,是何等的煊赫;如今人亡情散,门可罗雀,孤儿寡母,无依无靠,寄寓寺院,难返故乡;今非夕比,好不凄凉。几番寄书给女婿郑恒,至今杳无音信。本想女婿是自家侄儿,亲上加亲,晚年有靠,现在却不知他在哪里?想到这里愈发伤心,不觉失声痛哭起来。哭了一会儿,丫环们上前将老夫人扶起,老夫人看了看身边的那个男孩儿道:"欢郎,去给你爹爹烧香。"欢郎由奶妈领着到神位前上香跪拜。然后红娘搀扶莺莺过来跪拜。莺莺还未走到荐亡台前,早已珠泪滚滚,她亲手点燃三炷香,插在香炉内,缓缓跪在拜垫上,嘤嘤泣拜。

　　此时立在殿角的张生早已直着双眼,对法聪低声说道:"小和

all the time. He whispered to Fa Cong: "Young monk, your piety has brought an angel down to earth."

"It is your own merit that has done that," replied Fa Cong.

Zhang ignored him, and returned to gazing at Oriole. He noticed that her lips were cherry-red, her nose jade-white, her face like the flower of the pear-tree, and her figure as slender as a willow branch. Having time to ponder her charms, Zhang found himself falling deeper and deeper in love.

Abbot Fa Ben, conducting the ceremony from the pulpit throne, also could not tear his eyes away from Oriole. Fa Zhi, the head monk, who took the lead in chanting scriptures, was so fascinated with the girl's beauty that he absent-mindedly struck Fa Cong's head instead of the bell. The acolyte forgot which candles to light, and the monk in charge of the incense had to be constantly reminded to keep his mind on his duty.

Zhang, deaf to every other sound, heard Oriole weep like a stricken bird in a deep and gloomy forest, and saw her tears running down like pearly dewdrops on flowers. He longed to call out, "Miss Oriole, please don't be too sad!" Seeing Oriole shedding tears made Zhang's heart ache unbearably. But he dared not go to comfort her. Instead, he went back to the sacrificial table set up for his parents, dropped to his knees and began to sob. What was going through his mind was: "I am alone in the world, and drifting here and there. I have neither married, nor started my career. Though I've found my true love, it seems unlikely that I will ever be able to marry her...." The more he thought about his apparently hopeless situation, the more upset he felt, until eventually he could not help wailing out loud. Everyone in the hall heard him cry out. Rose recognized the voice at once. "Oh, it's that foolish scholar!" she thought to herself. What's he doing here? Oh, I remember: They said that he had paid 5,000 cash to be included in the service. But it's too bad that he should be making such a show of himself."

Oriole too was startled by the disturbance. She stopped weeping, and turned her head to see what the matter was. Perceiving Zhang crying bitterly in front of a sacrificial table, she remembered that Rose had told her that the young scholar was to be included in the service, as he wished to burn incense to the memory of his parents. Seeing him in this state, she was impressed by what a dutiful son he was. Rose went over to help Oriole get up and return to her place.

56

尚,只为你志诚,引得个神仙下凡来。"

　　法聪也压低声音说道:"是秀才心诚,须看仔细些。"

　　张生无心理睬法聪的调侃,只顾紧盯着莺莺。只见她檀口点樱桃,粉鼻儿倚琼瑶,淡白梨花面,轻盈杨柳腰,满脸儿俊俏,浑身儿娇柔,苗条妖娆,果真是"窈窕淑女,君子好逑"!

　　且不说张生在这里如醉如痴,就是高居法座诵经的法本长老,也不禁被莺莺的美貌所折服,直勾勾地盯着小姐。再看那带头诵经的法智和尚,手中击磬,眼睛却直怔怔地看着莺莺,竟将法聪的光头当作金磬敲起来。其他诸和尚,敲钹的停了手,诵经的住了口,添香的头陀忘了添香,剪烛的行者剪灭了香烛。一时间,法鼓铙钹、金磬木鱼,没谱没点,没腔没调,乱哄哄好似正月十五闹元宵。和尚们无论老的小的、村的俏的,神魂颠倒,把个道场乱作一团。

　　张生对周围的一切视而不见,听而不闻,眼里只有小姐一人。那小姐哭声似莺啭乔林,泪珠儿似露滴花梢。张生心痛莺莺,又不能上前去劝阻,便跪到父母荐亡台前抽抽咽咽哭将起来,想自家孤身一人,湖海飘零,既未成家,又未立业,虽然目下有了心上人,可不知何年何月方能结成眷属?真正前途渺茫,不觉心灰意冷,悲从中来,恸哭失声。这哭声立即传到了在场的每个人耳朵里。红娘一听,哦,这不是那个二十三岁未曾娶妻的傻角么?那日他花了五千大钱要附斋一份,此时在场也不足为怪,只是堂堂须眉,不该如此号啕大哭。

　　莺莺一听,止了悲声,泪眼一瞥,见张生俯在一侧的荐亡台前哭拜,想起来红娘曾说过这秀才要附斋荐亡,心想这倒是个至孝之人!红娘见莺莺哭声止了,忙及时劝慰道:"姐姐休哭坏了身子。"说着将莺莺扶了起来。

Madame Cui, meanwhile, was most annoyed at the disturbance. "Where on earth did this man come from, causing this most unseemly row," she thought, with indignation. "How dare he take such liberties?" It was then that she noticed the other sacrificial table. "Good Heavens, another family is taking advantage of our funeral service to perform a sacrifice for themselves! This is most outrageous! The things some people will do to save money!" Madame Cui then demanded of the abbot what the meaning of this outrageous behavior was.

Fa Ben, startled at Zhang's outburst, hurried over to Madame Cui with a hurried explanation: "I hope Madame will forgive me. A relation of mine, who is a scholar on his way to the capital, asked me to include him in the service to show his gratitude to his deceased parents when learning that Miss Oriole would make an offering for the soul of the late Prime Minister Cui. Moved by his filial piety, I promised him I would. But I did not find time to report it to you. I am afraid I have incurred your displeasure."

Madame Cui, somewhat mollified, said, "How could I be displeased to see anyone show his gratitude to his deceased parents? Why don't you introduce him to me, since he is your relative?"

"I certainly will, Madame," said Fa Ben, breathing an inward sigh of relief. He went to Zhang, thinking that since the young man had a pleasing appearance and polished manners, there would be no harm in his meeting Madame Cui. "Sir, please restrain your grief," he urged. "Madame Cui wishes to meet you."

Zhang was delighted to hear this. He wiped away his tears, and followed the abbot to the center of the hall, where he was duly presented to the widow of the late prime minister.

The funeral service proceeded. All through the night and until dawn the next day, candles flickered, incense burned, gongs boomed and chants resounded. Zhang kept himself busy attending to Oriole as she went through the prescribed rituals.

Finally, Fa Ben recited some prayers, and burned paper money as a symbolic gift of wealth for the deceased in the afterlife. Then he said to the mourners: "It is dawn now. The service is done. Please return to your quarters, Madame and young mistress."

Madame Cui got up: "Thank you, abbot, and your monks too. You've worked hard. I'll take my leave now." So saying, she led her entourage back to their quarters in the western bower.

　　老夫人一听有男子的哭声，眉头便是一皱，心想："我家做道场，怎么平白跑出个大男人来号啕大哭，太放肆了!"循声看去，只见殿中一侧另设了一座荐亡台，看来这功德堂里尚有一家与我家同时做道场，真真是岂有此理! 要做道场，可以另选日子，何必要挤在一起呢? 老夫人想到这里，脸往下一沉，向长老问道："请问长老，那边是什么人家? 为何安排两家挤在一处做道场? 这恐怕有些不大妥当吧!"

　　法本长老听到张生哭声，又见老夫人脸生不悦之色，向自己询问，忙从法座上下来，紧走两步，来到老夫人面前应道："老夫人请宽恕老僧专擅之罪，老僧有个敝亲，是个饱学秀才，父母亡后，无可相报。听得小姐追荐相爷，触动了思亲之心，故恳求老僧附带一份斋。老僧念他一片孝心，再者也是亲情难却，故而答应了他，还未禀明老夫人，万望老夫人恕罪则个。"

　　老夫人见事已至此，埋怨也于事无补，不如顺水推舟，送个人情，便道："长老何罪之有? 难得这秀才一片至诚孝心，长老的亲戚，便是我的亲戚，何不请来相见?"

　　长老见老夫人如此通情达理，也就放心了。又想那张生仪表出众，风度翩翩，见也无妨，便说声"遵命"，向张生那边走去，到了近前道："秀才节哀，崔老夫人命老僧前来请秀才相见。"

　　张生听到老夫人相请，心里高兴，立刻止了悲声，擦干眼泪，兴冲冲随长老过来。见老夫人端坐在荐亡台旁的一张太师椅上，正上下打量自己，便眼观鼻，鼻观口，目不斜视地立在一旁。长老将身一让，手一招道："秀才请过来，这位就是崔府相国夫人，上前见过了。"

Alone in the Hall of Merits and Virtues in the gray light of dawn, all the candles and incense sticks snuffed out, Zhang pondered in anguish: "Oh, Abbot, what am I to do now? Did you see Miss Oriole cast glances towards me time after time, her eyes full of love? She must know that I am dying for love of her."

张生近前深深一拜道:"晚生参拜老夫人!"

老夫人忙起身道:"先生行此大礼,老身万万不敢当,快快平身。"

"多谢老夫人!"

此时烛影摇曳,暮霭沉沉,众和尚早已看饱了莺莺,一个个忙收拾起心猿意马,各司其职,尽心尽力做起道场来。一时间,云板敲得叮当,法鼓擂得山响,行者嚷,沙弥哨,佛号震天。张生也跑前跑后点烛燃香,在莺莺面前献殷勤,直忙到月儿西沉,晚钟叩响。

长老摇铃宣疏,荐了亡灵,烧了纸钱后,对老夫人道:"启禀老夫人,荐亡功德已经圆满,天不早了,请老夫人和小姐、公子回宅歇息吧。"

老夫人起身道:"长老辛苦了,众位师父辛苦了,老身告辞!"说着带着众人回归寺后宅院。

一旁的张生听得长老请老夫人等起驾回宅,心里好生不悦,暗道:这佛事再做一会儿也不妨,长老呀,看你哪里发付小生也!你看那小姐屡屡顾盼小生,眉梢含情,秋水盈盈,我的心绪她知道;愁种心苗,她的心情我猜得到唉!有心怎似无心好,多情反被无情恼。真个是:玉人归去的疾,好事收拾的早。

功德堂里香消雾散,烛灭灯熄,只留下张生独自发痴。

CHAPTER FOUR

Letter Summons Help

After the funeral service, Oriole found herself so restless that she could scarcely do needlework, read books, or even eat or drink. She felt uneasy whether sitting or standing. What was more, she was distressed to see that the spring was departing — blossoms were falling in showers and ten thousand petals were whirling in the wind. White butterflies and willow down mingled, so that the air was filled with snow-like flakes, and swallows packed their nests with fallen blooms. Seeing the pond full of green weeds, but with only a few flowers, Oriole felt sadder still. When Rose saw her young mistress shed tears, pensive and melancholy, at the fast disappearance of the flowers, she determined to try to cheer her up by encouraging her to go out for walks.

However, Oriole did not appreciate her attendance, and petulantly upbraided her: "I do wish you would not hover around me like a shadow all the time!"

Rose protested that it was Madame Cui who insisted on her never letting her young mistress out of her sight.

At this, Oriole felt resentment well up inside her. "My mother is far too much of a tyrant," she thought to herself. "Especially in the past two years, she has been making sure that Rose keeps a particularly close eye on me. It seems that she is afraid that I will bring disgrace to the family. The very idea!"

Meanwhile, Rose was wondering what had come over her young mistress. She was bright enough, however, to realize that this melancholy and listlessness had started soon after she had first met that foolish young scholar. "Has she fallen in love?" she wondered.

One fine day, Oriole was gazing out of the window, lost in thought. Noticing that butterflies and swallows were fluttering about in pairs, she began to shed tears. She thought, "I'm already 19 years old, and unmarried. I am not satisfied with the fiance chosen by my late father. Though my

第四章
传书退贼

　　却说莺莺自做道场归来，与先前大不相同，针线懒拈，笔墨不近，坐也不安，睡也不稳，少言寡语，情思恹恹。况值暮春天气，或一阵雨来，打落梨花片片；或一阵风吹，飘下万点红英；便是艳阳高照之日，也是蝶彩轻沾飞絮雪，燕泥香惹落花尘。眼见得池塘萍满，枝头花稀，春光去也，愈加伤感不已。红娘见小姐对花落泪，知她心中忧愁，便想方设法为其解闷开心，不是陪着去花园散步，便是登高远眺。可谓时时在意，事事用心。

　　莺莺见红娘像影子般一刻不离自己左右，有时反倒烦她，便出言相讥："好个尽心职守的丫头，与我影子一般。"

　　那红娘是个千伶百俐的人儿，听话听音，便知小姐心中生怨，不由委屈道："这不干红娘的事，是老夫人着我跟着姐姐出来的。"

　　莺莺听了，心说："俺娘好没意思！近二年来，叫个梅香行监坐守，就怕俺女孩儿家失了名分，丢了相国人家的脸面。"

　　红娘也在一旁自忖："小姐这是怎么了？往常从不愿见客人，偶然撞见个外人也远远避开，可自从见了那个二十三岁不曾娶妻的傻角，便无情无绪，魂不守舍起来，莫非是小姐对他动了春心？"

　　这日，春光明媚，莺莺倚窗沉思，见窗外蜂双蝶对，燕侣莺俦，

cousin Zheng Heng is from an official family and is the son of a minister, he is ignorant and clumsy. He is not an ideal lifetime companion. He by no means compares with that scholar who recited a verse on the other side of the wall on that moonlit night. I fell in love with him at first sight. It was a masterful verse that he composed, using fine words and natural sentiments. Besides his handsome face and fine figure, he has such a gallant air about him! I think of him alone these days. He lives so near to me — we are only separated by a wall — but how can I let him know how I feel about him?" All of a sudden, there came a knock at the door. When Rose opened it, she found Madame Cui and the abbot standing there. "Miss, my mistress and the abbot have come," she informed Oriole.

The latter stood up, tidied her clothing and came forward to greet her mother. "Ten thousand blessings, mother. Ten thousand blessings, abbot," she said.

Both Madame Cui and the abbot looked grave and flustered. As she took a seat, and before Rose could offer the visitors tea, Madame Cui started to speak hurriedly. "There is terrible news, my child," she wailed. "The bandit known as Sun the Flying Tiger has besieged the monastery with 5,000 men. He has heard that your beauty is such that it outshines that of the fabled courtesans of old. He is determined to take you by force." Thereupon, she broke into uncontrollable sobbing.

The bandits were entrenched on Mount Leishou, in Mid-River Prefecture. Sun the Flying Tiger had been an officer under Ding Wenya, military commissioner of the prefecture, but when Ding Wenya proved incompetent, he soon lost control of the troops under his command. Finally, arrears of pay resulted in a rebellion, and Sun led a ragtag army of 5,000 men in a life of wandering banditry. They burned, killed and looted in the Mid-River Prefecture wherever they went. It was he who had prevented Madame Cui and her family taking the coffin of the late Prime Minister Cui to his hometown, as he had learned that in the entourage was the prime minister's beautiful daughter. He was determined to have Oriole as his wife. He thought to himself, "An old saying goes: A hero and a beauty is an ideal combination. Just as Xiang Yu, the king of Western Chu, had Yu Ji to keep him company, so should I, Sun the Flying Tiger, have Oriole as my wife."

One day, he donned his armor, gathered his men and said in a loud voice: "Officers and men, hear my command! We are about to make a silent night march to surround the Salvation Monastery. If I can have Oriole

又垂下泪来,想自家青春一十九岁,尚待字闺中,先父为自家订下的亲事又不称心。那表兄郑恒虽说是宦门出身的尚书之子,可斗鸡走马,不学无术,实在是难托终身。哪里能与那隔墙吟诗唱和的书生相比!他那咏月新诗,做得意境高远,念得字正腔圆,强似织锦回文。他脸儿清秀,身儿俊俏,性儿温存,心儿多情,着实爱煞人。虽说他住在寺中,只隔一墙,可是有谁肯穿针引线,替我向东邻去说一声。正在独自胡思乱想,就听有人敲门。红娘过去开门,见是老夫人和法本长老立在门外,便回过头说道:"姐姐,老夫人和长老来了。"

莺莺快步出来相迎,万福道:"母亲万福,长老万福。"

就见老夫人和长老神色慌张地进门,老夫人开口便道:"孩儿,你可知道么?如今孙飞虎将五千贼兵围住寺门,道你眉黛青颦,莲脸生春,有倾国倾城之容,西子太真之颜,要掳你去做压寨夫人。这可如何是好?"说着老夫人已泪下如雨,泣不成声……

原来,这河中府的雷首山上盘踞着一股贼兵草寇,头领叫做孙飞虎,本是河中节度使丁文雅的部将。丁文雅表面上飞扬跋扈,实际懦弱无能,失去军心,部下分崩离析,各自为政。孙飞虎本来奉命镇守河桥,因一来无油水可捞,二来朝廷经常欠饷,三来受制于人,不能明目张胆为非作歹,不得自由,便想道:主将尚然不正,我独廉何为?便一不做二不休,将自家统辖的五千人马拉了出来,占山为王,在河中府一带烧杀抢掠,骚扰百姓。近来听说先相国崔珏的女儿莺莺借居在普救寺,且生得眉黛含情,莲脸生春,似捧心颦眉的西子,倾国倾城的杨妃,便日思暮想若能与天姿国色的绝代佳人颠鸾倒凤,岂不快哉?何况自古英雄配美人,西楚霸王项羽有个虞姬陪伴,我堂堂孙飞虎也当有莺莺做妻,才不枉英雄一场,风云一世!

as my wife, then the desire of my life will be fulfilled, and I will reward you all handsomely."

All his men cheered in unison. Eager for booty, they lost no time marching on the monastery. They appeared before it at dawn the next day, and began to beat drums and gongs, wave flags and shout battle cries. The monks flew into a panic.

Sun's lieutenant stepped forward, and called out to the frightened monks: "Hear this! Sun the Flying Tiger demands that you hand over the young lady Oriole within three days to be his wife. If you refuse to comply with this order, we shall kill everyone in the monastery, and burn it to the ground!"

Abbot Fa Ben was horrified at this turn of events, and hurried to inform Madame Cui. The two decided that Oriole must be told of the situation at once.

Oriole fainted on the spot when she heard the grim news. Rose and Madame Cui after a long while managed to revive her, but Oriole could not be comforted. "An old saying goes," she thought, "that beauties are often ill-fated. This is certainly true in my case. Now I can neither stay nor depart. Where can we find a friend on whom we can rely? Without my blessed father, we are completely helpless!"

At this moment, the drums started beating outside until they reached a crescendo, and the dust from the bandits' stamping feet raised a cloud of dust which floated to the heavens. Oriole stood up, and wiped away her tears, thinking: "What's the use of weeping in front of those bandits, who kill people without even batting an eyelid? I must think of a way to divert this calamity from my family members and the 300 innocent monks of the Salvation Monastery."

Madame Cui was surprised to see her daughter suddenly become so calm. Thinking Oriole was scared out of her wits, Madame Cui cried, "I am nearly 60 years old. For me, death would not be premature. But you, my dear child, are still young and not yet married. How can I bear to see you fall victim to this beast of a bandit?"

"Mother, I have an idea," said Oriole, with determination.

Upon hearing this, the others felt relieved, thinking, "Oriole is a worthy daughter of the late prime minister. She betrays no fear in an hour of danger."

"I think that all that can be done is to hand me over to the bandit, so that the lives of our family and the monks can be saved, and the monastery

主意拿定，这天披挂整齐，集合了手下兵马，吼道："大小三军听我号令：饱餐一顿，喂好战马，人皆衔枚，马尽勒口，连夜进兵河中府，围困普救寺！掳莺莺为妻，偿我平生愿足，奋勇当先者赏！"众喽罗齐声欢呼，摩拳擦掌，都想趁此番下山之机多掠些财宝女子。不日，众贼兵风卷残云，扑向普救寺。孙飞虎将营盘扎在寺前广场上，鸣锣击鼓，呐喊摇旗，将寺里僧众吓得紧闭山门，不知所措。

孙飞虎压住阵角，令一些嗓门大的喽兵到山门前叫阵，道："寺里的秃驴们听着，限你们三日之内把莺莺小姐献出来，与俺家将军成亲，则万事皆休，若有半个不字，定将这寺院一把火烧个干净！"

长老听到后吃惊不小，想此事重大，关系着小姐的名节、寺院的安危，应该速告老夫人，所以他先到老夫人处告急。老夫人听了，惊得说不出话来。法本长老见状忙道："不如速去与小姐商量。"

莺莺听罢母亲的话，惊得顿时灵魂出窍，昏厥过去。红娘连忙扶住，急用手不住地在小姐胸口轻轻揉搓，老夫人急得哭道："儿呀，你快些醒来！"莺莺经红娘一阵揉搓，悠悠缓过气来，暗思：人常言红颜薄命，红颜祸水，今日看来果是这样，眼下真是进退无门，到哪儿去寻一个能保护自家的亲人？

此时，听得寺外锣鼓震天，喊杀阵阵，莺莺将眼泪拭干，心中盘算：对付这些杀人不眨眼的强盗，便是哭干了眼泪又有何用？不能因为自家连累了崔氏一门和这普救寺的三百无辜僧人，须想个法子出来。老夫人见女儿苏醒过来，神情镇定，真让人出乎意料，以为女儿过分恐惧而吓痴了，便哭道："老身是快六十岁的人了，就是死了也不算夭寿，只是孩儿你年纪轻轻，尚未嫁人，老身和先夫未了向日之愿，死不瞑目，却如之奈何？"

protected," said Oriole.

A cry of dismay arose, and Madame Cui was heartbroken. "My dear daughter," she cried piteously, "in our family no man has ever broken the law and no woman has ever been sullied. How can I bear to hand you over to that bandit and disgrace our family?"

Oriole was convinced that what her mother said was right. She reflected, "I am a daughter of the exalted Prime Minister Cui. How could I become the wife of a bandit? It is better that I die to maintain my chastity. That way, the bandit will have no further reason to harass the monastery, and my family members and the monks will be saved!"

She turned to her mother and said, "Mother, you'd better hand me over to the bandit."

"My dear, that is out of the question! How can you suggest such a thing?" cried Madame Cui in despair.

"My dear mother, in my opinion there are five advantages to handing me over. Firstly, your safety will be ensured; secondly, the temple will escape being razed to the ground; thirdly, the priests will be able to continue to pray for me and our ancestors; fourthly, my father's coffin will be allowed to reach its final resting place; and fifthly, Merry Boy will survive to be the scion of our family...."

Merry Boy, who was clinging to Madame Cui, interrupted at this point: "Elder sister, don't worry about me. I am not afraid," he assured her.

Oriole stroked the boy's head gently, and said, "You are the only one who can continue our family line. Should I disobey the bandit and fail to make this sacrifice, the temple and our father's coffin will be turned into ashes, and the monks who offer prayers for us will be slaughtered. How could I be so selfish?"

Upon hearing this, Madame Cui was deeply grieved. "I will never hand you over to the bandit," she said crying bitterly.

With tears in her eyes, Oriole said, "Mother, you must sacrifice me. I will take my own life with a white silk scarf. You may have my dead body presented to the head of the brigands. The bandit who wants me to be his wife will surely not accept my dead body. When I die, the bandits will withdraw, and you will all be saved...."

The others were all moved by her words. But Madame Cui shook her head, saying, "No, it won't do."

"Mother, you must bear to be separated from me. You should

　　莺莺此时将心一横道:"母亲,孩儿倒有一计。" 大家一听小姐有计可退贼兵,悬着的心都放了下来,无不钦佩小姐终究是相府千金,名门才女,临危不乱,故都倾耳静听。

　　莺莺道:"只有将我送与贼汉为妻,庶可免一家儿性命,保寺院完好。"众人一听全都泄了气,老夫人原本听得女儿已有妙计,心中暗自高兴,及至听完反倒愈发伤心,哭道:"咱崔家世无犯法之男、再婚之女,你叫为娘怎舍得将你献与贼汉,却不辱没了咱相国家谱。"

　　莺莺一听母亲的话也不无道理,自家堂堂相国千金,如何肯从了盗贼? 倒不如自己死了,倒还可以保全一个清白之躯,也让贼兵没了想头,便道:"母亲,你就将女儿献与贼人吧。""万万不能。"

　　"娘啊,将女儿献与贼人,其利有五:一可以免得老母亲受摧残;二免得寺院堂殿化为灰烬;三可以保得众僧侣性命;四不惊动父亲的灵柩;五欢郎弟弟还没成人,可留崔家一条根苗……"

　　依在母亲身边的欢郎插嘴道:"姐姐,俺不当紧,俺不怕! "

　　莺莺摸摸欢郎的头,道:"你是咱崔家的香火传人。若姐姐只爱惜自家声誉,不从贼人,众僧侣就要遭杀戮,伽蓝将被焚烧,先父灵柩也要化为灰尘,爱弟之情,慈母之恩,全都玉石俱焚。"

　　老夫人闻言悲痛欲绝,道:"把你送与贼人,为娘实是不肯! "

　　莺莺含泪道:"母亲,休爱惜莺莺这一身,儿现在就白练绕颈寻个自尽,母亲可令人将儿的尸身献与那贼人,那贼人要抢的是孩儿的活身子,死了就不要了。那时,他们定会退兵,既保全了儿身清白、相府名声,也救了大家性命……" 这番话一出口,在场的人无不为之动情。老夫人连连摇头道:"不可! 不可! "

　　莺莺哭道:"娘就舍了女儿吧,就譬如当初没生我这个女儿,

convince yourself that you never had a daughter. I will have to repay all your kindness of bringing me up in the next life," the weeping Oriole begged.

Seeing both mother and daughter so heart-broken, Abbot Fa Ben said, "Madame and young mistress, don't be upset. Let us go to the Hall of the Dharma and inquire of the monks and laymen there if they have any suggestions to offer, so that we can devise a plan. An old saying goes: 'For every 10 steps there must be grass, and for every 10 houses there must be someone of talent.' In addition, Madame may offer a generous reward to anyone who is able to induce the bandits to withdraw. For another old saying goes: 'When a high reward is offered, brave fellows are bound to come forward.' What do you say, Madame?"

"That sounds reasonable, abbot. Let's go at once," Madame Cui agreed.

Both inside and outside the Hall of Dharma there were throngs of people, alarmed and bewildered. Abbot Fa Ben escorted Madame Cui and Oriole into the hall, and he stayed outside to confer with the monks. However, no one could offer an acceptable proposal.

After a long while, the abbot stepped into the hall to report to Madame Cui: "Madame, no one is able to present a completely safe plan. What can we do then?"

Oriole cut in calmly: "Mother, at this very moment you must make up your mind to sacrifice your daughter. I have an idea. You should proclaim that if anyone in the monastery is able to induce the bandits to withdraw, you will present me to him as his wife, and give him a handsome dowry."

Madame Cui at first refused to hear of such a thing, but after having thought about it for a while, she came to believe that it was a good proposal after all. Though an uneven alliance, such a match would be better than Oriole's falling into the hands of the brigand Sun. At this critical moment, it was the only thing they could do. So she said, "Abbot, please proclaim to all the priests and laymen in the monastery that if anyone is able to induce the bandits to withdraw, I will give him my daughter's hand in marriage, together with a handsome dowry."

Fa Ben went out to proclaim this offer, which aroused great interest among both monks and laymen. They all admired the beautiful Oriole, but it seemed that no one had any idea how to drive away the bandits. Eventually Zhang stepped forward. "I have a plan for getting rid of the

72

娘的养育之恩，孩儿只有来生来世再报答了。"

法本长老见她母女俩哭成一团，也没个良策，便在一旁劝道："老夫人小姐，且休伤悲了。不若咱们一起到大雄宝殿去，传示两廊僧俗人等，古人云：'十步之间，必有芳草；十室之邑，必有俊士。'老僧认为一定有高见者出来帮助出谋划策。另外，老夫人也可以立下重赏，常言道：'重赏之下，必有勇夫。'老夫人意下如何？"

老夫人听了，觉得事到如今，也只能这样了，便点头道："长老言之有理，咱们这就去罢。"

一行人来到大雄宝殿，大殿廊下已挤满了人。法本长老将老夫人小姐红娘等让进大殿，自己亲自到两廊与众僧商议。一时你言我语，也没个正经主意。半晌长老回到大殿，面呈难色，对老夫人道："老夫人，此时，谁也拿不出个万全之计来，这可如何是好？"

莺莺在一旁冷静地说道："母亲，事到如今，须横下一条心来，舍了儿这一身。孩儿别有计策，不拣何人，只要能杀退贼兵，扫荡妖氛，建立功勋，咱家倒陪家门，儿情愿与英雄缔结婚姻，结为秦晋。"

老夫人先是一个劲儿地摇头，后来又思量思量，觉着这个计策倒也可行，虽然不是门当户对，也强如给强盗做妻。便点头道："也罢，只是委屈我儿了。长老请在法堂上高叫，两廊僧俗，但有退兵之策的，老身情愿倒陪妆奁，将莺莺送与他为妻。"

长老领了老夫人之命，出殿宣唱，话既出口，犹如一石激起千层浪，引起了僧俗人等的极大兴趣，一时议论纷纷。众人皆慕莺莺小姐美貌，但是又苦于并无退贼良策，只能是望美兴叹而已。这时猛然听得有人击掌欢呼，众人循声望去，却见张生正鼓掌向前走来，边走边说："我有退兵之策，何不问我？烦请长老通报老夫人，说张珙求见。"

bandits," he declared in a ringing voice. When the abbot asked him what it was, the young man said, "Could you please inform Madame Cui that I want to see her?"

Fa Ben lost no time returning to the anxious Madame Cui in the Hall of the Dharma. "Heaven has extended a helping hand to you, Madame," he cried. "Someone has offered to drive away the bandits!"

"Buddha is merciful, Abbot! Who is this bountiful person?"

"I beg to inform you, Madame, that he is my relative who joined in the funeral ceremony. He is a young scholar by the name of Zhang Gong, and styled Junrui."

Madame Cui nodded her approval, and Oriole was delighted to hear it. She prayed in her heart: "May the brave young scholar drive away the bandits and keep us all safe."

"The young man is waiting outside. He wants to meet you, Madame," the abbot said.

"Please bring him in," Madame Cui urged.

The abbot thereupon hurried out to summon Zhang. In no more than a moment, the young man entered the hall, calmly and gracefully. He readjusted his hat, stepped forward and made a deep bow to Madame Cui.

The latter was impressed by the young man's dignified demeanor, and signaled to Rose to bring a chair for him. She lost no time explaining her dilemma: "Sir, a disaster has fallen on my family. Sun the Flying Tiger has surrounded the monastery with his troops. He demands my daughter Oriole for his wife. We, a widow and orphans, have no one to rely on. An old saying goes: 'Everyone has a sense of pity.' I hope you will rescue us from the danger. All the members of our family will be deeply grateful to you, and will never forget your kindness."

Upon hearing this, Zhang thought to himself: "What about her reported promise to give Oriole as wife to anyone who can drive the bandits away?" And he decided to keep silent until she made the offer in person.

Seeing that Zhang did not give an answer straightaway, Madame Cui immediately guessed the reason. She said, "Sir, just now I asked the abbot to convey my intention to give my daughter Oriole to anyone who can drive the bandits away."

Zhang was overjoyed to hear that it was true after all. "Do you really mean that?" he cried.

"What has been said cannot be unsaid," replied Madame Cui

法本长老于是兴冲冲地回到大雄宝殿。老夫人正在大殿上急得头发昏,忽见老和尚奔来,想是事情有着落了,忙问道:"怎样了?"

法本长老道:"禀告老夫人,已经有人挺身而出,愿退贼兵。"

老夫人大喜,双手合十,对着佛像膜拜道:"菩萨保佑。长老,不知这位恩公高姓大名?"

法本道:"此人与老夫人有一面之识,乃老衲的亲戚,前番附斋的秀才,姓张名珙,字君瑞。"老夫人听了点点头。莺莺小姐听了,芳心一动,心中暗自祈祷:但愿这书生能平安退贼。

长老道:"那秀才尚在外面,等候拜见老夫人。"

老夫人连声道:"长老,赶快出去,说老身有请。"

长老道声:"遵命。"就到大殿外去请张生。倾刻,张生潇洒自如地迈步进来,深深一揖道:"老夫人在上,晚生这厢有礼了。"

老夫人见张生风度翩翩,神彩飞扬,气宇轩昂地走进来,又大大方方地施礼,忙用手虚扶一扶道:"不敢,不敢,老身还礼了,先生请坐。"一旁的红娘搬了一个机子放在下手,请张生坐下。老夫人道:"先生,老身家门不幸,祸从天降,强盗孙飞虎兵围寺院,要抢小女莺莺。可怜我们孤儿寡母,无依无靠,古人云:恻隐之心,人皆有之。万望先生伸手援救,则老身一家感恩戴德,没齿不忘。"

张生听了老夫人的话,心想,皆是些客套,为何不提许婚之事?适才老和尚在廊下当众宣告,可毕竟不是老夫人亲口说出,多半靠不住,只是自家不好当面问明,便一声不吭,做出洗耳恭听的样子。

老夫人说完,见张生不搭腔,就明白了张生的心意,于是道:"刚才老身托长老传话,但有退得贼兵的,将小女莺莺与他为妻。"

张生心花怒放,又追问一句:"老夫人此话当真?"

solemnly. "If you can get rid of the bandits, you may marry my daughter right away. The abbot will be the witness."

Zhang stole a glance at the beautiful Oriole, then said, "If that is the case, please let my future bride go back to her chamber. I have a plan for driving the bandits away."

Upon hearing this roaming scholar call Oriole his 'future bride,' Madame Cui was somewhat displeased. But in this critical situation, she had no choice. So she said to Rose: "Escort your young mistress back to her chamber."

Oriole too, hearing Zhang call her his 'future wife,' was disconcerted, but by no means displeased. Blushing, she allowed Rose to guide her back to her chamber.

"Now, sir," said Madame Cui, turning to Zhang, "what is your plan?"

"My plan, Madame, first of all requires the assistance of the abbot."

"An old priest is no fighter. I must ask you, sir, to find someone else to replace me," said Fa Ben, shaking his head.

Zhang smiled and said, "Do not be afraid. I do not want you to fight. Just go and tell the rebel chief that it is the decision of Madame Cui that her daughter in mourning cannot marry a general in arms. Moreover, the young mistress has been pampered since childhood. It would be a great pity if she was frightened to death by the sound of drums and gongs. If he wishes to marry her, he must take off his armor, lay down his arms and withdraw as far as an arrow can fly. Then he must wait for three days, until the funeral service is finished. After she bids farewell to her father's coffin and changes into her bridal robes, she will be escorted to him. If she should be escorted at once, it would be unlucky for his army because she is still in mourning. Hurry and tell him that."

"But what is to be done after the three days?" asked the abbot.

"Don't worry, Abbot. I am prepared for that contingency."

Sun the Flying Tiger was pacing up and down, consumed with impatience. Normally he would have simply stormed the monastery and seized his prey. But as Oriole was the daughter of the late prime minister, he felt that he had to employ some finesse in the matter. Unexpectedly, one of his men came in to report: "The abbot is requesting a parley with the general." Sun the Flying Tiger strode to the front gate of the monastery. Not being a man to beat about the bush, he roared, "Listen to me, you bald-headed old ass. Send Oriole out here at once, or I'll burn your monastery to the ground!"

老夫人郑重地说道:"老身一言既出,驷马难追。先生若能退贼解围,待得太平,便立即完婚,更有法本长老作证。"

张生听了,看一眼千娇百媚的莺莺,便道:"既是这样,休唬了我浑家,请回闺房里去,俺自有退兵之策。"

老夫人见张生俨然以莺莺丈夫自居,心中略有不快,但形势紧急,迫在眉睫,也顾不许多,便对红娘道:"红娘先扶小姐回去吧。"

莺莺听张生以"浑家"相称,脸儿不禁一红,心中暗自祈祷:"但愿他有诸葛孔明之才,笔尖儿横扫了五千贼兵。"

老夫人待莺莺红娘走后,对张生道:"先生,退敌之计安在?"

张生道:"老夫人莫急,小生有计,先须用着长老。"

法本一听,头摇得拨郎鼓一般:"老僧不会厮杀,请另换一个。"

张生笑道:"长老休慌,不是要你上阵厮杀,只需你出去对那贼汉说老夫人本待将小姐即刻送与将军为妻,无奈小姐尚有父丧在身,恐与将军不利。再者,小姐自幼娇生惯养,何曾见过这等阵势,若是鸣锣击鼓惊死了小姐,岂不可惜?将军果若诚心做女婿,可按甲束兵,退出一箭之地,待三日功德圆满,脱了孝服,定将小姐倒陪妆奁送与将军。我想那贼汉断无不允之理,长老快快去说。"长老心想这是什么良策,便脱口道:"三日后又当如何?"

张生道:"这个不劳长老费心,小生自有妙计。"

法本长老只得带了法聪到山门处的钟楼上,开窗叫道:"各位好汉通报一声,请孙将军前来答话。"孙飞虎正在军帐中暴跳如雷,依他素日习性,早就撞破山门冲进寺中,将小姐抢来。只因莺莺是相国千金,须得客气些,听得喽兵来报,寺中钟楼上有个老和尚要自家去答话,便大踏步出了军帐,怒冲冲来到山门下,冲着钟

The abbot adopted a conciliatory tone, saying, "Please do not be hasty, General. I am ordered by Madame Cui to inform you that...." He repeated what Zhang had said.

It sounded reasonable to Sun, who said, "All right. But if Oriole is not sent to me when three days have passed, I will have you all put to death. In the meantime, go and tell Madame Cui what an excellent son-in-law I will make." Then he turned to his men, and shouted, "Withdraw as far as an arrow can fly!" Thereupon, all the bandits retreated out of sight.

Returning to the hall, the abbot reported to Zhang: "Sir, all the bandits have withdrawn. But if Oriole is not sent to him after three days, Sun says, he will kill all of us."

"Sir, what's your plan? Please tell me," the anxious Madame Cui urged Zhang.

The young man said calmly: "I have a friend whose name is Du Que and whose title is White Horse General. He is now in command of an army of 100,000 men, guarding the Pu Pass. He and I are sworn brothers. If I write a letter to him, he is sure to come to our rescue. But the pass is about 40 miles away. Who can deliver a letter there for me?"

"If the White Horse General comes, we need not be afraid of even a hundred so-called Flying Tigers," Fa Ben said, with great enthusiasm. "Sir, I have a disciple called Hui Ming," he went on. "He is most trustworthy. He can deliver the letter for certain."

"Excellent," exclaimed Zhang. "Please have a writing brush and some paper brought to me."

Upon being presented with the four treasures of the study, Zhang took up the brush and began to write. In only a few minutes, the letter was ready to be dispatched.

However, the abbot said, "There is one thing, young sir, which I forgot to mention. This man Hui Ming is a person of peculiar temperament. Remiss at reciting the scriptures and praying, his predilections are fighting and drinking. If you ask him to send the letter, he is sure to refuse, but if you can challenge his perverse spirit, nothing will deter him from going."

Zhang thought to himself: "He sounds like a real stubborn donkey. He will refuse to go when asked, but will volunteer to go if he is beaten. Well then, I will lead him a merry dance today!" Then he folded the letter, put it in an envelope, walked out of the hall and proclaimed to the assembled monks and laymen: "Sun the Flying Tiger has the monastery

楼上的法本吼道:"咄,那老和尚听着,快快送莺莺小姐出来,万事皆休,若有半个不字,本大王一把火烧了你个普救寺,叫你片瓦不留。"

长老稳稳心神,壮着胆子道:"将军,请暂息雷霆之怒,且听老僧说来。"接着就照张生所教说了。

孙飞虎听罢,觉得倒也在理,便道:"既是如此,就宽限你三日,三日后若不送来,我叫你人人皆死,个个不存。你对老夫人说去,像这般好性儿的女婿,到哪里去找,就让她快些招了俺去吧。"说罢转身号令道:"大小三军,后退一箭之地!"贼兵潮水般退了下去。

长老回到殿上,对张生道:"秀才,贼兵已经退了,三日后不把人送出去,便都是死。"老夫人也问道:"先生之计倒底是什么?"

张生不慌不忙地说道:"小生有一故人,姓杜名确,号为白马将军,现统十万大军,镇守着蒲关。小生写一封书信去,此人必来救我。只是此间离蒲关四五十里,写了书信,怎么派人送去?"

长老道:"若是白马将军肯来,何虑孙飞虎。秀才只管写信,俺这里有一个徒弟,法名惠明,此人定能将信送出。"

张生听罢,便道:"如此,拿笔砚来。"

法聪忙将文房四宝呈上,张生提笔在手,笔走龙蛇,倾刻写成一封书信,道:"长老,信已写好,就叫惠明师父去吧。"

长老道:"适才老僧尚未把话讲完。我这个弟子惠明,平日不念法华经,不礼梁王忏,就喜欢喝酒厮打。如今若求他去,他定然不肯,须将言语激他,他一定肯去。"

张生心想:"这倒是一头犟驴,牵着不走,打着倒回。我张珙今日倒要逗逗你。"便将信叠好,装进信封,出了大殿门向廊下高呼道:"强盗孙飞虎现兵围寺院,我等岂能坐以待毙?小生有一故友,

surrounded. How can we just sit here waiting for death? I have a friend known as the White Horse General, who is guarding the Pu Pass. I have written a letter begging him to come and save us from the brigands. Who dares to take it to him?" All the monks and laymen looked at each other, none of them daring to volunteer. "Isn't there a single brave man in such a large monastery?"

"I will go!" All of a sudden, a tall, strong monk came forward, with an iron club in his hand and a sword in his belt. "Sir, give me the letter. I'll take it to the White Horse General."

Zhang was inwardly delighted, but pretended to be quite unimpressed with the offer. He spoke deliberately: "This is no trifling matter. If this letter should fall into the hands of the bandits, we will all be put to death and the monastery razed. Are you sure you have the courage and skill required to deliver such an important letter?"

Hui Ming patted his chest proudly and said, "The quiet life in this monastery irks me, and a meatless diet is not to my taste. I am eager to pit my wits and strength against these 5,000 churls who have dared to be so insolent."

"Are you sure that you really have the courage to go?" the abbot asked.

Hui Ming retorted with a flurry of oaths that nothing would stop him delivering the letter, least of all a handful of ragged robbers. And so, Hui Ming departed on his mission. He left the monastery by the back door, where only a handful of brigands had been left on guard. They shot arrows at the monk as soon as they saw him, but he simply knocked the arrows aside with his iron club. When this incident was reported to Sun the Flying Tiger, he thought that one of the monks must have panicked and fled. So he gave it no more heed.

Hui Ming reached the Pu Pass before daybreak. He found General Du reviewing his troops. Granted an audience with the general, Hui Ming reported as follows: "The Salvation Monastery is surrounded by Sun the Flying Tiger and his 5,000 men. He demands that the daughter of the late Prime Minister Cui be handed over to him. I have brought a letter from Zhang Junrui, who requests Your Excellency to come to their rescue as soon as possible."

"Hand his letter to me," ordered General Du, frowning.

Hui Ming took it out, and handed it to the general.

General Du opened the letter and read: "Zhang Gong, your former

人称白马将军,镇守蒲关,我已修书一封求救于杜将军,这可是生
死攸关的大事,谁敢突围前去蒲关投书?"大殿下僧俗众人,你看
我,我看你,都不吭声,张生又道:"难道这偌大一座寺院,就没有
一个有胆量之人?"

"我敢去!"猛然间炸雷般的一声吼,不待众人回过神来,一个
豹头环眼,膀大腰圆,身高八尺的莽和尚,手提一根精铁打磨的乌
龙棍,腰挂一柄戒刀,分开众人,直冲到张生面前,伸出蒲扇般的
大手,道:"秀才,将信拿了来!洒家送与那白马将军去!"

张生见惠明被激出来了,心中十分欢喜,却故意道:"此事可
非同小可,万一你冲不过去,信落在贼人手中,这一座寺院便要生
灵涂炭,你有没有这个能耐,敢也不敢呢?"

惠明将胸脯拍得山响,道:"师父休问俺敢不敢,俺问你们是用
不用咱?洒家只为了你这济困扶危的书生和那能文能武的杜将军,
定将这信送到!"说罢提了铁棍,背了戒刀,从后山门出去,趁着天
黑,一溜风地冲了下去。孙飞虎的大部分人马扎在寺前,寺后只派些
喽兵巡逻。巡哨喽兵见从寺内冲出个大和尚,便开弓放箭一阵乱
射。惠明舞动大铁棍拨打箭矢,不一会儿,就闯了过去。喽兵赶紧禀
报孙飞虎,孙飞虎不以为意,心想,逃走个把和尚无关大局。

惠明突围后,不敢怠慢,撒脚如飞直奔蒲关而去。天刚放晓已
到蒲关,正赶上杜元帅阅兵点卯。惠明到得辕门,对守门军卒道:
"军爷为洒家通报一声,普救寺僧人惠明有急事求见元帅。"军卒
忙入内禀报。杜元帅听禀后令军卒立即宣其进见。惠明闻宣,即与
军卒一同来见元帅。杜元帅道:"不知和尚到我军中所为何事?"

惠明道:"元帅容禀,今有贼寇孙飞虎作乱,将半万贼兵围困

fellow student and sworn brother, kowtows to you over and over again and presents this letter to Your Excellency General Du. Two years have passed since we met last, and I can never forget the windy and rainy nights when we shared lodgings together. On my way from my home to the capital, I came to Mid-River Prefecture and intended to pay you a visit. But the journey had so exhausted me that I fell ill. Now I am better, and there is no cause for worry. I have taken up quarters in a quiet monastery which has unexpectedly became a place of calamity. The widow of the late Prime Minister Cui brought her husband's coffin to the monastery on her way to its last resting place. But a bandit nicknamed Sun the Flying Tiger has besieged the temple with 5,000 men, determined to seize the late prime minister's beautiful daughter. Anyone who could see their pitiful and helpless state would feel indignant and try by all means to drive the bandits away. But, to my regret, as I am a mere scholar unable even to truss a chicken, I can do nothing to help them, even if I sacrifice my life. Then I thought of you, who have command of a huge army of gallant troops. You who follow the tradition of the heroes of old are in no way unworthy of them. I am now in grave danger, along with the kin of the late prime minister and the monks of this monastery. I beseech you to come to our aid as soon as possible. We would be as grateful to you as a fish stranded on dry land to the person who brings it water from the far-off West River. The late Prime Minister Cui, though in the eternal shades below, would also be grateful to you for your timely assistance. Anxiously awaiting your timely arrival, Zhang Gong salutes you again."

After having read the letter, General Du flew into a rage. "I heard that Ding Wenya lost control of the prefecture and that Sun the Flying Tiger has been running amok, causing all kinds of havoc," he thought to himself. "But this is outrageous! There is nothing else for it but to punish that scoundrel of a bandit once and for all." He said to Hui Ming: "I understand that the matter is urgent. Go back to the monastery and tell them to be of good cheer, for I will set off this very night to relieve the siege."

"The monastery is in a perilous situation," said Hui Ming. "I beg Your Excellency to make all haste."

"Don't worry. Though I have not received an imperial order, it is my duty to save the people from disasters. Adjutant, select 5,000 of my crack troops, and tell them to get ready to march to the Salvation Monastery in Mid-River Prefecture. Their mission is to crush Sun the Flying Tiger."

普救寺,欲劫故臣崔相国之女莺莺小姐为妻。有游客张君瑞,奉书令贫僧拜投于将军麾下,欲求将军以解倒悬之危。"

杜元帅听罢,剑眉紧锁,道:"把书信拿来。"惠明从怀里掏出书信,双手呈上。杜元帅拆开展看,只见上面写道:"珙顿首再拜大元帅将军契兄麾下:伏自洛中,拜违犀表,寒暄屡隔,积有岁月,仰德之私,铭刻如也。忆昔联床风雨,叹今彼各天涯。客况复生于肺腑,离愁无慰于羁怀。念贫处十年藜藿,走困他乡;羡威统百万貔貅,坐安边境。故知虎体食天禄,瞻天表,大德胜常;使贱子慕台颜,仰台翰,寸心为慰。辄禀:小弟辞家,欲诣帐下,以叙数载间阔之情;奈至河中府普救寺,忽值采薪之忧,不及径造。不期有贼寇孙飞虎,领兵半万,围困山寺,欲劫故臣崔相国之女,小弟之命,亦危在旦夕。兄长倘不弃旧交之情,兴一旅之师,上以报天子之恩,下以解苍生之危,使故相国虽在九泉,亦不泯将军之德矣!鹄候来旌,造次干渎,不胜惭愧!伏乞台照不宣!张珙再拜。"

杜确看罢,不由怒从心头起,前些时已风闻丁文雅失政,孙飞虎不守国法,剽掠黎民,因不知虚实,未敢造次兴师,如今孙贼竟于光天化日之下,大动干戈,强抢官眷,侵扰佛家圣境,实在是不加讨伐,不足以平民愤。他对惠明说道:"情况本帅已经明了,和尚你可前行,本帅点齐兵马,随后就到。"

惠明道:"时间紧迫,将军是必要快些。洒家先行一步。"

杜元帅道:"和尚放心,虽说并无圣旨,但将在外君命有所不受。解救黎民于水火也是本将军份内之事。中军官,传我将令:大小三军,速点齐五千人马,人尽衔枚,马皆勒口,星夜出发,直捣河中府普救寺,剿灭孙飞虎。"

Before long, General Du, resplendent in full armor and mounted on his white charger, set out at the head of 5,000 picked troops for the monastery. Sun the Flying Tiger was taken by surprise and, after a brief skirmish, captured. The other bandits fled or surrendered.

It had been a time of great tension and worry for the people in the monastery. After Hui Ming had left to seek help from General Du, Zhang tried to instill hope into everyone by assuring them that his sworn brother would come galloping to their rescue in no time at all, and give that villain Sun the Flying Tiger his just deserts. Nevertheless, he was consumed with worry: If anything should go wrong, all the people in the temple would die and he himself would lose a beautiful wife.

Two days of the three-day respite that Sun the Flying Tiger had given them had dragged by, when Madame Cui and the abbot came to see Zhang. As soon as she entered the room, Madame Cui said, "The letter was sent two days ago, but no reply has come yet. There is only one day left before that monstrous brigand comes to claim my poor Oriole. What are we to do?"

At that moment, a deafening commotion was heard outside the gate of the monastery. Zhang was beside himself with joy: "My sworn brother must have arrived," he cried out in exultation. "Abbot, let's go to the Bell Tower and take a look." So saying, he clambered to the top of the Bell Tower, followed by the abbot. From there, they saw that the area in front of the gate was a bedlam of dust and smoke, and hundreds of battle flags waved. Among them there was a large one on which the surname of the general, Du, was embroidered. The enemy were in great disorder, and before long they laid down their arms, fell to their knees and surrendered. Sun the Flying Tiger was captured alive. General Du had won a great victory.

Zhang and the abbot hurriedly descended the tower, and opened the gate of the monastery to welcome General Du. Zhang made a deep bow to Du: "It is so long since we parted that our meeting seems like a dream," he gasped.

General Du saluted him in return. "I am so pleased to see you," he said. "May I ask why you did not come to pay me a visit?"

"I happened to be indisposed, and besides I was busy trying to protect Madame Cui and her entourage. I hope you will forgive me."

Upon learning that the bandits had been eliminated, Madame Cui was so relieved that tears ran down her cheeks. She immediately ordered

惠明走了，中军官传令出去，蒲关上人喊马嘶，只一会儿功夫，三军集合完毕，整装待发。披挂整齐的杜元帅骑一匹白龙马，一声号令，带领五千人马直奔河中府而来。夜幕初降，已来到普救寺，把正在大帐中做着成亲美梦的孙飞虎和他的贼兵围了个铁桶一般，不消半个时辰，就将孙飞虎生擒活拿。众喽兵见大王被捉，也无心恋战，纷纷缴械投降。

再说普救寺内，自惠明连夜突围以后，全寺上下都提心吊胆，盼望着官军早些打来，真正是度日如年。张生表面上谈笑风生，安慰着不时前来问讯的僧众，一副稳操胜券的样子，其实心中也如翻江倒海，生怕事情万一有个闪失，断送了一寺僧俗的性命不说，自家还白搭个娇滴滴的娘子。

这天，老夫人与长老来张生处商议，进门便道："下书已两日，如何还不见回音？"

张生正欲安慰两句，就听寺外金鼓大震，喊杀连天，不禁喜上眉梢，哈哈大笑道："莫不是俺哥哥到了。长老你我速去钟楼观望。"说罢，拉了法本长老急忙爬上钟楼，临窗眺望，只见烟尘滚滚，旌旗蔽日，当中一杆帅旗上绣着一个斗大的"杜"字，果然是盟兄来了。再看贼营中人仰马翻，乱做一团，不一会儿，又见贼兵纷纷缴械，孙飞虎被擒，官军大获全胜。

张生、长老忙下楼大开山门迎接杜元帅。

张生长揖道："自别兄长台颜，一向有失听教；今日一见，如拨云睹日，快何如之。"

杜元帅抱拳道："贤弟见外了，敢问贤弟，因甚不至为兄军帐？"

a banquet prepared to celebrate the victory of the White Horse General.

General Du bowed to Madame Cui, and said, "I had not taken proper precautions against these bandits, and as a consequence you have been needlessly troubled, for which I should bear the blame."

"I will not hear of it, General Du," said Madame Cui. "We were in such a hopeless situation that we deemed death inevitable. It is due to you that we are able to continue our lives. I do not know how to repay your kindness."

"It is merely my duty," said General Du.

Zhang explained: "I wrote you that letter to ask you to rescue us from the siege, because Madame Cui had declared that if anyone were able to induce the bandits to withdraw, she would present him with her daughter as his wife."

Du Que said, "My heartiest congratulations and best wishes to you." Then he said to Madame Cui: "Zhang proposed a plan for defeating the bandits, and you, Madame, made a promise. If you keep your promise, your beautiful daughter and this talented young man will make an ideal couple, I think."

Madame Cui smiled, saying: "I am afraid my daughter is not worthy to be his wife. Anyway, I have still other arrangements in mind. Let dinner be served."

Du Que declined, "It is unnecessary to go to such trouble for what was merely a matter of duty. Besides, as the bandits have just surrendered, I must go and deal with the matter. Moreover, I am in charge of guarding the Pu Pass, so I must not be away from my regular post for too long. But I will certainly come on the wedding day of my sworn brother. I hereby take my leave. I hope you, Madame Cui, and Zhang will forgive me."

"I dare not detain you, lest it should interfere with your duties," said Zhang.

They saw the White Horse General off at the gate of the monastery, and together with all his officers and men returned to the Pu Pass in triumph.

The horsemen leave the temple 'mid the cymbals' sound;
The soldiers sing victorious songs, for the Pu Pass bound.

After they had gone, Madame Cui said to Zhang: "We are deeply grateful for your invaluable help. From now on, you should no longer

张生道:"小弟原本是要去拜谒的,无奈小疾偶作,不能动止,所以失敬,还望兄长海涵。"

老夫人得知贼兵剿灭,激动得老泪直流,忙吩咐厨房安排酒宴,为白马将军庆功。

杜元帅见了老夫人,施礼道:"杜确有失防御,致令老夫人受惊,切勿见罪是幸!"

老夫人道:"将军言重了,老身母女的性命,皆是将军所赐,真不知如何补报才是?"

杜元帅道:"不敢不敢,此乃末将职责所在,何须言报。"

张生一旁言道:"此次愚弟作书请兄长兴师解围,皆因见老夫人受困言道:凡退得贼兵者,以小姐妻之。"

杜确一听,笑道:"既然有此姻缘,真是可喜可贺!"又对老夫人言道:"张生建退贼之策,老夫人面许结亲,若不违前言,淑女可配君子,倒是天作之合呀!"

老夫人微微一笑道:"恐小女有辱君子,配不上张先生。杜元帅,老身已令人备下酒宴,请入席。"

杜确道:"不必了,贼寇尚有余党未尽,末将还得剿灭,况军务在身,不能久离蒲关,异日贤弟洞房花烛,愚兄定来庆贺。就此告辞,请老夫人和贤弟勿罪!"

张生道:"兄长军务繁忙,小弟也不敢久留,有劳台候了!"

众人将白马将军送出山门,官军人马得胜回关。正是:

马离普救敲金镫,人望蒲关唱凯还。

送走白马将军,老夫人对张生道:"先生大恩,老身馀生不敢忘记,自今日起先生休在寺里住了,老身命人为先生寺内养马,先

dwell in your present quarters, but move to our library, which has been cleaned and made ready. You may move in at any time. A special dinner will be prepared tomorrow, and Rose will come to invite you. I insist on your presence." So saying, she and her maids left.

Zhang was overjoyed at this turn of events. He said to Fa Ben: "I thank you for everything you've done for me. But I am not sure about my marriage."

"It is all settled," said Fa Ben. "Oriole is destined to be your wife. You're very lucky. The disaster posed by the bandits has turned out to be a blessing after all! Get ready to be a bridegroom."

In high spirits, Zhang packed his things, and moved to the library of Madame Cui's quarters.

生则来家内书院里安歇。书院已收拾好了，便搬过来。到明日略备草酌，着红娘来请，先生是必前来一会，别有商议。"说罢由丫环扶着回去了。

张生听了，心花怒放，对法本道："小生之事全仗长老了，也不知小生的亲事如何？"

长老道："这事不是明摆着么？莺莺定是君妻。好你个有福的秀才，只因兵火至，引起雨云心。准备着做新郎去吧。"

张生满心欢喜，收拾行李到西厢书院去住。

CHAPTER FIVE

The Promise Broken at a Family Feast

Now that the danger had passed, Madame Cui started to have second thoughts about her rash promise. First, Oriole had been betrothed to her nephew Zheng Heng at the express wish of her late husband, and she feared to face the wrath of her elder brother if she broke off the engagement. Second, and just as important in her eyes, was the fact that Zhang came from a family that gone down in the world, and as yet he had no official title. All that day, Madame Cui was so perturbed that she could neither eat nor rest. She was forlorn and tearful as she thought, "When my husband was alive, he took care of everything. Now I have to make all the decisions. As a widow and an orphan, I and my daughter are prey to bullying by all sorts of rascals."

Nevertheless, to thank Zhang for his help, Madame Cui had a feast prepared in the guest hall of the monastery, and sent Rose to the library to insist on Zhang's attendance.

Rose thought to herself: "Madame does not need to worry about that; the foolish young man is only too eager be anywhere where Oriole is likely to be present." So off she went to find Zhang.

After the White Horse General had crushed the bandits headed by Sun the Flying Tiger, Zhang moved to live in the Western Bower at the invitation of Madame Cui, fully expecting her to keep her promise and allow him to marry Oriole. He had already been informed of the upcoming banquet, and was unable to sleep that night for excitement. Long before dawn, he woke his page, and started to wash and dress. With the help of the page, he scrubbed himself till his skin shone, using up two pieces of soap and two buckets of water. He then put on a black silk hat and a scholar's robe of pure white with a gilt-buckled belt. No sooner was he ready than he heard a knock at the door.

"Who is it?" he asked eagerly.

"It's me," said Rose.

第五章
家宴赖婚

　　却说老夫人自打张生修书,惠明送信,白马将军解围后,虽说心里一块石头落了地,却又思谋起来,悔不该前几日一时情急,听信了莺莺之计,当众言明,谁有退兵之计,便将女儿倒赔妆奁,与人为妻。一则,莺莺是相爷在世时许与侄儿郑恒的,自家怎能违背夫命,私自毁约,日后回到京师也不好与兄长见面;二则,张生家道中落,尚在白衣之列,门户不当,贻人笑柄!只因有此两条,老夫人整日里食不甘味,寝不安眠。想起丈夫在时,万般皆由其作主,何须自己费一点儿心思,如今客居萧寺,孤苦无助,方受人欺凌,惹出诸多麻烦。每思至此,不由得潸然泪下,啜泣无声。……

　　这日,老夫人为酬谢张生解围救命之恩,特意于中堂上安排好一桌酒席,命红娘到书院去请张生。

　　再说张生自白马将军解围之后,应老夫人之请,住进西厢书院,就等老夫人实现诺言,自家与莺莺早成婚配。昨日红娘告诉他老夫人将请他今日赴宴,把他欢喜得一夜未眠。今晨起来,叫醒琴童,侍候梳洗,皂角用两个,水也换了两桶,洗得浑身上下清清爽爽,头戴揩刷得光亮亮的软脚乌纱小帽,身穿浆洗得干干净净的白襕衫,腰围黄橙橙的角带,正在坐立不安之际,听到敲门声。张

93

Zhang invited her in, and lost no time asking, "Rose, why is Madame Cui holding this banquet?"

Rose smiled mischievously: "In the first place," she said, "it's being held to celebrate our escape from danger. And in the second place, it's being held to thank you for your kindness." Then, after a moment of hesitation, she said, "Oh, I almost forgot! It's also being held in honor of your marriage to Oriole."

Zhang was overjoyed. He made a deep bow to Rose and said, "Tell me, is it really decreed by fate that I am to marry Miss Oriole today?"

"Indeed it is," Rose said. "A truly happy union cannot be decreed by mortals, but by fate alone. Just as plants and trees grow together naturally in the spring breeze, you and Miss Oriole are meant for each other."

Zhang was even more pleased than ever. "Rose, will your young mistress be faithful and true?" he asked.

"You two will have to decide for yourselves who is faithful and who is not. But I want to warn you, Master Zhang, that you must be gentle to my young mistress tonight. She is very delicate."

Scarlet-faced, Zhang replied, "Don't worry, Rose; I have a tender heart. Now, tell me what arrangements have been made and how the chamber is decorated."

"The bed curtains are embroidered with a full moon and pairs of love birds, and there are two screens of the finest jade adorned with images of peacocks. There is also an orchestra, which will play *The Song of Happy Union*. You must prove yourself worthy of these lavish preparations tonight."

Though Zhang knew that Rose was making fun of him, he was pleased to hear this. But then it occurred to him that he had nothing to offer as a gift for the bride and her family. He mentioned this worry to Rose, who assured him that in the circumstances, with no other guests at the banquet — not even the abbot — the normal etiquette would not apply. So it was with a feeling of relief that he allowed Rose to depart.

No sooner had the door closed behind her than Zhang fell into a pleasant reverie. He imagined his reception by Madame Cui. "She will say, 'Here you are, Master Zhang. You and my Oriole will make a happy couple, so drink a cup of wine each before you retire to the bridal chamber.' Then we two will go to the bridal chamber. After Oriole

生心中激动,一边忙问:"是谁来了?"一边把门打开。

"是我。"门扇开启处,红娘含笑立在门前。

张生连忙深深一揖道:"拜揖姐姐,今日老夫人为何摆下筵席?"

红娘调皮地一笑道:"这一来么,为了压惊;二来么,为了谢恩。不请街坊,不会近邻,避开了和尚,单请你先生,和莺莺匹聘。"

张生听罢,心花怒放,欢天喜地地躬身一揖道:"小生自寺中见了小姐之后,日思夜想,不曾想今日得成婚姻,这难道不是前生注定?"

红娘忙道:"说得在理,姻缘的确非人力所为,皆是天意所定。"又道:"这人一事精,百事精;一无成,百无成。世间草木本无情,可自古云:地生连理木,水出并头莲。秀才和小姐便是一对儿。"

张生听了心中愈加喜欢,又问道:"红娘,你家小姐果有信行?"

红娘道:"谁无一个信行?你俩个今夜里自去对证。我说张先生,张秀才,今宵你和小姐成婚,可要温柔些,我家小姐娇软得很。"

张生脸一红道:"红娘姐姐尽可放心,小生自会怜香惜玉。敢问你们那里有什么景致?"

"俺那里准备了鸳鸯同销帐,孔雀春风软玉屏,有凤箫象板,锦瑟鸾笙,演奏着《合欢令》,真正是落红满地胭脂冷,秀才可不要辜负了良辰美景。"

张生听了心下欢喜,知是红娘戏他,猛地惭愧起来,道:"小生书剑飘零,无以为彩礼,这可怎么是好?"

红娘道:"秀才休要自寻烦恼,凭着你举将能、灭寇功这两件,就足可抵得上红定聘礼了。老夫人之命,足下不须推辞,和贱妾立马便行,才是正理。"

张生道:"红娘姐姐请先行,小生随后便到。"

removes her clothes, we shall be as close as fish and water. In the dim lamplight, I will gaze on her black hair cascading over her shoulders, and her star-like bright eyes will gaze into mine. I can see them now — the jadeite-colored quilts and the socks embroidered with mandarin ducks!"

Meanwhile, Madame Cui was wracked by impatience, waiting for Rose and Zhang. When Rose finally returned and reported that the young man was on his way, she sent her to fetch Oriole.

Zhang appeared soon afterwards. He straightaway saluted Madame Cui: "Madame, I have come to pay my respects to you."

"Please don't stand on ceremony, Master Zhang," Madame Cui said. "If it had not been for your timely assistance, we would not have lived to see this happy day. As you know, I have had a banquet prepared for you. Although it can in no way requite you for your splendid service, I hope you will not scorn this little token of my appreciation."

Zhang waved his hand dismissively, and said, "You are too kind, Madame. It is said that on the good fortune of one person often depends that of multitudes. The defeat of the bandits was due to your good fortune, Madame. Nothing else is worthy of mention."

"Your modesty becomes you as a scholar," his hostess rejoined, and urged him to be seated at his ease.

But Zhang continued to play the role of the self-effacing scholar in front of his prospective mother-in-law: "I should remain standing, Madame, as prescribed in the ancient rites. How could I presume to sit down in your presence?"

"Do you not know the old saying that politeness is not as good as compliance? Please sit down, sir," Madame Cui urged him.

"You are right, of course. I will take my seat." Zhang said, ingratiatingly, and proceeded to do as he was bidden.

Madame Cui ordered wine to be brought, personally filled a cup, and offered it to the young man with both hands, a singular honor.

Zhang, feeling extremely flattered, stood up to receive it, and said, "This is very kind of you, and though I'm not used to drinking wine, I remember that it says in *The Book of Rites* that younger people should unhesitatingly obey the orders of their elders." He thereupon drained the wine cup.

　　红娘走后,张生忙把门关上,闭着眼睛设想一会儿拜见老夫人的情景:老夫人定然说张生你来了,饮几杯酒,去绣房里和莺莺做亲去罢。自家到了卧室内,和那莺莺解带宽衣颠鸾倒凤,同谐鱼水之欢,共效于飞之乐。灯下观她定然是云鬟低坠,星眼微朦,被翻翡翠,袜绣鸳鸯,到时不知性命如何? 张生飘飘然自我陶醉在幻想中。

　　再说老夫人,把酒筵摆在中堂上,单等红娘请张生来。正心焦着,见红娘一人回来了,不待她开口,红娘便上前禀道:"老夫人,张生叫红娘先行一步,他随后便来。"

　　老夫人听禀,点点头道:"如此,你去请小姐过来,与张先生行礼。"红娘一听老夫人吩咐,便应声"是",飘也似地出了中堂。

　　红娘刚走,张生就到了,一见老夫人,便上前施礼道:"老夫人在上,晚生这厢有礼了。"

　　老夫人忙道:"先生不要拘礼! 前日若非先生,焉得有今日,我崔家满门之命,皆是先生救活,今日聊备小酌,请先生勿嫌简慢。"

　　张生摆手道:"老夫人客气了,书云:'一人有庆,兆民赖之。'孙贼之败,皆老夫人之福。万一杜将军不来,我辈皆无免死之术,此皆往事,不必挂齿。"老夫人道:"先生真乃谦谦君子,快快请坐。"

　　张生愈发谦恭道:"晚生侍立座下,尚然越礼,焉敢与老夫人对坐!"老夫人道:"先生不必客气,常言道'恭敬不如从命。'但坐无妨。""既然如此,晚生就谢坐了。"

　　老夫人冲一旁侍立的丫头道:"将酒来。"自家双手捧杯,递在张生面前:"先生请满饮此杯。"

　　张生见老夫人如此盛情,受宠若惊,恭恭敬敬站起来道:"晚生多谢老夫人抬爱,虽说晚生不善饮酒,但《礼记》云:'长者赐,少

97

He then poured wine for Madame Cui. These formalities completed and all the normal polite formulae exhausted, an oppressive silence reigned in the banquet hall. Zhang sat fidgeting, and wondering when Oriole and Rose were going to put in an appearance.

All this time Oriole was doing embroidery in her room, unaware of the banquet which had been arranged. She was startled when Rose burst into the room, crying, "Miss, miss!"

Oriole paused in her work, and asked the girl: "What is it, Rose? What are you so excited and flustered about?"

"Madame is entertaining a guest in the main hall of the monastery. She asks you to join them."

"Go and tell my mother that I'm not feeling well today, so I beg to be excused."

Rose pouted. "You'll be sorry you refused to go when you find out who the guest is," she murmured.

"I don't care who he is; I won't go."

"That's what you say now, but wait till you hear who the guest is!" Rose said, archly.

"All right, tell me who it is."

"None other than that young scholar!" cried Rose triumphantly. "He isn't married, remember?"

Oriole was delighted to hear this, but she was careful not to make this obvious to Rose. She thought to herself: "Master Zhang was the one who saved us from those savage bandits. The least we can do to show our appreciation is to hold a feast for him." She thereupon told Rose that, on second thoughts, she had decided that it was only right and proper that she should attend the banquet after all.

Upon hearing this, Rose teased her, saying, "Whenever the young scholar is mentioned, you become agitated. Aren't you ashamed?"

Oriole blushed and muttered, "Stop talking nonsense, Rose," aiming a playful slap at her.

Rose then helped her mistress to wash and dress herself, taking extra pains so that she would look her best when she met Zhang. She combed her hair into an elegant pile on the top of her head, and in it inserted a green peony which had just been picked from the garden, holding it in place with a gold hairpin. Oriole then painted her eyebrows, powdered her face and put on some lipstick. Then she changed into a pink jacket

者不敢辞。'晚生从命就是。"说罢端起酒杯，一饮而尽。

张生饮过酒，也为老夫人斟了一杯酒道："晚生为老夫人敬酒一杯，以介眉寿。"老夫人听了暗自惊叹，这秀才用《诗经》中"为此春酒，以介眉寿"之句，倒也吉庆，便微微点头，端起酒杯抿了一口。张生与老夫人应酬一番，不觉心生疑惑，为何不见俺那浑家与红娘？

不说张生心中生疑，单表莺莺小姐今天尚不知母亲宴请张生。正在闺房中刺绣，忽听得红娘气喘嘘嘘连声唤道："小姐，小姐！"

莺莺停针望去，见红娘脸红气喘撩帘进来，以为发生了什么事，忙问道："红娘，为何这般大呼小叫的，发生了什么事？"

红娘笑道："老夫人在中堂请客，令我来请小姐出去哩。"

莺莺听了，一颗悬着的心这才放下，心想：母亲请客，我出去做甚？便冷冷道："红娘，你去回老夫人，说我身子不适，不能出去。"

红娘冲她扮了个鬼脸道："姐姐不出去，过后可不要后悔啊？""我有什么可后悔的？""小姐啊，你先别嘴硬，你可知道请的是谁？告诉你吧，请的是那二十三岁不曾娶妻的张秀才呀。"

莺莺闻听，芳心大悦，心想：若不是张生交游广，朋友多，换个人怎能退了干戈！是他救了俺全家命，礼当敬重他，早该摆酒筵款待他。不由得脱口而出："若是请那张生，扶病我也当走一遭。"

红娘听了，挤眉弄眼冲着莺莺直刮脸道："一说请那酸丁，姐姐就来了精神，羞也不羞。"

莺莺话一出口，顿知失言，不禁霞飞双颊，绷着粉脸道："小蹄子，看我不撕了你那张嘴。"说着，佯装做势要打。

红娘忙道："姐姐息怒，饶过奴家这回吧，你还是快快梳妆打扮做新娘吧。"说着命小丫头准备洗脸水，待莺莺净面后，先将一

decorated with small flowers and with buttons down the front, a silk skirt, and a pair of pink shoes with a phoenix pattern. When her toilet was complete, she looked a veritable vision of loveliness.

"Your face looks so delicate that it seems even a puff of wind would hurt it, Miss!" said Rose. "What a lucky man Zhang is! My Young Mistress, you were indeed born to be the wife of a grand official!"

Though inwardly pleased, Oriole frowned and said, "How you talk, Rose! I have nothing but a friendly interest in that kind young man. Wife of a grand official, indeed!"

But Rose kept on teasing her: "Both of you are lovesick for each other. And now, finally, your long days of suffering have come to an end."

Oriole lowered her head, and thought to herself that Rose was absolutely right.

Suddenly, Rose thought of something, and said, "Miss, isn't it strange that your mother did not decide to throw a big banquet and invite relatives and friends, if you and Zhang are to be married today? It isn't like a wedding banquet held by a prime minister's family at all!"

"Rose, you don't understand the situation," Oriole said. "My marriage to the impoverished young scholar will bring a financial burden upon our family. My mother's only concern right now is to save money."

"Yes, I suppose you're right," Rose agreed. "Well, now that you are ready, let's go to the main hall."

As soon as Oriole entered the hall, her eyes met Zhang's arduous gaze. She hurriedly looked at the ground, trotted up to her mother, and paid her respects to her.

The sight of Oriole in her holiday best, and groomed and made up like a bride brought a frown to her mother's brow. "My dear," she said coldly, "Now pay your respects to your elder brother."

All the people in the hall were aghast at hearing Madame Cui refer to Zhang as Oriole's "elder brother."

The two words, indeed, hit the young man like a thunderbolt. Oriole was only prevented from falling down in a swoon by Rose, and she thought, "My mother must have decided to call off the marriage. Everyone knows that a sister and brother may not marry."

Rose herself was flabbergasted too.

With a vacant smile, Madame Cui said, "Rose, bring heated wine for your young mistress to fill the cup of her elder brother."

This was duly done. Sad and indignant, Oriole lifted the wine cup

头乌云梳理成望仙高髻,髻侧簪上一支刚从花园摘来的绿牡丹,
紧傍牡丹的是一支金步摇。脸上轻抹蛾黄,淡匀脂粉,贴了花钿,
点了樱唇,描了柳眉,愈显得春山涵黛,秋水盈盈。又换了一件淡
粉洒花对襟通衲衫,系一条七破暗彩绫裥裙,脚穿一双淡粉红凤
头小弓鞋,走起来婷婷袅袅,回眸一笑,百媚俱生。

红娘在一旁看了啧啧笑道:"瞧俺姐姐这张嫩脸儿,真真吹弹
得破。张生好福气也。姐姐天生一个夫人模样。"

莺莺心里得意,口中嗔道:"小蹄子休要信口开河乱嚷嚷,谁
知他福命如何? 不过么,像俺这样的,也做得个夫人了。"

红娘笑道:"往常你二人害足相思病,今天可算是熬到头了。"

莺莺娇羞地低头思量:"红娘这鬼丫头说得对。"

红娘又突然说道:"小姐,今日这事有些蹊跷,若是给小姐和张
生成婚,老夫人怎生不做大筵席,会亲戚朋友,全不像咱相府人家办
喜事的排场?"莺莺道:"红娘,你不解老夫人的心思。俺娘只图省钱,
不想张罗。"红娘点头道:"也许是吧,姐姐,咱们赶紧去吧。"

莺莺来到上院中堂,一进门便与张生那火辣辣的目光相遇,
不禁芳心狂跳,忙垂了眼帘,轻轻走到老夫人面前,深深福了一福
道:"孩儿参见母亲。"老夫人见女儿喜盈盈盛装到来,微微蹙了一
下眉,转而不动声色地道:"我儿快去拜了你那救命的哥哥。"

老夫人这一声"哥哥"出口,顿时惊呆了所有在场的人。张生就
觉得仿佛是被人当头给了一闷棍,暗叫:"呀,这口气可不妙哇!"莺
莺有如受了雷击一般,向旁一歪,被红娘扶定,心说:"不好,俺娘变
了卦! 如何叫我做妹妹拜哥哥,谁不知兄妹不能成婚配?"

红娘心上也是一惊,暗忖:"不得了啦,老夫人要赖婚! 这事可

slowly, but did not fill it. Her mother urged her: "My dear daughter, you must present a cup of wine to your elder brother."

At this moment, Zhang stood up, and declined the wine. "I beg to be excused," he said. "But I cannot drink any more wine."

Oriole understood his reticence very well. With tears in her eyes, she ordered Rose to remove the wine. She wanted so much to pour out her feelings to Zhang, but with her mother at her side it was impossible. Although her lover was but a foot from her, he seemed as far off as the Milky Way. How could they have expected that the delight enjoyed beneath moonbeams would turn into empty dreams?

Madame Cui flew into a rage at this turn of events, yelling, "Rose, fill a cup of wine, and let your young mistress to present it to her elder brother."

Rose cursed Madame Cui in her heart: "You're an unfeeling old woman who is only interested in riches and decorum. You care nothing for the tender feelings of young people in love!"

"Rose!" Madame Cui shouted, seeing the girl hesitate.

"Yes, Madame," Rose answered. She filled a cup and gave it to Oriole, who immediately pushed it aside, spilling the wine. Angry that Oriole refused to bend to her will, Madame Cui ordered, "Rose, conduct your young mistress to her bed chamber."

Rose did as she was bidden.

Seeing Oriole leave in sadness and anger, Zhang felt as if a knife were piercing his heart. He went up to Madame Cui, and made a bow, saying, "Madame, I wish to consult you on a matter which I am not sure if it is proper to ask you about."

"If you have anything to say, please speak out," Madame Cui replied with a self-satisfied smile.

"Do you still remember the promise you made when the bandits were surrounding the monastery?"

"Ye..es...."

"At that time, you promised to give the hand of Miss Oriole to anyone who could make the bandits withdraw. Is that not what you said? Hence I wrote that letter in haste, requesting General Du to come and save the lives of your whole family. When Rose came this morning to summon me, I thought you were going to fulfill your promise, and I was to marry your beautiful daughter. I cannot for the life of me imagine what has made you suddenly change your mind and call me her 'elder brother.'

做得太不像样了,没些些信义,这两个相思又有得害了。"

老夫人见莺莺倚着红娘呆立不动,嘴角溢出一丝冷笑,道:"红娘,将这热酒斟上,莺莺快去与你那救命的哥哥敬酒!"

莺莺悲愤交加,慢慢捧起酒杯,却迈不出一步。老夫人在一旁催促道:"儿呀,快去给你那救命哥哥敬酒!"

张生见状,忙起身推辞道:"小生量窄,委实不能饮了。"

莺莺明白,这杯中便是玉液琼浆,他也饮不下这"妹敬哥"的破婚酒。莺莺粉泪盈盈,对红娘道:"红娘接了这杯盏!"有心对张生倾诉衷肠,怎奈老母亲在座,又如何启齿?真是咫尺如天涯,谁曾想月底西厢,变做了梦里南柯。老夫人见莺莺把酒杯递与红娘,心中大恼,便对红娘道:"你再去斟一杯,让小姐敬与哥哥。"

红娘心中骂道:"你个积世的、狠心的、无情无义的恶婆婆。看来佳人自古多薄命。"

"红娘!"老夫人厉声唤道。

"哎!"红娘忙应道,急又斟了一杯酒,递与莺莺,背过老夫人悄声说道:"姐姐这可怎生是好?你敬也不敬?"莺莺也不说话,只用手一推,那酒都洒在地下。老夫人见莺莺执意不肯敬酒,知女儿恨自己赖婚,硬着心肠道:"红娘,送小姐回卧房里去。"

红娘应声"是",便将酒杯放下,扶起莺莺就往外走。

张生见莺莺含悲带恨地走了,真是心如刀绞,看着老夫人气不打一处来,稳了稳心神一拱手道:"老夫人,小生有一事不明,想请教于您,不知当讲不当讲?"老夫人含威不露,微微一笑道:"请教不敢当,先生有话,但讲无妨。"

"老夫人可还记得贼寇相迫,兵围寺院之时,您亲口所言?当

103

But, if you think I am unworthy of being your son-in-law, I request that you allow me to leave your presence for ever, here and now."

Madame Cui heaved a deep sigh, and said, "It is you to whom we owe our lives. However, my daughter was betrothed to my nephew Zheng Heng when my late husband was still alive, and I have written to summon him here. So you see, it is out of the question for you to aspire to my daughter's hand. Now I think the best thing I can do is to reward you with a large sum of money, so that you may select another lady of noble birth and that both of us may carry out our matrimonial arrangements to our own satisfaction."

Zhang said: "What use have I for your money if Oriole is denied me? An old saying goes, 'There are gilded palaces in books, and there are beautiful ladies in books.' I will now bid you farewell." So saying, he turned to leave.

"Pray do not be so hasty, sir. I fear the fumes of the wine you drank have gone to your head," said Madame Cui. "Rose, see the young gentleman to the library. Tomorrow we will discuss the necessary arrangements."

Leaning on Rose, Zhang stumbled from the hall, his head reeling from the wine, but more so from the shock he had just received.

"Alas, Miss Rose, I am afraid that I was born unlucky. I am doomed to pass lonely nights. And to think that I expected to pass this night in the bridal chamber!"

Rose uttered some words of comfort, but Zhang fell to his knees before her: "Miss Rose," he cried, "you must know that since I first set eyes on your young mistress, I have neither eaten nor slept properly. My sufferings have been unbearable. I thought I would marry Miss Oriole today. But to my utter consternation, Madame Cui changed her mind! I am devastated with grief."

"Please do not despair, sir," Rose interrupted him. "I will do my best to help you."

This caused a ray of hope to gleam in Zhang's heart. "But what can you possibly do to save a lovelorn wretch like me?" he asked, pleadingly. "But if there is anything you can do, I will be grateful to you to the end of my days."

Rose said, "I have noticed that you possess a lute, so I suppose you are adept at playing that instrument. Now, my young mistress also loves the music of the lute. She will go with me to the garden to burn incense

时老夫人说，但能退贼者，以莺莺妻之。如此小生方挺身而出，作书与白马将军，请兵前来，得免老夫人一家之祸。今日小生奉命前来赴宴，原以为有喜庆之事，不知老夫人何见，竟以兄妹之礼相待？小生非图哺啜而来，婚事果若不谐，小生即当告退。"

老夫人无可奈何地长叹一声道："先生纵有活我之恩，无奈先相国在日已将小姐许下老身侄儿郑恒，且老身也作书赴京师唤他去了。如若他来了，这事可怎生是好？老身也是夫命难违，不得已而为之。还请先生救人救出水，帮人帮到底。老身绝非薄情寡义之人，莫若多以金帛相酬，先生只管拣豪门贵宅之女，别求姻缘，不知先生台意如何？"

张生道："既是老夫人不肯将小姐许配于我，小生又何慕金帛？岂不闻：'书中自有黄金屋，书中自有颜如玉？'小生今日便告辞了。"说罢转身就走。

老夫人忙道："先生暂且住着，你现在喝多了。"又冲着刚送小姐回来的红娘吩咐道："红娘，快扶将哥哥去书房里歇息，到明日咱别有话说。"

红娘过来扶着张生往外走，一出门，张生便软下来，步履蹒跚，如同醉了一般。红娘嗔怪道："先生也该少吃一盏。"

张生道："我吃什么来？"又长叹一声喃喃道："想小生命悭，有分只熬萧寺夜，无缘难遇洞房春。"

红娘劝道："先生凡事当想开些才是。"

张生听到红娘这一声劝解，真是百感交集，双膝一软，跪在红娘面前道："红娘姐姐明鉴，小生为小姐废寝忘食，魂劳梦断，常忽忽如有所失。自寺中一见，隔墙酬和，迎风待月，受无限之苦楚。刚

tonight. When you hear me give a cough you should start playing your lute. I will observe her reaction closely, and at the right moment I will tell her your sentiments. I will let you know early tomorrow morning what she says."

Zhang shed grateful tears and thanked the girl over and over again. But Rose cut him short, and departed to attend to her young mistress.

刚以为能成就婚姻,却不曾想老夫人又变了卦,使小生智竭思穷,此事何时是了?姐姐怎生可怜见小生,将此意申与小姐,令她知我这一片赤诚之心,小生便是死了也无怨了。现就当着姐姐之面解下腰中之带寻个自尽,倒也干净。"说到此早已泪下如雨。一边动手解带,一边呜咽道:"可怜刺骨悬梁志,今作离乡背井魂。"

红娘伸手阻拦道:"街上好贱柴,烧你个傻角!你倒死了个痛快!秀才休惊,此事自有红娘为你谋之。"

张生听了,神情为之一振道:"姐姐计将安出?小生当筑坛拜将。"

红娘道:"俺见先生有囊琴一张,想你必善于此。俺小姐深慕于琴,颇通音律。今晚俺与小姐同到花园内烧夜香,秀才但听咳嗽为令,动手操琴,将你之心愿弹出,俺小姐定能知晓。到时看她说些什么言语,若有话说,明日红娘定来回报。"

张生感激涕零道:"多谢红娘姐姐为小生指点迷津。"

红娘道:"罢了,罢了,时候不早了,怕老夫人找我,我回去了。"

CHAPTER SIX

The Love Message of the Lute

Zhang was delighted with Rose's suggestion, and could not wait for nightfall. He passed the time tuning his lute and preparing himself for a new expression of his love for Oriole. As the drumbeat announced the onset of the night hours, he sat before the instrument and addressed it thus: "Oh, lute, you have accompanied me through thick and thin for many years. I depend on you for the success of tonight's venture." Then he turned his eyes heavenward, and prayed, "Oh, Heaven, graciously lend me a fair breeze to waft the music of my lute to Oriole's ears."

Meanwhile, Oriole was sitting dejected in her bed chamber, devastated by her mother's harsh treatment of Zhang and despairing of ever finding happiness. Unexpectedly Rose suggested, "Miss, how bright the moon is tonight! Let's go and burn incense in the garden. There we can pray for better fortune."

Oriole sighed, and wailed, "My mother's mind is made up. What's the use of burning incense now?"

"The Moon Goddess is always ready to lend an ear to the petitions of young lovers, Miss," said Rose, coaxingly.

Oriole was reluctant to go, feeling that everything was hopeless, but eventually she allowed herself to be led out into the garden by Rose.

Just as the girl had said, it was a brilliant moonlit night. The moon itself dazzled the eye, and fragrant flowers, wafted by the breeze, filled the air like a snow shower.

Rose lost no time setting up the incense table. Oriole picked up three incense sticks, and said in her heart: "Oh, Moon, what can I do now? *The Book of Odes* says, 'Good in the beginning, but usually bad in the end.' Mother, you are the widow of the late prime minister. How could you go back on your word? Why should something well begun be in the end undone? Zhang will now be to me but a dream lover. And I shall be to

第六章
君瑞琴挑

　　却说张生听了红娘所献计策,心中复又升起希望,单等天黑月儿升,好以琴声传情,表心达意。当下先令琴童将几案拭净,瑶琴摆好,自家洗手焚香,调弦定音,安排停当。就听钟楼击鼓撞钟,夜色降临。张生正襟危坐,双手抚琴,暗自祈祷:"琴呵,小生与足下湖海相随数年,今夜这一场大功,都在你这神品、金徽、玉轸、蛇腹、断纹、峄阳、冰弦之上,浩浩苍天呀,待会儿子怎生得一阵顺风,将小生这琴声吹入俺那小姐玉琢成、粉捏就、知音的耳朵里去呵。"

　　红娘为张生献计后,匆匆回到闺房,见莺莺一脸不悦,知她为老夫人赖婚之事伤心烦闷,便欢声道:"小姐,今晚月色好明,咱花园里烧香去来。"莺莺怏怏道:"唉,事已无成,烧香何济?"

　　"姐姐,事成不成在天,心诚不诚在己,想是苍天不负有心人,咱一味地敬她月神娘娘,总会有好报的。再者说,便是不烧香,到花园里散散心也好。"说着红娘连扶带搀将莺莺搡出闺房。

　　挑帘但见云敛晴空,冰轮乍涌,残红纷纷,香阶乱拥,果真好月色也。红娘手脚麻利地设好香案,莺莺拈起三烛香,抬头望月,心中暗道:"月儿呵,你是团圆了,俺可怎生是好?《诗经》曰:'靡不有初,鲜克有终?'可你身为堂堂相国夫人,却做了个言而无信,有

him merely a beloved image. I can only long for him in vain. We cannot meet, except in sweet dreams. Oh, my heart breaks when I think how I was attired in my bridal array! So close to happiness!"

Seeing Oriole wipe away tears, Rose said, "Look, there is a halo around the moon! It will probably be windy tomorrow."

"It will probably rain tomorrow also," Oriole sighed. "There is the moon and the wind in Heaven, but there is not a happy thing on Earth."

"What do you mean, Young Mistress?" asked Rose, puzzled.

"There is also the halo of the moon on earth too," replied Oriole. "A lovely jade-like face is locked up within embroidered curtains of lace. It fears to be profaned by the touch of a mortal hand. Just like the Goddess of the Moon traversing the sky from west to east, all alone. Her lover cannot visit her palace again, which is surrounded by screen on screen, lest she be seen and her heart above be moved to love."

Hearing this, Rose thought to herself: "Oh, Miss, you are seriously lovesick! Zhang must be waiting in great anxiety on the other side of the wall. I'd better give him a signal." Then she coughed lightly.

Zhang on the other side of the wall heard the cough, and a surge of excitement ran through him. He straightaway began to play his lute. The melody flowed in an exhilarating medley of sounds. Now like the clash of cavalry sabers; now soft like flowers dropping into smoothly flowing streams. At one time high like the cry of a crane in a breezy moonlit sky; at another, low like lovers' whispers. Oriole, who had been in no mood to appreciate the moon, was fascinated by the beautiful music.

Rose was happy to see her young mistress listening to the strains of the lute with great attention. She said, with a smile: "Please stay here and listen to the music, Miss. I am going to see if your mother needs me."

Oriole gave an absent-minded nod.

Rose's voice was heard by Zhang, who immediately thought to himself that he must seize this chance when Oriole had been left alone to express his love for her. He remembered that an ancient scholar had wooed a beautiful lady by playing a tune called "The Phoenix Seeks His Mate." So he began to play this old romantic tune, at the same time singing:

始无终，害得张生他做了个影儿里的情郎，女儿我做了个画儿里的爱宠。到如今，只落得女儿我心里念想，嘴里空说，梦中相逢。谁曾想娘啊，您主人情重，让女儿与张郎兄妹相称，把一段婚姻便葬送了。"想到此珠泪夺眶而出，怕红娘窥见，便急以袖拭泪。

红娘见小姐对月发痴，便道："姐姐，你看月亮外有圆圈。"

莺莺道："那是月阑，又叫月晕，谚曰：月晕而风。也可能是雨。"转而又悲叹道："风月天边有，人间好事无。"

红娘眼睛一转，问道："姐姐这是何意？"

莺莺道："你看这人世间，也有月阑。多少淑女佳人，深锁绣帏之中，生怕有人挑逗起春心。遥想那月宫嫦娥，西落东升，有谁陪同？这云层，好似我这里罗帏数重，怕嫦娥心动，因此围住了广寒宫。"

红娘心中暗道：你这相思可害得不浅，想那张生早就隔墙等得猴急，待我快些给他个信号。便提高嗓子一连咳了三声。

再说隔墙张生听到了红娘的信号，顿时精神大振，轻舒双臂，十指翻飞弹奏起来。琴声悠悠传出。只听那琴声雄壮时，如铁骑刀枪铿锵；幽咽时，若落花流水潺潺；高亢时，像风清月朗鹤唳长空；低吟时，似儿女喁语小窗中。原本无心赏月的莺莺，被这悦耳动听的琴声拨弄得耳聪目悦，如痴如醉。

红娘见莺莺专注听琴，抿嘴一笑，连连轻唤几声。莺莺都顾不得答应，只顾侧耳倾听，便道："姐姐你这里听，我瞧老夫人去，一会儿便来，"莺莺胡乱答应了一声，仍然凝神倾听琴声。

再说张生听得红娘言语，知莺莺就立身窗外。这真是天赐良机，此时不表明心迹，更待何时，便将弦改过，奏起《凤求凰》的曲子来。和着琴声，张生又唱道："有美人兮，见之不忘。一日不见兮，

"There is a lady I cannot forget, I swear.
Not a single day but she puts me in despair.
Hither and thither see the phoenix fly,
Seeking his mate low and high.
Alas! Where is the lady fair?
I cannot find her anywhere.
I sit forlorn and strum my lute
To help relieve my pain acute.
When will you give your word
To the wandering phoenix bird?
When will we two soar,
Wing to wing, evermore?"

Oriole's heart was touched by the exquisite pathos of the tune and the bitter longing expressed by the words. Suddenly, the music stopped, and she heard the player lament from the other side of the wall: "Alas, I, Zhang Junrui, am unlucky in love. Your mother may be ungrateful and unjust, but you, my dear Miss Oriole, how can you deceive one who believes in the sincerity of your feelings?"

But Oriole could not answer him. Now the moonlight seemed to shed wan beams of desolation all around, and what had been a delightful vista was now a heart-breakingly lonely scene.

From then on, Oriole languished in her bed chamber, unable to apply herself any more to her needlework. At the same time, Zhang found himself unable to concentrate on his studies. Both of them pined for each other, not knowing what to do to end their heartache.

One day when Oriole went to pay respects to her mother, Abbot Fa Cong came to tell them that Zhang was sick. Hearing this, Oriole was so distressed that she had difficulty restraining her tears. Upon returning to her room, she prevailed upon Rose to go and see how Zhang was faring, enjoining her to be as discreet as possible.

Rose tiptoed up to the outside of the young man's quarters, and peeped through a tear in the paper which covered the window. She saw the young scholar lying fully dressed on his bed. He looked pale and sickly. His breath came in labored gasps. Rose knocked lightly on the window frame.

"Who is there?" Zhang asked, in a creaking, strangled voice.

"The spirit of lovesickness," answered the mischievous Rose.

思之若狂。凤飞翩翩兮,四海求凰。无奈佳人兮,不在东墙。张弦代语兮,欲诉衷肠。何时见许兮,慰我彷徨?愿言配德兮,携手相将!不得于飞兮,使我沦亡。"

却说莺莺听得入了迷,心中暗叹:"张郎弹得是好啊,琴声美妙,歌词哀怨,情真意切,凄然如白鹤唳天。"就听张生长叹一声道:"唉,想我张君瑞好生命悭,老夫人做得个出尔反尔也就罢了,小姐,怎么你也说谎呢?"莺莺却无法诉说,只能是对着窗棂默默叹息。抬头望月,冷月无声,愈发凄凉难耐。

却说自那夜听琴后,张生莺莺两个人各自在居所长嘘短叹。一个糊途了胸中锦绣,睡昏昏不待观经史;一个珠泪涟涟,懒洋洋无力弄针黹,两下里梦魂牵绕相思难忍,不知如何才好。

这日,莺莺到老夫人处问安,恰巧长老使法聪传过话来说张生病了。莺莺听了心疼万分,险些当着娘的面滴下泪来,勉强回到绣阁,思来想去,还是得叫红娘去书院探望一遭。便吩咐一个丫环去老夫人处唤红娘回来。红娘听说小姐召唤,也不知有何事,便停下手中活计回绣阁来,进门就问:"姐姐唤我何事?"

莺莺霞飞双颊,嗫嚅半响道:"你与我望张生走一遭。"

红娘出来,一路往书院而来。来到书院,静悄悄的无些儿声息。近窗前,将窗纸润破,朝里一看,往日里风流倜傥的白面书生现已是面黄饥瘦,气血涩滞,声息微弱,和衣而卧,睡在榻上,罗衫皆是褶皱。红娘看了张生这副狼狈相,自言自语道:"今日俺方信了这世间的'情义'二字。"说着拔下头上金钗轻轻敲打门环。

张生正在朦朦胧胧似睡非睡之时,听到门环声响,忙睁眼问道:"是谁?""是我,散相思的五瘟神。"

Pleased to hear Rose's voice once more, Zhang struggled to his feet and opened the door. "Have you brought a message, Rose?" said the young man eagerly. "Did your young mistress say anything to you last night after having listened to me playing the lute?"

Rose pretended to be angry: "My young mistress has been feeling uneasy since she heard your lute playing last night," she said. "She does not attend to needle and thread, nor take any care of her appearance. She sheds tears as she gazes upon the flowers, and is sad and weary as she looks up at the moon. Her appetite has vanished, and all day she thinks only of you, Master Zhang. "

"Since Oriole loves me, it is worth suffering from lovesickness," thought Zhang. Then he said out loud: "Miss Rose, I have a letter to send to your young mistress; may I trouble you to deliver it for me?"

"Oh, no," Rose protested. "A letter is too dangerous! What if somebody should find it later? However, I can pass on a message by word of mouth."

But Zhang balked at this suggestion. "My message is only for your young mistress' ears," he explained.

"Even so, I am not sure how my young mistress will react upon receiving an intimate letter," Rose said. "Maybe she will pull a long face and say, 'Rose, from whom is this message you dare to bring to me? You little minx! How dare you be so impudent?' Then she will tear the letter to pieces without even reading it. What could I do then?"

"I'm sure you will think of a way to get your young mistress to read the letter."

"You're good at manipulating others."

"I will give you a handsome reward for your trouble," Zhang offered.

But this had the opposite effect to what he had intended. "What a disgraceful thing to say!" snapped the girl, flaring up. "Don't think that just because I'm a maid I can be bought to further your sordid little affairs!" And she turned to leave.

"Don't be angry, Miss Rose," the young man pleaded. "It was silly of me to say such a thing. Please forgive me."

"If you say, 'Have pity on poor, lonely me, I pray,' I may try to find a way for you. But if you presume on your wealth, I'll be treacherous and ruthless," Rose said.

"As you say, Miss Rose, have pity on poor, lonely me, I pray. Will

　　张生一听便知是红娘，真正是喜出望外。想是小姐有话让她捎来，便下地趿鞋过来开门。红娘闪身进来道："俺小姐想着风清月朗夜深之时，令红娘来探你。"张生忙请红娘坐下，道："姐姐既来，小姐必有言语，不知那日你家小姐听琴后怎样？"

　　红娘佯怒道："只因午夜调琴手，引起春闺爱月心。我家小姐回去后，整日价无心拈针，脂粉懒添，观花落泪，对月伤情，茶饭少咽。"

　　张生心想："果然小姐钟情于我，我这番相思也算值得。"便对红娘道："小姐既有见怜之心，小生有书信一封，烦请姐姐代劳捎与你家小姐，也好让小姐知小生肺腑。"

　　红娘连忙摆手道："不行，不行，捎个口信尚可，万一事情败露，白纸黑字留下凭据，可不是耍的。"

　　张生道："此事天知地知，你知我知，绝不会败露的。"

　　红娘道："即便是瞒过众人，可俺小姐的性情捉摸不定，万一她见了你的书信翻了面皮，看也不看，将信扯了，那该咋办？"

　　"你若是费心尽力帮时，自有主意让小姐看信。只要姐姐鼎力相助，日后小生一定多以金帛相酬。"

　　不待张生把话说完，红娘"呸"地啐了一口道："好你个馋穷酸徕没意儿，卖弄你有家私，莫非俺红娘到此是图谋你的钱财东西来了？你也太门缝里看人将人看扁了吧。俺虽是个丫头，可做人的志气不少，你留着你的钱财另找人去，我走了。"说着起身就走。

　　张生知道自家伤了红娘的心，忙起身相拦道："姐姐息怒，小生一时性急，说错话了，小生焉敢小看姐姐？姐姐饶恕小生吧。"

　　红娘缓了口气道："看你这副可怜相。若你说可怜见小子只身独自，俺到愿帮你，若再说出那财大气粗的话来，可别怨俺翻脸无情。"

that do?" Zhang said.

"Yes, that's better. Now write your letter, and I will deliver it for you," Rose said, smiling.

On hearing this, Zhang felt an enormous sense of relief. He lost no time preparing paper, a brush and ink. Even though she could not read, Rose was impressed by Zhang's penmanship. She could not help saying, "How nice your handwriting looks! Read it to me, please."

Zhang was most reluctant to read out his love letter to Rose, but as he was eager to stay in her favor he had little choice. So, after a great deal of throat clearing, he began:

"With a hundred salutes, Zhang Gong humbly presents this letter to Miss Oriole. The other day your mother rewarded my service, slight as it was, with undeserved unkindness. When the feast was over, I could not fall asleep. So I played my lute to express my helpless feelings and so that you might know that both the lute and its player would soon be gone forever. I am taking advantage of Rose's visit to send you a few lines in the faint hope that you, who are so near and yet so far away, may have pity on me and come to my rescue. While awaiting your decision, I add a poem which I hope you will condescend to read:

Gnawed by lovesickness,
I play on my lute.
Spring is happiness.
Can your heart be mute?
Love can't be disobeyed.
Of vain fame make light.
Pity the flower's shade;
Don't miss the moon bright."

Though Rose could not understand the elegant language this missive was couched in, she thought that its contents were charming.

"Miss Rose," Zhang enjoined her, "You must be very careful not to let this letter fall into the wrong hands," he said as he handed it to her.

"I will take this letter for you, sir," Rose said. "But you must not forget your ambition to become a top scholar and a high official. You should concentrate now on your studies, and be prepared to postpone

张生忙道："好姐姐,可怜见小子孤身独自,客居萧寺,怎生拉扯小子一把。"

红娘"扑嗤"笑道："这还差不多,你快写来,我与你捎将去。"

张生见红娘转怒为喜,一颗悬着的心方落到肚里,忙研墨醮笔,展笺于案上,提毫悬腕,刷刷点点,宛若行云流水。红娘立在一旁,大睁两眼,不识一字,只见张生笔走龙蛇,字写得好看,不由脱口赞道："写得真好呀! 快读一遍我听。"

张生听了头一句,以为红娘称赞自己的信写得好,尚有些不好意思。待红娘第二句话出口,方知这丫头不识字,心略放宽些,思量这情书如何给人念得,可是不念,又怕得罪了这位穿针引线的雁使,便恭恭敬敬地说道："姐姐果真想听,小生就献丑了。"说着清了清喉咙,朗声念道："珙百拜奉书芳卿可人妆次:自别范颜,鸿稀鳞绝,悲怆不胜。孰料老夫人以恩成怨,变易前姻,岂得不为失信乎? 使小生目视东墙,恨不得腋翅于妆台左右,患成思渴,垂命有日。因红娘至,聊奉数字,以表寸心,万一有见怜之意,书以掷下,庶几尚可保养。造次不谨,伏起情恕! 后成五言诗一首,就书录呈:

相思恨转添,谩把瑶琴弄。乐事又逢春,芳心尔亦动。

此情不可违,芳誉何须奉? 莫负月华明,且怜花影重。"

红娘虽听不太懂,但大意到也明白,便点头道："哦,先写下几句问寒问暖的客套话,再叙相思之情,最后是五言八句诗,不错,不错!"张生听了红娘这番品评,双颊潮红,不好意思地连连摆手道："见笑,见笑。"说着将信封好交与红娘道："可千万在意呀!"

"放心罢学士,这简帖儿我给你送去,今后先生当以功名为念,可休为这儿女情长堕了志气,你须将那双偷香手,准备着蟾宫

your happiness until you have succeeded in passing the civil service examination."

These words made Zhang think, "Though Miss Rose is young, she has lofty thoughts. She is really a girl of exceptional ability."

"You must take good care of yourself, sir. Don't let worries take a toll on your health," said Rose.

"I will bear in mind your kind words. But as to the letter, dear Miss Rose, you must be careful."

"You can rest assured, sir," said Rose. "I will be very careful to convey it straight to my young mistress. I'll also use my own eloquence to convey your true feelings and get my young mistress to pay a visit to you."

Rose thereupon tucked the letter in her sleeve and left.

All this time, Oriole was waiting impatiently for Rose to return with news of Zhang. Night fell, and there was still no sign of the girl. Oriole went to bed, but tossed and turned all night long, and only fell asleep at daybreak.

It was not until after Madame Cui had finished her breakfast that Rose found time to go to see Oriole. She opened her young mistress' bedroom door, and saw that the room was lit by a single candle which had burned low. She gently drew aside the bed curtain, and gazed on Oriole's tousled hair, with its hairpin askew.

Rose took out Zhang's letter. She thought, "It would be better to put it in her make-up case, and let her find it herself." So she put the letter in the case, leaving a corner of it sticking out, so that it would be quickly noticed. She went to stand behind the screen, and coughed.

Oriole woke up. She rose, stretched and sighed deeply. "Who's there?" she called out. But there was no answer. She got out of bed and sat at her dressing table. The first thing that caught her eyes was the corner of the letter sticking out of her make-up case. She took it out, opened it and read it. As she did so, her heart beat faster and her cheeks turned red. She read it over and over again. Then it suddenly occurred to her that Rose must have put it where she had found it. "I'll bet she is peeping me and giggling inwardly right now," she thought. "Rose!" she cried. "Come out from wherever it is you are hiding!"

"What can I do for you, Miss Oriole?" Rose said, emerging from

去折桂;也休教那淫词儿沾污了好端端一手龙蛇字。常言道:好男
儿当有鸿鹄之志,可休为了翠帏锦帐一个俏佳人,耽误了你这玉
堂金马三学士的锦绣前程,待挣得一个状元回来,成亲不迟。"

张生听了心想,到不能小看了这红娘,她年纪虽轻,可胸中不
乏丘壑,是个女中丈夫,实在难得。红娘又叮咛道:"先生自家要保
重些,不可这般愁损了身子,清减了精神。"

张生道:"姐姐的话小生记下了,只是你可千万小心在意些!"

红娘道:"你自管放宽心,只为你与我家小姐这段情,红娘也
会加心在意。凭着俺这三寸不烂之舌和你简帖里的心意,管教那
人儿来望你一遭儿,你就听好吧。"说罢袖了简帖,飘然而去。

再说莺莺自昨日打发红娘去书院探视张生,量那张生定有话捎
给自己,单盼着红娘前来回话。可左等不来右等不来,想是红娘伺候
老夫人不得空便。一夜辗转反侧,不曾合眼,及至天亮却睡意涌来,
拥衾倚枕,沉入梦中。及至日上三竿,红娘伺候老夫人吃罢早饭后,
这才得空过绣阁来看莺莺。院子里静寂无声,绿叶成荫,进得门来,
只见阁内瑞香缭绕,暖帐帘垂,过来轻掀帘角,但见莺莺钗横鬓偏,
酣然沉睡,心中暗道:"好个懒散的小姐。"掏出张生那封信,回头环
视见梳妆台上的梳妆盒,眼睛一转,心说有了,将信放进去,合上盖
子时故意压了一个角露在外面,尔后退到屏风后咳嗽一声。

那莺莺被这咳声惊醒,问道:"是谁?"不见有人回应,便下得
床来,坐在梳妆台前,揉眼展目,就见梳妆盒着一角信笺,忙启
盖抽了出来,撕开封口展看,看着看着不由心突突地跳,这才想到
定是红娘将信简儿送了过来,可这半天怎不见她的影子,定在这
屋里藏着窥视,便绷紧粉面,皱了黛眉,唤道:"红娘,红娘!"

behind the screen.

"You little minx!" barked Oriole. "Why were you skulking behind that screen? Where has this come from, Rose? I am the daughter of the late prime minister; how dare you make fun of me with such a letter? I've a good mind to report this misbehavior to my mother, and get her to give you a good thrashing."

"You were the one who sent me to the young gentleman," Rose retorted tartly. "And he gave me the letter. You know quite well that I cannot read. So how could I know what he has written? Anyway, it's nothing to do with me. In fact it would probably be better for me than for you to take this letter to your mother and tell her all about it." So saying she snatched the letter from Oriole's hand, turned and walked towards the door.

Flabbergasted, Oriole chased after her, and grabbed hold of her gown. "Rose, Rose, Rose, Rose, Rose! I was only joking. Don't take it seriously. Now give me back that letter, there's a good girl."

"Let go of me Miss, if you please," said Rose coldly.

Oriole dared not let her go. "Dear Rose, could you please tell me how Zhang's health is?"

Rose cast a glance at Oriole, and then tossed her head, saying, "I don't know. His health has nothing to do with me."

"Oh, Rose, do tell me! You don't know how I feel...."

"I don't care how you feel. You're much better off than that foolish young scholar anyway. He has no desire to drink or eat. Facing the eastern wall, he sheds tears day and night. He has become so pale and wan that I fear he is in a state of terminal decline."

Rose's words made Oriole's heart ache. "We should call a doctor!" she burst out.

"No medicine can cure him; only his lover," said Rose.

Oriole, whose face had turned bright red, pretended not to hear. She took the letter from Rose and said, "Although my family is under an obligation to him, the relations between us are merely those of brother and sister, and nothing more. You are always discreet, Rose. If others get to know of this letter, what will become of the honor of our family?"

"Miss, you are the person who has made Zhang suffer so much. What do you really want? You encouraged him to climb up the tree, and then you removed the ladder and gazed upon him with indifference. How

躲在屏风后面的红娘忙应声站出来道:"小姐有何吩咐?"

莺莺紫胀了面皮嗔道:"为何躲在后面?这是从哪里来的? 我是堂堂相国小姐,谁敢将这简帖儿来戏弄于我,看不告过老夫人。"

红娘冷笑一声道:"小姐让我将去,他着我送来,我个不识字的丫头,知他写了些什么? 再者说了,这事也不关我的事,分明是小姐的过犯,你不曾看惯这等东西,谁又看得惯? 姐姐也休要这般不依不饶地闹个没完,不等你对老夫人说去,我就把这拿到老夫人处出首去。"说着伸手从莺莺手中将书简抽了过来,转身就往外走。

莺莺没料到红娘有这么一手,忙一把揪住红娘的衣襟,转嗔回喜道:"嗳呀,还当真了,我逗你耍呢。"

红娘气呼呼冷着脸道:"放手。"

莺莺不敢松手,央求道:"好姐姐,这两日张生他怎样了?"

红娘白了莺莺一眼,将头一扬,道:"我不知道。"

莺莺道:"好姐姐,你就告诉我吧,你不知人家心里……"

红娘鼻子里哼了一声道:"你心里怎么了? 不像那个傻角茶不思、饭不想,将自家好端端的身子弄得不成样子,病得不行了。"

莺莺听了心疼万分,脱口道:"那就快些请个太医给他看看。"

红娘道:"他那病,恐怕吃药是不济事的,依我看,若想治愈,除非是出几点风流汗。"

莺莺脸红心跳,装做没听懂,从红娘手中又将那书简扯了来,说道:"虽说我家有些亏他之处,可我与他只是兄妹之情,焉有其他? 红娘,也亏你口稳哩,若是让别人知道了,早嚷了出去,可成甚体统?"

红娘道:"姐姐就别转圈儿了,你哄谁哩? 你把那个饿鬼弄得

can you and your mother be so heartless?"

Oriole's face turned now red, and now white. She lowered her head and picked up a writing brush. "Dear Rose, stop talking. Let me write a letter to him, telling him not to be so foolish."

After having written and sealed the letter, Oriole said to Rose: "Give him this letter and say, 'When my young mistress sent me to see you, sir, it was simply a matter of courtesy between sister and brother; it meant nothing else. If you persist in your nonsense, my young mistress will be obliged to tell her mother.' And Rose, you will have to answer for this!" So saying, Oriole threw the letter on the ground, and went to lie down on her bed, ignoring Rose.

Rose thought to herself: "You don't know how to restrain your tongue, you vixen, abusing others and making them feel sad by giving vent to your own bad temper. When you heard the lute beneath the bright moon, you didn't fear the cold on a dewy spring night. Was it because you were devoured by your flame for the scholar so that you felt no shame? You weren't afraid of freezing into stone for that crazy, gallant man. You are a flower thirsting for rain."

Rose picked up the letter from the floor, but hesitated. She was afraid of what her young mistress would say and do if she disobeyed her and refused to deliver the letter. But she was afraid that the letter would hurt Zhang. She thought about it over and over again. Finally she tucked the letter into her sleeve, and left for the library.

Zhang was waiting impatiently for Rose to bring him an answer to his own letter.

Accompanied by a clatter of jade pendants, Rose entered the library. Zhang was glad to see her: "So you have come, Miss Rose. What about the letter?"

Extremely worried, Rose heaved a deep sigh: "It failed to touch my young mistress' heart, I'm afraid, sir. I must advise you to put an end to your foolishness."

"My letter was a talisman to make lovers meet. How can it have failed? It must have been your fault, Miss Rose; you were not zealous enough," Zhang said.

Rose was stung by this remark. "To tell you the truth, sir, your letter was impertinent. It could have got me into trouble, too. From now on, meetings will be rare, and there will be no more moon viewing in the Western Bower."

七死八活的，究竟想要怎样？亏你说得出口，把人家撺掇得上了竿，又撤了梯子看好看，你们母子也真做得出来！"

莺莺脸儿红一阵，白一阵，垂了粉颈，拈起描眉笔，就一页洒金帖子上写了起来，边写边说道："好姐姐，别说了。我给他写个字条儿，让他下次休要这般，也就是了。"写罢，封了，又对红娘说："红娘，有劳你再去一趟送给他，就说我令你看他，皆出于兄妹之礼，非有他意，今后他若再敢如此无礼，写来淫词秽语，必告知老夫人，到时可别怪我翻脸无情。"说罢冷冷将帖子掷在地上，起身又到绣帐中躺了，朝里扭转身子，不理红娘。

红娘心说："那夜听琴不畏春寒，为了那疯魔汉，险些做了望夫石，是你用心拨云撩雨，不肯思自己的不是，专寻别人的破绽。"

红娘拾起简儿好生犯难，赌气不去吧，又怕小姐怨自己违拗她；待去吧，又不忍让这无情信伤了那眼巴巴等着自己回话的痴情秀才。思量再三，还是得去，便袖了书简出了绣阁朝书院走去。

张生正在书院里单等红娘的回话。心想小姐若见自家昨日那封书信，必定高兴，自然会让红娘回话，今日定有好消息来。

伴着一阵环佩叮咚声，红娘进得门来，不等她开口，张生便惊喜地叫道："是红娘姐姐来了，擎天柱，大事如何了也？"

红娘愁容满面，长叹一声道："不济事了，先生休傻起劲了。"

张生道："小生的简帖儿是一道会亲的符咒，怎会不济事？"

红娘委屈道："还说你那简帖呢？如今那简帖儿到做了你的招状，险些把我拖累了。从今后你们相会少，见面难。想是月暗西厢，凤去秦楼，云敛巫山。你也省心些儿，我也省力些儿。咱们大家早些各自散了，省得麻烦。"

As she turned to go, Zhang fell on his knees before her. "Miss Rose," he cried, "If you abandon me, who will there be to plead my cause? You must help me to win back my lover, and save my life."

"You are a learned scholar, sir. Can you not perceive how the matter stands? My young mistress is fickle. I can hardly understand her moods. I could easily be beaten for my involvement in your love affair."

Zhang wept. "If you won't help me, Miss Rose," he cried, "there can be no hope for my life."

Rose was in a quandary, hearing this. So she took her young mistress' letter from her sleeve, and handed it to him. "I can say no more," she said, with a sigh of resignation. "Here is her answer to your letter. You can read it for yourself."

Zhang took the letter, wiped away his tears, and began to read it. Suddenly he leapt up from the ground, exclaiming, "Today is indeed a happy day!" Then he placed the letter on the table, and bowed to it time and again: "I should burn incense and make three bows to this letter. If I had known your young mistress' letter was to arrive, I should have prepared an honored reception. Now it is too late, so I hope I may be excused."

Rose thought the young man must have taken leave of his senses. "Perhaps the strain of disappointed love has been too much for him," she thought. "Sir, please pull yourself together," she urged him.

Zhang emitted a cackle of laughter. "Miss Rose, you will rejoice too before long," he assured her.

"I am afraid you must have lost your mind, sir, as a result of your lovesick grief. What does she say in the letter?"

"The meaning of her letter is the very opposite of what she says, you see," answered Zhang, with a crafty smile. "What she really means is that we should meet in the garden again tonight."

"I don't believe it," snorted Rose. "Be so kind as to read me the letter."

Zhang cleared his throat, and began to read:

Wait for moonrise in the Western Bower,
Where the breeze blows ajar the door.
The wall is shaded by dancing flowers;
Then comes the one whom you adore.

张生被红娘这通话说得天旋地转，六神无主，怔怔道："姐姐此一遭去了，还有谁肯与小生分剖，必得做一个道理，方可救得小生一命。"说着双膝一软跪在红娘面前，揪住红娘裙裾苦苦哀求。

红娘道："先生是读书人，岂不知此意。那边小姐性儿撮盐入火，一天十八变，你这里又可怜兮兮的，甜言热话说下一大筐，倒叫我两下里做人难。先生快快起来吧。男儿膝下有黄金，我可担待不起。"

张生哭道："小生这一条性命，都在姐姐身上，你若不管，我就不起来。"

红娘哭笑不得，从袖里抽出书简往他面前一递道："我跟你也说不明白，唉，这是小姐回与你的书信，你自己看了，便清楚了。"

张生急接了过来，抹泪展简观看，猛地欢叫一声从地上站起来道："呀！有这场喜事。"又将那简儿恭恭敬敬放在书案上连连作揖道："撮土焚香，三拜礼毕，早知小姐简至，理当远迎，接待不及，勿令见罪！"

张生这一连串的动作，把个红娘弄得丈二和尚摸不着头脑，以为这秀才气成失心疯了，便道："先生，先生，你醒醒，醒醒。"

张生脸上泪痕尤在，哈哈大笑道："姐姐，你也当欢喜才是。"

红娘更加不解道："你该不是气糊涂了吧？信上怎么说？"

张生摇头晃脑得意洋洋道："小姐骂我都是假的，这书信里写的才是真的。她书中之意是让我今夜到花园里去，和她哩也波哩也罗哩。"

红娘道："我不信。你读与我听听。"

张生清一清嗓子，吟道："待月西厢下，迎风户半开。隔墙花影动，疑是玉人来。"

127

"What does it mean? Please explain it to me," Rose said.

Zhang explained, " 'Wait for moonrise in the Western Bower' tells me what time to go to the garden. 'Where the breeze blows ajar the door' means she will open the door and wait for me. 'The wall is shaded by dancing flowers' tells me to climb over the wall screened by the shadows of the flowers lest I should be seen. And 'Then comes the one whom you adore' of course needs no explanation."

Rose began to laugh: "Are you sure she wants you to climb over the wall?"

"What else can she mean if not that, Miss Rose? I am a master at solving romantic riddles. I have made no mistake," Zhang said with great confidence.

"Then my young mistress has made a fool of me," said Rose angrily. "Who has ever seen a messenger fooled by the sender? Five words hint at the time; and four lines appeal to the lover missed. Oh, Young Mistress, you have treated me like a puppet on a string, playing your crafty games!"

"I'm sorry to have made you go through all this. I offer my deepest apologies to you on behalf of your young mistress," Zhang said, bowing to Rose.

Rose said: "My young mistress has shown affection to you, but she makes light of me. Her honeyed words will warm you in the depth of winter; but her frown makes me shiver even in midsummer."

"Don't be angry, Miss Rose. I still need your help. I have visited the garden twice, without any result. I am not sure how she will treat me," said Zhang, with a worried frown.

Rose offered words of encouragement: "This letter is proof of her sincerity, I'm sure."

Zhang was overjoyed to hear this. As he watched Rose depart, he thought, "All things are fated. Who could have anticipated the happiness Miss Oriole would send me in her letter? I'll hold my young lady in my arms soon...." He read the poem time and again, regarding it as a treasure. Looking forward to their happy meeting, he resented the lingering daylight; the sun seemed motionless in the sky. He pointed at it, and complained:

When I talk with a happy friend,
The sun will soon westward descend.
But today, when I am to meet my love;
The sun seems glued to the sky above.

128

红娘道:"怎么见得是她让你来? 你解与我听。"

张生眉飞色舞道:"待月西厢下, 让我待月儿上来时; 迎风户半开, 是说那时她将开门待我; 隔墙花影动, 疑是玉人来, 是让我跳墙过去,和她……"

红娘听了笑弯了腰道:"她让你跳过墙来? 是你自家想的吧! 果真有此一说么?"

张生把头一晃自信地说:"俺是个猜诗迷的行家, 风流隋何, 浪子陆贾,哪里有猜错的时候!"

红娘道:"你看看, 小姐在我这儿也使这般道儿, 你几曾见过寄书的颠倒瞒着鱼雁。好个小鸡肚肠转圈子的主子, 原来那诗里包笼着三更枣,简帖里埋伏着九里山,俺小姐倒真会闹中取静。放心罢学士,稳情娶金雀鸦鬟。"

张生作揖道:"让姐姐受屈了,俺替小姐给姐姐陪情。"

红娘道:"不是我背后怨她, 她对别人甜言美语三春暖, 在俺跟前恶语伤人六月寒。如今更做出这孟光接了梁鸿案。我到要看看她这个离魂倩女,怎发付你这个掷果潘安!"

张生道:"姐姐休生气, 诸事还得姐姐费心帮忙才是。小生也曾到那花园里两遭了。尚不见一星半点儿好处, 这一遭知她又将怎样?"

红娘道:"如今不比往常, 今日这一次才结成正果, 你可一定要赴约呀!我走了。"

张生目送红娘离去, 欣喜若狂, 心想:"万事自有分定, 哪曾想小姐有此一场好处。今夜里到那里与我那小姐扎帮地倒地, 成就了好事……"想着, 不时将小姐的简帖颠来倒去地观看, 一遍又一

He was chagrined to note that it was still only noontime. After another hour, he berated the Heavens again:

> *No cloud in the azure sky,*
> *No fragrance drifting by.*
> *Who can shorten the day,*
> *Driving the sun away?*

Then he struck him that perhaps Heaven was offended with him, and had stopped the sun in its tracks deliberately. So he changed his tactics. Bowing skyward, he prayed, "Oh Heaven! You give everything to everyone. Why won't you give me a single day? Oh Sun! Please go down quickly!" He went back to the library, sat at a desk, and tried to read. The minutes dragged by one by one. Finally the sun began to sink in the west. Frowning at it for its tardiness, Zhang recited:

> *The sun's a golden crow*
> *In Heaven's palace high.*
> *I'd shoot it with a bow*
> *Down from the western sky.*

At last, the drums and bells announcing nightfall brought this welcome news to Zhang's eager ears. Gulping down his supper, the young man hurriedly changed his clothes, closed the door of the library and ventured forth to meet his lover.

遍地吟着那四句诗,如获至宝,爱不释手。想着今夜便成就好事,便盼着夜幕早垂。只是天公不作美,太阳好像被胶粘在天上一般,半晌挪不了一寸,心中顿生恨日之心,指天怨道:"读书继暑怕黄昏,不觉西沉强掩门。欲赴海棠花下约,太阳何苦又生根?"张生抬头望日望得脖酸眼花,嘴里自言自语道:"呀,才晌午呵,只得再等一等。今日这颓天百般的难晚,真真要了小生的命了!"过了不到一个时辰,张生复又看天道:"碧天万里无云,空劳倦客身心,恨杀鲁阳贪战,不教红日西沉。"骂了几句又觉自家有些过于不恭了,便对日拜道:"天呀,你有万物于人,何故争此一日?小生求你就快下去吧!"再回书房看书,却魂不守舍,怎么也看不进去,如同热锅上的蚂蚁,坐卧不宁,真正是度日如年。好不容易熬到红日西斜,可看着夕阳就是不肯落下,心中愈发恼火,不禁指了夕阳斥道:"无端三足乌,团团光烁烁;安得后羿弓,射此一轮落。"眼盯着金乌不情愿地渐次落下,耳听前边寺院传来暮鼓晚钟,张生这才松了口气道:"谢天谢地,你总算下去了。"忙吃了晚饭,洗漱换衣,收拾利落,出了书房,喜滋滋前去赴约。

CHAPTER SEVEN

Repudiation

On her way back to her young mistress' room, Rose was wondering how she should report what had happened to Oriole. "If I tell her the truth," she reasoned, "she will be too shy to keep the appointment, and Zhang will be very disappointed. But since she did not tell me the truth, I will simply suggest that she burn incense in the garden, and watch her reaction when the young man appears."

Oriole, meanwhile, was on tenterhooks, wondering what Zhang's reaction to her letter had been. She was hoping that he had not revealed their illicit love to Rose. Just then, Rose entered the room. Oriole looked carefully at the girl, trying to guess if she knew how matters stood between her and Zhang. But Rose showed no sign of having become privy to any secrets.

"Oh, you're back, Rose," said Oriole, feigning nonchalance.

"Yes, I am."

"Have you been to the library?"

"Yes."

"Did you give my letter to Master Zhang in person?"

"Yes."

"Did he read the letter?"

"Yes."

"Did he say anything?"

"Nothing much. And he didn't shed any tears either. I told him that you wanted him to regard you as a sister, as you told me. He seemed quite content with that idea."

At this, Oriole felt relieved. She let Rose go to attend her mother, while she prepared her make-up.

After Rose returned, she started to prepare the supper, knew quite well what was in her young mistress' mind on noticing her dressed and made up for a lovers' tryst.

第七章
莺莺赖简

再说红娘从书院出来，回绣阁复命，一路上暗忖如何回复好做假的小姐，若实话实说，还不把她羞煞，今夜断不肯赴约，如此又岂不害了那情种张生？小姐既不肯让我知道，我也不捅破这张窗户纸，只请她花园里烧香，成就二人好事。

此时，绣阁内莺莺坐卧不宁，惦记着那张请柬，不知张生看罢如何？张郎心通七窍，聪明绝伦，这点道理还是懂的。自家倒是庸人自扰了，正在患得患失，就见红娘进来了。莺莺见红娘表情平平，与往常无异，也没看出什么破绽，便问道："那封简帖可曾亲手交给张先生？"红娘道："交与他了。""他可有甚话说？""俺一去，就先将姐姐交待的话对他说了，好好地羞臊了他一番，后来又给了他姐姐的信，反正那信上说的与俺说的都一样，可他看了却不再哭了。"

莺莺这才将一颗心放下，便令红娘去老夫人处支应，自家独自重匀脂粉，淡扫蛾眉，刻意打扮起来，及至红娘回来，忙传晚饭。红娘知她心急赴约，不由得心中暗想道：小姐定与那张生一般，早就盼不得天黑，挨一刻好似过一夏，你今日晚妆打扮得与往日不同，别样精神，为了今夜的云雨巫山，你控制不住意马心猿，你自家以为做得天衣无缝，我倒要看看你怎样瞒过我红娘？

Overwhelmed with anxiety, Oriole pushed open the window, to find the sunset clouds gone and the land covered in darkness. Already the moon was high above the eastern wall.

"What a beautiful evening for burning incense in the garden!" exclaimed Rose.

Oriole had been thinking long and hard of an excuse to go to the garden to meet Zhang, but didn't want Rose accompanying her. Nevertheless, she couldn't very well order the girl to stay behind without arousing her suspicions. So she pretended not to want to go to the garden, protesting that the night dew was bad for her health.

At this, Rose played her part excellently. "Miss, you have prayed to the full moon for many years without fail," she reminded Oriole. "You should not break your rule today."

Oriole had no choice but to comply.

As she proceeded to the garden of the Western Bower, she found the zigzag path hard to negotiate. The dewy moss was slippery under her feet. She gave a start as her jade hairpin caught in the grape trellis, and her heart leapt into her mouth when the ducks in the pond woke with an ear-splitting cackle at her approach.

Rose set the incense table under the poolside rockery in a grove of poplar and willow trees. With the excuse of catching glowworms, she walked to the other side of the rockery to open the side door linking the monastery with the garden. She stepped through the door, and looked around. There was no sign of Zhang. She gave a low whistle, which was answered from nearby. Instantly, Zhang in a black silk headdress appeared from behind a tree. Zhang asked: "Miss Rose, where is your young mistress?"

Rose said, "My young mistress is over there in the garden burning incense and praying to the moon. But are you sure that she asked you to come here tonight? If not, I fear that I will be punished for letting you in."

"Didn't I tell you that I am a master at solving romantic riddles? So I am sure to captivate her. Now, don't delay me any longer, Miss Rose."

Rose felt relieved upon hearing this. She then said, "Don't go through the door, or my young mistress will say that I have let you in. You must climb over the wall, using that old apricot tree over there. Isn't it a beautiful

莺莺心事重重，推窗望去，只见天边晚霞散尽，暮霭笼罩，月上东墙，不由启一点樱唇吟道："花阴重叠香风细，庭院深沉淡月明。"

红娘忙在一旁接言道："今夜月明风清，好一派景致也。姐姐，咱花园里烧香拜月去来。"

莺莺正在苦思冥想如何到花园去赴约，听红娘一说，心中不觉发虚道："夜深露重，不去也罢。"

红娘心说，你到此时还在做假，再不去时，那呆子如何受得了？便道："还是去吧，姐姐多年规矩，月圆则拜，今日焉能破了？"

莺莺想了想，便点头道："就依你，准备香案，咱这就去。"

主仆二人沿花径迤逦而行，夜凉苔滑，露湿绫袜，莺莺心慌意乱，一会儿金莲蹴损牡丹芽，一会儿鬓上玉簪钩住了荼蘼架，扰起了池塘睡鸭，柳丛栖鸦。红娘把香案设在湖山下，杨柳边，请小姐焚香。自家便以扑萤为名，转过假山去开了寺里通往花园的角门。出去一看，不见人影，便嘬了樱唇"咻咻"吹了几声口哨。就听不远处也传来"咻咻"的口哨声，便知道张生来了。定睛借月光看去，只见槐树下闪出一个人来，乌纱角带铮亮，穿过花径一路小跑奔了过来。

张生道："红娘姐姐，小姐在哪里？"

红娘一指道："你瞧，正在湖山下焚香拜月。我且问你，小姐果真约你来吗？你绝不可有半句谎言。不然我可是吃罪不起呀。"

张生一扬头自信地说道："这个自然，小生不是告诉过你吗，我是猜诗谜的行家，哪里会错！今夜一准成就好事。姐姐快闪开，让我过去。"

night for a lovers' meeting?"

Zhang bowed to the girl. "Thank you very much for your help, Miss Rose," he said.

"But I have something else to tell you," Rose said.

"I'll listen with respectful attention."

"My young mistress is a pure maiden. You must be gentle and use sweet words. You must not take her for a flaunting flower!"

"Don't worry about that, Miss Rose," the young man assured her. "How could I treat the most beautiful creature in the world with anything but the gentlest consideration?"

Then Rose closed the side door and went back to the poolside rockery.

At midnight, all was quiet. A fleecy cloud veiled the bright moon, causing everything to be bathed in silvery candlelight. With Heaven as a quilt and the earth as a bed, the world seemed to be changed into a huge bridal chamber.

After she finished praying to the moon, Oriole paced back and forth, restless and whimsical. Her heart was beating fast. Suddenly she heard the shaking of tree branches, and the thud of feet on the grass. Before she had time to think, the ardent Zhang was standing before her. He took Oriole in his arms. But to his consternation, Oriole struggled free in an instant.

"Have you no shame, sir?" she cried. "If my mother finds out that you have trespassed in the Western Bower like this, and thrust your attentions upon me, we shall both be ruined for life!"

This took Zhang completely by surprise. He was flabbergasted at this cold reception, and thought, "The young lady has changed her mind."

Rose, who was hiding behind the rockery, was outraged at Zhang's impetuous behavior. "What a bad memory you have!" she fumed inwardly. "You have forgotten everything I told you. You're too rude and too eager. Why don't you tell her that it was she who invited you here?"

At this moment, Rose heard Oriole call to her: "Rose, there is an intruder in the garden."

Rose, pretending to be flustered and alarmed, hurried to her young mistress' side. "Who is it? Who has dared to sneak into the garden of the Western Bower?"

　　红娘见他说得如此肯定，也就放心了，便说："你等等，且休从门里进去，你这样过去，小姐肯定说是我放你进来的。小姐想瞒着我，这样反会坏事，你还是跳墙过去。今夜我一准助你两个成亲。不过，我还有几句话要事先嘱咐。""姐姐请讲，小生洗耳恭听。""俺小姐可是个娇滴滴的金枝玉叶，你可要温柔体贴些。万不可鲁莽行事，把她当作残花败柳。""姐姐只管放心，小生怎敢唐突西施。""好了，我这就回去，你就跳墙过去。"说着，指了指墙边的一株老杏树。张生心知红娘是让他攀着此树跳过墙去，便点了点头。红娘安顿好张生，忙关好角门返回湖山。

　　此时良夜迢迢，万籁俱寂。淡云笼月，似红纸护蜡；柳丝垂挂，似帏幕珠帘；芳草茵茵，似绿毯铺榻。浑然天作盖，地为床，自然一个洞房。莺莺拜罢月，芳心狂跳，不知今夜如何做事，正在心猿意马之际，就听墙角"扑腾"一声，似有人跳进，花枝摇动了几下，猛地窜出一个人来。不等莺莺看清，那人便冲了过来，展臂将莺莺抱了个满怀。莺莺惊叫："是谁？"张生急切里喘息未平，道："是小生。"莺莺四下里望望，用力挣脱，怒道："张生，你是何等身份之人。我在这里烧香拜月，你无故至此。若老夫人闻知，你有何理说？"张生不提防莺莺有这么一招，顿时如遭雷击，痴呆呆说不出一句话来，心中暗叫："不好，小姐她变卦了。"

　　隐在山石后的红娘看了这个场面，心里直骂张生："好个无记性的秀才，也太鲁莽了些。事已至些，何不索性向前搂住滚翻在地，成了好事，就是告到衙门里，还怕羞了你？照直说出是她约你'待月西厢下'，怕她吃了你不成？"红娘正心中着急使不上劲儿之际，就听莺莺叫道："红娘，你快来呀，有贼！"

"It is I, Miss Rose," Zhang said, appealing to Rose, as if he had found a savior.

"What is your business here, Master Zhang?" Rose cast a stern glance at him.

Afraid that Zhang would tell Rose that she had invited him, Oriole cut in: "Don't bandy words with him. Have him taken before my mother!"

But Rose said, "Don't be angry, Young Mistress. Master Zhang is not a stranger; he has saved our lives. If we drag him off to my mistress, it would ruin his reputation. Let me deal with him for you." Oriole said nothing. "Master Zhang, kneel down," Rose ordered.

Like a wooden image, Zhang knelt down in front of Oriole, with tears in his eyes.

Rose interrogated him: "Since you've studied the classics, you should be aware of ethical behavior. Why have you come to the garden in the dead of night? Tell me the truth!"

Zhang could not think of how to answer this question without implicating Oriole, so he simply knelt there dumbly, his eyes pleading.

Rose thought, "So you're still trying to protect my young mistress, are you? Well, I'm going to give you a hard time!" She questioned the young man again. "Do you know what your crime is?"

Zhang, trembling all over, said, "No."

"You're a scholar who does not know how to behave in a delicate situation. Who told you to jump into our garden at midnight? You should be a distinguished guest, but now you are a man who wants to steal sweet flowers."

Rose then proposed that he be let off, as it was certain that he would never do such a thing again.

Oriole said, with a snort of contempt, "If it was not for Rose's sake, you would be dragged to my mother's place without leniency. Then how could you face your elders in your hometown? Stand up!"

Rose gave Zhang a push, motioning him to stand up.

"We are bound to repay your kindness for saving our lives," said Oriole icily. "But since we have become brother and sister, how can you have any further desire? What if my mother should get to know of this? Let this be a lesson to you." So saying, she stalked away.

Rose remained behind, and as soon as her young mistress had

红娘只得紧走几步过来,装作什么也不知道,问道:"是谁?敢入园作贼?"张生见红娘过来,似见了救星一般忙道:"是小生。"

红娘瞪了张生一眼道:"张生,你来这里作甚么?"莺莺怕张生说出自家约他之事,忙道:"不用问,先将他送到老夫人那里去。"

红娘知小姐好作假,也该给他们个台阶下,便对小姐道:"姐姐息怒,张生也不是外人,何况有恩于咱,若扯到老夫人那里,也怕坏了他的行止。我替姐姐处分他一场也就是了。"见莺莺不吭气,便一指张生道:"张生,你还不过来跪着!"张生到此,如木偶一般,脑子里一盆浆糊,不由得双膝一软,眼泪汪汪跪在莺莺面前。

红娘道:"你既读孔孟之书,必达周公之礼,深夜来此何干?"

"这……这……这……"张生张口结舌,半晌说不出话来。

红娘心想:"都到这份儿上了,你还替小姐包着,屈死活该!"又看看莺莺,说道:"老实说,不是俺一家儿乔做衙门审你,俺原以为你文章学问海样深,谁知你色胆倒有天来大!你可知罪吗?"

张生气得浑身乱颤道:"小生不知罪。"

红娘道:"好个不识趣的秀才,谁教你深夜跳入人家花园,你本是个折桂客,偏做了偷花汉。"又对莺莺道:"姐姐,且看红娘的面上饶过这秀才吧。"莺莺哼了一声道:"若不是看在红娘面上,定扯你到老夫人那里,看你有何面目见江东父老?起来吧。"

红娘推了张生一把,示意张生快起来。莺莺依旧冷着脸说道:"先生虽有活人之恩,恩则当报,你我既为兄妹,怎能生此非份之念?今后再要如此,与足下决不干休!"说罢甩袖而去。

红娘对张生说道:"以后再休题什么'春宵一夜千金价'了,好好准备着'寒窗更守十年寡',猜诗谜的行家,想差了'迎风户半

disappeared said to Zhang: "I thought that you were supposed to be a master at the art of solving romantic riddles!"

Zhang seized Rose by the sleeve, and begged, "Please listen to me, Miss Rose. I want to write another letter to express my love for Oriole. I need your help just one more time."

But the girl shook him off. "Your amorous scheme has come to naught; my young mistress has no tender feelings for you. The road ahead for you is clear. You should concentrate on your studies from now on."

"But your young mistress will be the death of me," he wailed. "When I was sick yesterday, it was her letter which revived me. But I suffered such a rebuff today that I'm afraid that I will never recover."

There was nothing for it but to return to the library. Zhang slept not a wink all night, thinking how Madame Cui had prevented his marriage to Miss Oriole, how the most beautiful girl in the world had denied the sentiments in the letter she had sent him, how thoroughly wretched and miserable he was.... At daybreak, he felt dizzy and could not get out of bed.

His page, who did not know what had happened the night before, got up early as usual. He carried a basin of water to the library for his master to wash his face. But when he lifted the mosquito net around the bed, he was alarmed at the sight of his master's pallid complexion and the tear stains on his cheeks. He found that Zhang's forehead was blazing hot. "Sir, what's the matter with you?" he cried.

Zhang groaned. With his eyes screwed tight, he grunted, "Boy, I'm dying." Then he fainted. His terrified servant rushed to the abbot for help. The abbot sent Fa Cong to report the matter to Madame Cui, and Hui Ming to fetch a doctor. Then he followed the page to the library.

Madame Cui was chagrined at the news that Zhang was very ill. She thought to herself: "This is terrible! That young man saved my family, but, after all, I had no choice but to stop the marriage from going ahead. I had planned to give him a large sum of money so that he would be in good circumstances to marry another girl. However the young man failed to appreciate my kindness, and continued to hang around the monastery. Now he is ill. What a bother! I'd better send Rose to see him." So she said, "Rose, go to the library and find out what is wrong with that young man."

开',山障了'隔墙花影动',绿惨了'待月西厢下'。自此后,你快将那尤云殢雨的心晒干,速把那窃玉偷香的胆收起,再把那倚翠偎红的话句删除了,好好读书做人吧。"

张生一把抓住红娘的衣袖,央求道:"小生再写一简,烦姐姐送与小姐,以尽衷情如何?"红娘甩脱他的手道:"你怎么还看不穿、想不透这风流戏法。你就收心养性给我游学去罢!"

张生万分委屈地说道:"你家小姐送了人的命了!昨日得简方喜,故今日强扶病身至此,又值这一场怨气,眼见得我命休矣。"

话说张生昨夜攀树跳墙、花园赴约受尽屈辱,回到西厢,一夜思绪翻滚,未曾合眼,一会子忆及老夫人赖婚,一会子想到小姐赖简,一会子又想到已故的爹娘,真是百感交集,及至天亮,头晕目眩,起不来床了。琴童不知夜里之事,早起似往常打水端盆,来侍候主人梳洗,撩了帐帘一看,不由大惊失色,只见张生面若黄蜡,涕泪不干,伸手往额上一试,滚烫灼人,忙道:"哥哥,你这是怎么了?"

张生强睁双目,少气无力地呻吟道:"琴童,我命休矣!"说罢,眼一闭竟昏厥过去,把个琴童吓得连呼:"哥哥醒来!哥哥醒来!"张生只是不出一言。琴童心急无奈,只得跑到方丈,去求长老相救。长老一听张生病危,十分焦急,一面派法聪报与老夫人,一面派惠明去请郎中,自家则随了琴童到书院来看张生。

再说老夫人一早听得法聪来报,说张生病重,心里也是一惊,毕竟张生有恩于崔家,先前赖婚本是出于无奈,原是要多酬些金帛钱财,令其另择名门闺秀成婚也就罢了,只是这秀才住在书院里,不肯离去。如今病了,怎么也该派个人去问候一下。便叫红娘过来吩咐道:"红娘,你速去书院,看看君瑞哥哥病情怎样?"

Rose realized that Zhang had not been exaggerating when he had said that Oriole's rebuff would be the death of him. But she pretended to make light of the situation. "Oh, he's nothing but a shameless fellow who is trying to win your sympathy, Madame. I think you should pay no attention to him."

As she expected, Madame Cui was annoyed at her brazenness. "Don't talk back. How dare you refuse my order?" she barked.

"It is just that I don't understand why he should be allowed to ensnare you with his nonsense, Madame, just because he saved our lives," Rose said, cunningly.

This was a sore spot with Madame Cui. Even more ruffled than before, she ordered Rose to go to see Zhang right away. Rose then went straight to the Embroidery Pavilion, where Oriole was waiting.

"Rose, what did my mother want you to do?" Oriole asked.

Afraid that her young mistress would be worried, Rose said, "Nothing important. It seems that last night's intruder is dying, that's all."

This news struck Oriole like a thunderbolt. "It's all my fault," she thought to herself. "I must somehow go to comfort him. But it would never do for my mother to find out." Suddenly she hit upon an idea. She turned to Rose and said, "Rose, if Master Zhang is very ill I have an excellent prescription for you to take to him."

"No, no!" Rose shook her head. "You are at it again. My dear young mistress, you will be the death of him!"

"Rose, I do believe that I am the only person who can save his life."

Rose sighed, and said, "Well, as your mother has just ordered me to go there, I will take your prescription to him."

Oriole was delighted to hear this. She went straight to her desk, picked up a brush and began to write. When she finished, she handed the piece of paper to Rose. Now, the girl may have been illiterate, but she had seen medical prescriptions before, and this did not look like one. "I hope you haven't forgotten to include the medicine," she said archly.

Oriole's face turned red. "This prescription is just what he needs," she said.

"I'm sure it is," retorted Rose, looking not at all convinced. Tucking the prescription or whatever it was in her sleeve, she skipped off to the library. Just outside, she bumped into the abbot and a doctor coming out. Rose greeted them, and the abbot informed her that the doctor had diagnosed nothing more important than a severe chill, which would be

红娘听了老夫人的话,心中暗叫:"不好。想是张生昨夜里吃了小姐和我那一场气,病愈发重了。小姐呀,你可把他的小命送了。"嘴上应道:"那个没脸皮的酸秀才病死也就算了,老夫人理他做甚?"

老夫人将脸一沉道:"死丫头休得胡说,老身叫你去你就去,嘴皮子刀子似的,成何体统?""红娘不敢,只是那酸秀才仗了救了咱一家子的性命,当真做起哥哥来了,他是俺哪门子的哥哥。"

老夫人最怕提起张生救命之事,忙道:"死丫头,怕人不知道你有张嘴!休得多言,快去!"红娘便出来三绕两绕回到绣阁。

莺莺一见红娘,便问道:"红娘,老夫人唤你去为何事?"

红娘怕小姐着急,道:"那个昨夜里跳墙入园的贼快要死了。"

莺莺心下一惊,知道张生定是为昨夜之事病体加重,自家昨夜也是不得已而为之。有心去书院看他,又怕母亲知道了责怪,猛然间她眼睛一亮,对红娘说道:"张生病重,俺这里有一个好药方,烦劳姐姐送与他。"红娘听了,头摇得像拨郎鼓一般,道:"不不不,又来了,小姐呵,可不要送了他的小命。"

莺莺道:"救人一命,胜造七级浮图,你就给他送去吧。"

红娘无奈地叹道:"唉,除非你,谁也救不了他。如今老夫人正派我去书院探病,你当真有良方,俺也就再冒一次险。"

莺莺见红娘答应了,忙坐到书案前,展笺拈毫,认认真真写罢交与红娘。红娘虽不识字,但药方是见过的,见小姐的方儿开得整整齐齐,也不太像,便问道:"这便是方子,可不要少了哪一味。"

莺莺脸儿一红道:"俺这方儿配伍齐全,保他药到病除。"

红娘半信半疑,将方子袖了,去西厢书院看望张生。进门正碰上长老和郎中出来,红娘道了万福。长老还礼道:"阿弥陀佛,老僧

easy to cure once Zhang's young servant returned with the medicine the learned physician had prescribed.

As they departed, Rose thought to herself: "What a charlatan that old quack is! Master Zhang is suffering from a malady that no doctor can cure." She pushed open the door, and saw Zhang lying in bed with his eyes closed and his face ashen. Rose coughed lightly.

Zhang opened his eyes. Seeing Rose, he said, "Oh, it's you, Miss Rose. Thank Heavens you've come!" And tears coursed down his hollow cheeks.

Rose bent over him and asked, "How are you feeling?"

Zhang tried to sit up, gave a groan, and fell back in a faint. Rose pounded him on the back, and he eventually recovered consciousness. He grasped the girl by the sleeve: "Should I die, Miss Rose?" he croaked. "You must be my witness at the tribunal of the King of the Underworld."

Rose too began to weep. "I have never seen such a tragic case of lovesickness," she sighed.

Zhang moaned, "It is all because of your young mistress. Both the mother and daughter are good at telling lies. Last night, when I returned crestfallen to the library, I burned with anger. How could a savior be wronged by the people he saved? An old saying goes that the maiden dotes, while the swain is unfaithful. But in my case the reverse is true."

"You should blame yourself," Rose retorted. "If you had concentrated on your studies and become the No.1 Scholar, you would certainly have a beautiful wife, and not found yourself in this grief-stricken state."

"There is only one Oriole on earth; I will never marry anyone else," declared Zhang.

Rose was glad for Miss Oriole. After so many troubles, the pathetic young scholar was still firm in his devotion to her. "Anyway," she said, "My mistress has sent me to see you and ask what medicine you, elder brother, are taking."

Upon hearing the words "elder brother," Zhang trembled with rage. "No doctor on earth can cure me, but Miss Oriole...."

Overcome with pity, Rose hastened to comfort him, "Master Zhang, my young mistress has written a prescription for you. She asked me to bring it to you."

已请太医为秀才诊过病开了药方，已命琴童出去抓药。张生不过偶感风寒，痰迷心窍而已，几副汤药下去，便会好转起来。"说罢携太医往前去了。红娘心说："真真庸医误人，什么偶感风寒，痰迷心窍？酸丁得的是心病，便是华佗再世、扁鹊重生也治不了。"她紧走两步，推门进去，只见张生拥衾倚枕，双目紧闭，歪在榻上，脸黄腮陷，无一丝光泽，着实可怜。便轻轻咳嗽了一声。

张生闻声抬抬眼皮，瞥见红娘，眸中放光，唤声"红娘"，便滴下泪来。红娘俯身问道："哥哥病体若何？"

张生强撑起身来，叫一声："害煞小生也！"便又昏厥过去。急得红娘口中呼唤："秀才醒来，秀才醒来！"忙为他抚胸捶背。半晌张生才苏醒过来，睁眼抓住红娘衣襟道："我若是死了，阎王殿里少不得姐姐做个干连！"红娘鼻子一酸，险些掉下泪来，拭了拭眼角，叹息一声道："唉，普天下害相思的都不似你这个傻角！"

张生委屈难平，愤愤道："还不是你那主子害的，娘母俩都好说谎，昨夜里回到书房，一气一个死。小生救了人，却反被害了，天理何在？自古道：'痴心女子负心汉。'如今到反过来了。"

红娘道："你也休怨天怨地的了，谁教你不管不顾没完没了地干相思，有这心劲儿用在功名上，得个状元，还愁甚如意娘子？"

张生喃喃道："天下更没有第二个莺莺，俺是非她不娶！"

红娘心中暗为小姐高兴，难得张生一片赤诚之心，便道："老夫人着我来看看哥哥，要什么汤药好叫太医抓去。"

张生听到"哥哥"二字，如遭电击，身子一哆嗦，说道："俺这颓病，非是太医所能治的。"红娘轻声说道："张生，俺小姐给你开了副药方，再三请求让俺将来与你。"

Zhang sat up at once. "Where is it? Let me have a look."

"Don't be impatient. Now listen to me." And she began to recite, "The laurel flowers cast their shadows when night is deep. The flowers should be soaked in Chinese angelica."

"But laurel flowers are warm by nature, and Chinese angelica is used to invigorate the circulation of the blood. How can the flowers be soaked in Chinese angelica?" asked Zhang.

"Hidden in the shade of the rocks by the poolside. It is very hard for you to find. If you can find it, you will recover after one or two doses," Rose continued.

This was all a mystery to Zhang.

Seeing his puzzlement, Rose chided him: "You say you are a master at solving romantic riddles. How is it that you can't understand my riddle? What 'The laurel flowers cast their shadows when night is deep' means that you may go to the garden to have a secret meeting with my young mistress. Hide yourself in the shade of the rocks by the poolside, and you may find your bride. I myself will be attending Madame Cui. Soon after you take my young mistress in your arms, you will recover." So saying, Rose took the prescription from her sleeve and handed it to Zhang. "Here is the prescription written by my young mistress for you," said Rose.

Zhang opened the letter, and read it. The letter's contents seemed to infuse new life into him, so that he was able to rise from his bed. Beaming with joy, he said in a rapturous voice: "Had I known that this was a poem from your young mistress, I should have received it on my knees. How happy I am!"

Rose was amazed at the sudden transformation in the young man's health, and even more amazed when she saw Zhang put on his shoes and start to dance.

"Miss Rose," he cried, "your young mistress has written a poem declaring her love for me!"

"It is a medical prescription, not a silly love poem," snorted Rose. "Don't get carried away again, I warn you!"

"You're wrong, Rose. It is a beautiful love poem. Listen."

And he read out the poem — for it was indeed a poem — that Oriole had written to him:

Trouble not your heart with trifles mere,

张生听得小姐亲自开方,坐起来急问:"在哪里? 快快给我!"

红娘失笑道:"看把你急的,你听我说,这方子是'桂花'摇影夜深沉,酸醋'当归'浸。"

张生脱口道:"桂花性温,当归活血,不知怎样炮制?"

红娘道:"面靠着湖山背阴里藏的,这方儿最难寻,但寻着,一服两服便治愈。"张生不解其中之意,问道:"须忌些什么?"

红娘道:"忌的是'知母'未寝,怕的是'红娘'撒赖。吃罢了,稳情取'使君子'一星儿'参'。"

张生沉思半晌道:"知母性甘微寒;红娘子苦平略有小毒,不可近目;使君子性甘温;人参么,性甘微寒。啊唷,红娘姐姐,此方这般配伍,怎会出自小姐之手?"

红娘心急:"亏你还自诩什么猜诗谜的行家,连俺红娘这几句话都猜不透,俺之意是让你在桂摇影夜深沉之时去赴约,与小姐成就好事。你问我忌些什么,自然是老夫人没睡,红娘跟你们捣乱。"见张生仍在沉思冥想,便从袖中拈出莺莺所写的药方,递到张生面前:"别胡思乱想了,这小姐亲自给你开的药方,你看了便知。"

张生接过展看,顿时一脸乌云散尽,抚床大笑道:"早知姐姐书来,合当远接,红娘姐姐,高兴煞小生也。"

张生这番举动倒把红娘吓了一跳,道:"先生又怎么了。"

张生直起身来,趿鞋下地,手舞足蹈,哈哈大笑道:"姐姐,你还不知这简儿里的诗意,小姐得要和小生哩也波哩也嘿。"

红娘见怪不怪,冷笑一声道:"明明是药方,怎么说是诗? 相公可别又看差了。"

张生笑道:"哪里会错? 这的确是一首诗嘛。我念与你听听。"

Nor extinguish your talent aglow!
To keep my modesty without a smear,
I knew not that it would bring you woe.
To pay my debt, convention I slight
But send a new verse to the Western Bower.
I'm sure to bring fresh showers tonight
For the long, long thirsting flower.

Though Rose did not completely understand the nuances in most of the poem, there was no mistaking the purport of the last sentence.

"Well, I'll tell you one thing," said Rose. "Your miserable chamber is like a monk's cell. I just can't imagine my young mistress being willing to catch her death of cold by spending a night here!"

Zhang was impressed by Rose's honest and forthright manner. Though she had a sharp tongue, she was always considerate about other people. He bowed to the girl, and said, "Here are 10 taels of silver. Could you please procure some suitable bedding for me?"

"I have pillows embroidered with pairs of lovebirds, and a coverlet of turquoise blue. But why should I lend them to you?" Rose said.

Zhang said, "If you can help me fulfill my love tonight, I will never forget your kindness."

"I don't want anything from you. Let bygones be bygones. I don't want white jade or yellow gold from you. If you have a suitable store of ambition, you should succeed in the imperial civil service examination, and make my young mistress an honored official's wife."

Zhang was overcome with gratitude. But then it occurred to him that perhaps Madame Cui would not allow Oriole to come out into the garden that night.

When he mentioned this to Rose, she dismissed the idea. "It all depends on my young mistress," she said. "If she is willing to come out to meet you, Madame will not be able to stop her even if she guards the door day and night. She will find a way to meet you."

As an old saying goes: Once bitten by a snake, one shies at a coiled rope for the next 10 years. Likewise, Zhang was still worried. "But what if what happened last night happens again...."

150

张生得意洋洋朗声吟道:"休将闲事苦萦怀,取次摧残无赋才。不意当时完妾命,岂防今日作君灾。仰图厚德难从礼,谨奉新诗可当媒。寄雨高唐休咏赋,今宵端的雨云来。"

红娘并未全听懂,但最后一句"今宵端的雨云来",还是听明白了。心想:好个小肠转圈子的小姐,又将俺耍了。便对张生道:"你可看仔细了?"

张生一拍胸脯道:"看仔细了,此诗非前日可比,小姐必来。"

红娘鼻子里哼了一声道:"你瞧瞧,身卧着一条布衾,头枕着三尺瑶琴,俺姐姐来时怎和你一处寝?果若你有心,她有意,昨日里花园中秋千下,你二人春宵一刻抵千金,何须今日又'诗对会家吟'?"

张生此时觉得红娘是个古道侠肠的好姑娘,话虽说得刻薄,但处处为自家与小姐着想,便躬身一揖道:"小生有花银十两,请姐姐为小生赁副铺盖。"红娘见张生当真相求,笑道:"俺那鸳鸯枕翡翠衾,如何肯赁与你个穷酸?"

张生连连作揖道:"姐姐就可怜可怜小生,成全了俺吧。今夜成了好事,小生怎敢忘记姐姐的大恩大德。"

红娘道:"俺可不图希你甚么,你若有志气,给俺小姐挣揣回个满头花拖地锦、五花官诰才是正事!"

张生感激涕零道:"姐姐的话小生全都记下了,多谢姐姐鼎力相助,不过… 只怕…只怕老夫人拘系得紧,小姐不能够出来。"

红娘道:"这事成与不成全在小姐身上,单怕她不肯,若是她肯时,就是老夫人日夜把门看着,她也自会对出空子,好歹与你相见!"

张生一次被蛇咬,十年怕井绳,心里难免生疑,巴巴地又道:"可休似昨夜……"

"You have only yourself to blame for what happened last night," Rose said. "If my young mistress comes tonight, it will be up to you to consummate your love. You don't need anyone to teach you, do you?" Then Rose took her leave.

Rose went to the Rear Hall to report on Zhang's state of health to Madame Cui before returning to the Embroidery Pavilion, where Oriole was pretending to be busy with her embroidery work.

"Get my bed ready, Rose," she told the girl. "I will retire early tonight."

"Oh, really?" exclaimed Rose. "He will be disappointed!"

"Who will?" asked Oriole, guilelessly.

"You know perfectly well who," said Rose. "If you keep secrets from me I will go and inform my mistress that you told me to arrange a rendezvous for you with Master Zhang."

"You little cat!" cried Oriole indignantly. "I simply asked you to take a prescription to him. What's all this nonsense about a rendezvous?"

"You wrote, 'I'm sure to bring fresh showers tonight.' What are 'showers'? I have never heard of a herbal medicine called 'showers.'"

Oriole blushed to the roots of her hair.

Without more ado, Rose helped Oriole to dress herself like a bride, and the two of them set off for the garden. Rose carried with her a brocade coverlet and a pair of pillows embroidered with love-birds. As they entered the gate, Oriole quickened her pace. Following behind, Rose thought, "You were shy a moment ago, and were hesitating whether to go or not. Now, the Fairy Queen is hastening to meet the Fairy King, who is waiting for her with dreams of spring."

红娘道："你打起精神来吧，今夜她若来时，肯与不肯由她，你见了时，亲与不亲在你，这事还须人教？"又叮嘱了几句，便告辞出来。

红娘先到后堂回了老夫人的话，而后才回到绣阁。莺莺正在埋头绣花，见红娘回来，便说道："红娘，你快收拾卧房，我想早些睡。"

红娘一听心中着急，脱口道："你若睡了，哪里发付那生？"

莺莺柳眉一挑，杏眼圆睁："什么那生？"

红娘道："姐姐，你又来了！送了人家性命可不是耍的，你今夜再翻悔，现在我就到老夫人那儿出首去，就说是你让我将简帖儿亲送了去约下他来。"

莺莺嗔道："你这小贱人，倒会放刁。俺让你去送药方子，怎反咬一口说是下简约他？"

红娘暗忖："好个爱做作的小姐，到现在了还跟我来这套。你若不瞒我，早就成了好事，干脆我先捅破这层窗户纸。"想到这里，便说："莫非俺吃了熊心豹子胆，敢给主子栽赃，你那药方上不是写着'今宵端的云雨来'么？这云雨是甚药，俺还从未听说过。"

莺莺一听，便知是那憨郎将诗读与红娘听了，羞得满面绯红。

夜深了，红娘对精心打扮停当的莺莺道："姐姐咱快去来，俺已打探到老夫人睡下了。"

莺莺踌躇道："羞人答答的，怎生去？"

红娘说："快走吧，到了那里把眼儿闭了，有什么羞的！"说罢，抱了锦被鸳枕，搀了莺莺便走。二人开角门进了花园，莺莺便加快了脚步。红娘跟在后面暗道："适才还嘴强哩，去呀不去呀的，现在脚下生风走了个快，也学那巫娥女赴高唐去会楚襄王。此时，那楚襄王想是早就候在阳台上了。"

CHAPTER EIGHT

The Tryst

After tidying up the library, Zhang waited for Oriole. The first watch of the night was already over, but there was still no sign of her. He was worried that she would play false with him again. In the bright moonlight, the wind stirred the bamboo groves, and the flowers danced. Zhang walked out of the library and, standing in front of the door, recited a verse: "The beautiful night on earth is silent far and nigh. When will the beautiful lady come from on high?" He thought to himself: "Since I first caught sight of Miss Oriole, I have been lovesick for her. But Oriole does not know how much I long for her. Had I foreseen that I would be obsessed day and night, I would have been afraid of meeting such a beauty. "

Zhang was as restless as an ant on a hot pan. It was already the second watch, and Miss Oriole still had not shown up. He went back to his room and lay down on the bed, thinking: "If she is willing to come, it is only a short distance between her chamber and the library. Why is it so hard for her to come?" Just as he was thinking of how much he had suffered over the previous six months there came a knock at the door.

Zhang jumped up from the bed as if at the sound of a fire alarm. He scurried to the door, opened it, and found himself face to face with Rose. "Has Miss Oriole come?" he gasped eagerly.

"Take her coverlet and pillows please. My young mistress is right behind me. How will you thank me, Master Zhang?"

The young man took the coverlet and pillows, and put them on the bed. Then he turned round and made a deep bow to Rose. "Miss Rose," he said, "words fail to express my feelings at this moment, but Heaven knows that I will be forever in your debt."

"Go to meet my young mistress. And remember to mind your manners, or you will frighten her," said Rose.

第八章
佳期暗度

再说张生在书斋里收拾爽利,单等莺莺到来。此时月明如水,清辉四溢,风弄竹声,花影婆娑。张生步出书斋,立在石阶之上轻声吟道:"人间良夜静复静,天上美人来不来?"又思道:"自家从佛殿惊艳以来,心中无一刻放下小姐,可小姐她哪里知道呵?早知道为了她无明无夜地害相思,倒不如当初不要遇上这倾国倾城的美娇娥。"张生这般忽喜忽怨,忽悔忽恨,忽疑忽猜,直到二更仍不见小姐来,便气得回房倒在床上,心里思绪翻腾:她若是肯来,这书院与绣阁也不过五百步的路程,如何这般难行?真是怪,小姐那般恶抢白,自家却并不往心里去,不知自家是怎样时时刻刻捱过来。

再说红娘抱着锦被鸳枕,与小姐从花园便门来到书院。红娘让小姐留在假山边上,自己先到书房敲门去叫张生。张生正在胡思乱想之际,听到敲门声,猛地从床上坐起,扑过去一把将门开了,喘息道:"红娘姐姐,小姐可来了么?"红娘将锦被鸳枕往张生怀里一推,道:"你快接了衾枕,小姐就在后面。张生你怎么谢我?"

张生忙将兰麝扑鼻的衾枕放在床上,转身对着红娘就是深深一拜,道:"红娘姐姐的大恩,小生一言难尽,寸心相报,惟天可表!"

红娘道:"还不快去接小姐。"

"But where is she?"

"Open your eyes wider. Who is the lady standing by the rockery?" Zhang was about to set off at a run, but Rose stopped him.

"What a bad memory you have! The last time you acted rashly too, and my young mistress was angry. Don't be so impetuous!"

"You're right, of course. But what shall I do then?" asked Zhang.

"You stay here; I will bring her in."

"Whatever you say."

Rose returned to the rockery and whispered to Oriole: "Master Zhang has been waiting for you for quite a long time."

Upon hearing this, Oriole covered her face with her sleeve, and was too shy to say anything. They walked towards the library slowly. Rose opened the door for Oriole, closed it after her, and remained outside.

Seeing Oriole standing in front of him, Zhang knelt down and said: "How fortunate I am to be favored with your visit. Am I in a dream?"

Oriole lowered her head and asked shyly: "Please get up. Are you feeling better now?"

"The very sight of your Heavenly countenance would banish every ailment," Zhang replied gallantly.

Oriole stretched out her hand to help him get up. Zhang took this opportunity to embrace her willow-slender waist. Her fragrant body was as light as that of a swallow. He carried her gently to the bed and examined her exquisite form closely under the light of the lamp. Zhang untied the silken belt that held her robe. Oriole felt soft all over, allowing Zhang to do whatever he wished. They made love to each other. Overwhelmed with ecstasy, they felt as happy and free as a pair of fish swimming in the sea.

Soon the moon sank in the west. In the lamplight, Zhang took a look at red blood on the white silk under their bodies.

Zhang said while fondling Oriole's breasts: "I have won your virgin purity. I have completed my happiness tonight."

Oriole got up to put on her clothes. "I must leave now," she said, "lest my mother discover my absence."

Zhang had no choice but to get up and put his own clothes on. "I'll see you off, my dear. Tonight, we have met behind the gauze bed-screen, but when shall I again untie your green belt?"

张生欣喜若狂,连连点头道:"是是是,俺那小姐现在何处?"

"你把眼睛睁大些,那假山旁立着的是谁?"

张生闪目一看,恨不得立刻冲上去,忙道:"俺这就去迎接。"

红娘拦住他,道:"好个记吃不记打的酸秀才,前番便是你鲁莽行事,臊恼了小姐,今日又……"

张生忙将脚儿收回,道:"姐姐说得极是,那小生应当如何?"

"好了,你等在这里,待俺把小姐扶来,你再接进去。"

"遵命,遵命。"

红娘回到假山旁,搀着莺莺缓缓行来,俯耳对莺莺说道:"姐姐,张生等你好久了。"把个莺莺羞得忙以袖遮面,说不出一句话来,及至门前,红娘轻轻一推道:"姐姐,你进去吧,我在门儿外等你。"说着反手把书房门带上。

张生见莺莺羞答答立在灯下,不觉双膝跪地,喃喃道:"想俺张珙有何德何能,敢劳神仙下凡,这该不是在梦里吧?"

莺莺粉颈低垂,娇羞不胜道:"还不快快起来,你的病可好些?"

张生道:"小生哪里得病来,姐姐一来,早医好了九分不快。姐姐这般用心,不才张珙,合当跪拜。"说着纳头便拜。

莺莺伸手相扶,张生顺势起来,将莺莺抱了个满怀,只觉她软玉温香,腰细如柳,身轻若燕,轻轻抱入帐中,灯下细瞧,则见她粉面桃腮,云鬓堆鸦,双目微闭,娇喘吁吁,美艳绝伦,不禁倍加爱怜,伸手轻轻为其宽衣解带。莺莺此时浑身酥软,无半两力气,只得任其摆弄。二人初试云雨,如鱼得水,意浓情切,自不必说。

及至月儿西沉,方云散雨歇。灯下张生偷瞧身下白绸,见腥红点点。

Oriole was too shy to say anything. They held each other tight. When they opened the door, they found Rose waiting outside. "Congratulations, Master Zhang," she said. "Now, how do you intend to thank me?"

"Miss Rose, I'm very grateful to you. I'll never forget your kindness."

"I should hope not," Rose said with a smile. Then she turned to Oriole: "Young Mistress, let's go back right away," she urged.

Zhang, who was reluctant to part from Oriole, said, "Please come earlier another night."

Oriole nodded slightly. Rose then led her away in the moonlight.

At this moment, there was a fragrant dew on the earth, the wind soughed over the lonely steps, and the moon shone its rays into the library.

张生轻抚玉人酥胸，口中赞叹："难怪唐明皇有'新剥鸡头肉'之叹，今日小生方信世间果有此物。"

莺莺羞答答掩胸起来穿衣，道："天色不早了，怕老夫人发觉，我该回去了。"

张生着实不忍其离去，可又不敢拖延，也整衣而起道："我送小姐出去，只是今宵同会碧纱厨，何时重解香罗带？"

莺莺含羞不语，与张生相拥至门前。刚一开门，红娘便迎了上来，道："张生你大喜了，快来拜你前世的娘。"

张生道："多谢红娘姐姐成就好事，小生没齿难忘！"

红娘笑道："罢了，罢了。"转身又对莺莺道："姐姐，咱快回去吧。"

张生依依不舍道："若小姐不弃小生，明夜破些功夫早点儿来吧。"

莺莺微微点头应允，红娘见她脚步挪不动，便上前搀起，乘着月色步苍苔出了便门。

此时露滴香埃，夜静闲阶，月映书斋，云锁阳台。

CHAPTER NINE

A Handmaid in the Dock

Soon the Mid-Autumn Festival came. Madame Cui noticed that her daughter seemed absent-minded and preoccupied these days. Moreover, her figure appeared different, with protruding breasts and a bulging waist. "What is the matter with her?" she wondered. The Mid-Autumn Festival, which falls on the 15th day of the eighth lunar month, is a day for family reunions. Madame Cui expected Oriole and Rose to arrive early in the evening to eat moon cakes and enjoy the full moon together with her. However, when there was no sign of Oriole and Rose after dusk had fallen, Madame Cui thought that something very odd indeed must have happened.

"Mother, I have something to tell you," piped up Merry Boy, who was standing near.

"What is it?"

"That night before last, after you had gone to bed, I went outside and saw my sister and Rose burning incense in the garden. Later, I found out that they did not come back until daybreak."

Madame Cui was astonished to hear this, and immediately her suspicions were aroused.

"Call Rose here right now!" she ordered the boy through clenched teeth.

Off the boy went on his fateful errand.

"What does she want?" asked Rose, when she heard the summons.

"Oh, she wants to know what you and Oriole were up to in the garden of the Western Bower the other night, that's all," answered the boy.

These words pounded Rose like hammer blows, but she managed to retain her composure, and said to Merry Boy: "Well, you run along now, and tell my mistress that I will be with her forthwith."

"You'd better hurry up; she's in a bad mood." So saying, he skipped back the way he had come.

第九章
夫人拷红

　　却说转眼到了中秋时节,老夫人发觉近些日子女儿莺莺春黛渐深,秋水凝眸,语言恍惚,神思徜徉,胸高腰圆,与以往不同,不由心中疑惑,莫非女儿做下什么事了?中秋月圆本该全赏月,可迟迟不见女儿与红娘来到,不由自言自语道:"这孩子也忒不懂事了,这个时候还不过来!"立在一旁的欢郎插言道:"娘,俺告诉您一件事。前日晚间,俺跑出去撒尿,见姐姐和红娘到花园里烧香,半晌不回来,俺便睡去了。听奶娘说第二天天快亮了她们才回来。"

　　老夫人心下顿时一惊:"女儿素有拜月习惯,只是如何能用了一夜时间,莫不是与书院那生……此事都在红娘身上,只问她便知根底。"想到这里,便对欢郎道:"你去叫那红娘过来。"

　　欢郎忙出来到绣阁呼唤红娘。红娘听到欢郎呼喊,探出头来问道:"小哥哥唤我做什么?"

　　欢郎道:"俺娘知道你和姐姐去花园里了,如今要打你哩。"

　　红娘一听,心中暗叫道:"呀!小姐,你连累我了。"又稳了稳心神对欢郎道:"小哥哥,你先去,我随后便来。"

　　欢郎道:"红娘你可要快些,俺娘气得很哩!我先去了。"说着一路蹦蹦跳跳地走了。

Rose ran into Oriole's bedroom and blurted out, " Young Mistress, I think your mother has found out about your affair with Master Zhang! She's sent for me, and I'm sure she's going to interrogate me about it."

Oriole was devastated. With tears in her eyes, she begged, "Dear Rose, you must not breath a word about it!"

"I kept telling you to be more discreet," said Rose. "I knew that the way you and Master Zhang were carrying on sooner or later someone would find out about your affair."

Oriole burst into a flood of tears. "What can we do? What can we do?" she cried. "Rose, you must be very careful when answering my mother's questions."

"You are the one who should be punished, Young Mistress, but instead I know that the blame will fall on me. While you two were snug and warm in your love nest, I was shivering outside all night. But anyway, I suppose that is the lot of a handmaiden. I will try to explain away your behavior, and if I cannot I am prepared to take the blows that should be directed at you." So saying, Rose left the Embroidery Pavilion, holding her head high. Her reception by Madame Cui was just as she had expected.

"Get down on your knees, you little wretch!" were her mistress' first words.

Obediently, Rose knelt down and lowered her head.

"Now confess your guilt!"

Rose raised her head and opened her eyes wide, "Your humble maid knows of no guilt to confess," she protested.

Madame Cui said, gnashing her teeth: "How dare you deny it! If you tell the truth, I will pardon you; if not, I will beat you to death, you little minx! Who told you to take your young mistress into the garden at midnight?"

Rose said: "Since her childhood, my young mistress has had the habit of praying to the moon. You always let me go with her on those occasions."

Madame Cui flew into a rage. "There was no moon the night before last, you impertinent slut!" she yelled. "Now, tell me: What were you doing in the garden?"

Rose realized that she was trapped, and if she had any more inclination to prevaricate it vanished as soon as she felt the sting of a bamboo cane across her thin shoulders.

红娘忙进卧室对小姐道："姐姐,姐姐,事发了呀,老夫人唤我去哩,这可怎生是好?"莺莺一听顿时没了主意,汪着两眼泪对红娘道："好姐姐,可要替我遮盖些。"

红娘道："俺的娘哟,俺早就叫你们做得隐密些。只让你夜去明来,倒还有个天长地久。谁让你停眠整宿?此时老夫人早猜到那穷酸做了新婚,小姐你做了娇妻,俺红娘做了牵头。姐姐你受责罚理所当然,我可图甚么来?你在绣帏里与张生颠鸾倒凤,共效于飞之乐,俺在窗外连咳嗽都不敢,整夜立在苍苔上,绣鞋儿都冰透了,今日里到落得个细皮肉挨顿粗棍儿抽。姐姐,你也别哭了,愁也没用,你在这里等俺的消息,俺这就去。说得过,休欢喜;说不过,休烦恼。"说罢挺胸抬头出门去了。

红娘出了绣阁,径到中堂之上,进门便对老夫人敛衽道了个万福。老夫人面沉似水,断喝道："小贱人,为甚么不跪下!"红娘道声"是",忙低头跪下。老夫人又道："你可知罪么?"红娘抬起头来睁大眼睛道："红娘不知身犯何罪?"老夫人恨得咬牙切齿道："你还敢口硬哩,我且问你,谁让你和小姐到花园里去来?"红娘道："小姐自小有焚香拜月的习惯,是老夫人您让俺同她去来。"老夫人一听,心说好你个伶牙俐齿的小蹄子,倒推了个干净,怒道："我让你陪小姐月明时焚香,谁着你整夜通宵拜月,更没让你没月时拜月。老实说,去花园干甚?""什么也没做,说俺们通宵整夜,谁见来?"

老夫人愤愤道："欢郎和他奶娘见来,还敢抵赖?看来不打你便不招。"说着站起来抓起竹棍儿劈头盖脸打来。

红娘急用双手护头,道："老夫人休闪了手,听红娘说!"

老夫人用竹棍狠戳红娘,道："快快从实招来。"

Rose explained: "One evening, when we had finished our sewing, we started to talk about her elder brother's plight. His health was becoming worse and worse. Alone there in the library, there was no one to take care of him. We felt sorry for him, and decided to inquire after his health without telling you."

"Bah! You're shameless! Then you went to the library?"

"Yes."

"What did the young man say?"

"He said that you had gone back on your word, returned evil for good and turned his joy into grief. He hates you because you stood in the way of his marrying Oriole."

"Oh, what an exaggeration!" cried Madame Cui. "What else did he say?"

"He told me to leave, but said my young mistress should remain."

Madame Cui's eyebrows shot up. "How could an unmarried maiden remain there unchaperoned?" she exclaimed. "I never heard of such a thing!"

"Well, I thought she was simply going to administer some healing medicine," explained Rose. "And then, before I knew it, they were spending every night together. There was nothing I could do about it, really Madame!"

Madame Cui trembled all over with anger. Pointing an accusing finger at Rose, she thundered, "This is all your fault. If you hadn't acted as the go-between this would never have happened."

"It is neither I nor Master Zhang nor Miss Oriole who is to blame, Madame. The fault lies with you yourself."

"What? Such impertinence! How can it be my fault?" Madame Cui yelled indignantly.

"It is fundamental for a man to keep faith. One who does not has no worth," said Rose, quoting *The Analects of Confucius*.

"Well, I never!" thought Madame Cui to herself. "I always thought that this girl was stupid, but although she is illiterate she knows how to pick up bits and pieces of wisdom from her young mistress' lessons and throw them in my face!"

"Why did you say I have not kept faith?" she asked aloud.

Rose said, "When the monastery was surrounded by the bandits, you promised to give your daughter as wife to anyone who could make them withdraw. If Master Zhang had not been an admirer of the beauty

　　红娘道:"那天夜里俺和小姐停了针绣,在灯下闲聊天,偶然说起张生哥哥病了好久,且一天重似一天,空斋寂寞,孤院萧条,近来不知怎样?药炉茶灶,谁去照应?万一不测,又有谁知道?一时心怜不过,便商议二人一道去书房问候。"

　　老夫人听到这儿,啐了一口道:"你们好不知羞,他说什么?"

　　红娘道:"他说老夫人言而无信,过河拆桥,令他半途将喜变做忧,把他与小姐好端端的婚事破了。他实是怨恨你哩!"

　　老夫人闻言心中发虚,道:"俺可没把他当外人,他还说些甚?"

　　"他还说红娘你且先行,教小姐权且落后。"

　　老夫人一听皱眉道:"她是个女孩儿家,着她落后做什么?"

　　红娘道:"老夫人说的是啊,俺原以为小姐神针妙手能医好哥哥的病,谁承想他们一双心意两相投,成就了燕侣莺俦,到如今他们双宿双飞,已一月有余。"老夫人气得浑身乱颤,七窍生烟,竹棍儿指点着红娘骂道:"没家亲引不出外鬼来,这件事都是你这个贱人窜掇的。"红娘道:"依俺看,此事非张生小姐红娘之罪,乃老夫人之过也。"老夫人道:"好你个小贱人,倒指下我来,怎么是老身之过?"红娘道:"信者人之根本,人而无信,不知其可也。大车无輗,小车无軏,其何以行之哉?"

　　老夫人听红娘背诵起《论语》来,心中暗自惊叹红娘的记忆力,难得她一个目不识丁的丫头,听小姐读《论语》,便能用心记下,且能拈来活用。只是平日太放纵她了,今日闯下大祸,反污我无信,这还了得?便打断她道:"小贱人,俺怎么无信了?"

　　红娘道:"当日孙飞虎兵围普救寺,是老夫人您亲口许下谁能退兵,便将小姐与他做妻。张生如不是爱慕小姐容颜,岂肯区区建

of my young mistress, would he, an outsider, have proposed a plan to rid us of the bandit plague? But when the bandits were routed and you were left in peace, you went back on your word. Was this not a breach of faith? If you found it impossible to consent to the match, you should have rewarded him with money and let him go far, far away. It was playing with fire to allow him to stay in the library near the young mistress' quarters in the Western Bower. Now what is done can't be undone. What is the use of blaming me? If you do not cover up this scandal, in the first place, the family honor of the late prime minister will be compromised, and in the second place, you will wrong Master Zhang, our benefactor. The best course for you to take is to keep the promise you made to unite them as man and wife. The young man has a bright future ahead of him, and your daughter is a radiant beauty. Besides, why make an enemy of a good friend who sent for the White Horse General to rescue you and your family when they were in distress? Why turn a benefactor into an enemy and bring disgrace to your own family?"

While listening to Rose, Madame Cui wrestled with mixed feelings of sadness, anxiety and anger. She thought: "Against innumerable hardships I struggled to bring up my daughter. I wanted her to marry my nephew, Zheng Heng, so that I could rely on them in my remaining years. To my surprise, my daughter has done such a disgraceful thing! But what this little chit of a handmaiden said makes sense after all. If the case were brought to the court, it would bring disgrace on our family. After pondering deeply for a while, she said, "There's no help for it but to sacrifice my beloved daughter to this unscrupulous schemer! Rose, go and tell Oriole to come here!"

"Yes, Madame," said Rose. She stood up, rubbed her knees and ran out of the Middle Hall. When she reached the Western Bower she saw that Oriole had been waiting on tenterhooks for her return.

Oriole was surprised and relieved to see that Rose was smiling after her ordeal of being interrogated by Madame Cui. She rushed to seize the girl by the hand. "Was it very terrible, Rose?" she asked solicitously.

"At first, yes. But after I gave her some straightforward advice, she came round to my way of thinking. She has agreed to let you and Master Zhang become man and wife. My mistress wants you to go to her straight away, together with Master Zhang, so that you can be married this very day. Congratulations, my dear young mistress!"

退兵之策？兵退身安,老夫人您却悔却前言,这难道不为失信？老
夫人既然不肯成就他二人婚事, 则当多多酬之以金帛, 令张生断
此念而去。更不该留张生住进老相爷西厢书院,使怨女旷夫早晚
相窥,咫尺相思。如今生米做成熟饭,你只管理怨俺个丫头有何
用？眼下老夫人若不平息其事,传扬出去,一来有碍于相国的声
望,败坏了小姐芳誉;二来张生日后名重天下,他岂肯白白施恩于
人而反受其辱？即便告到官府,老夫人亦得治家不严之罪。莫若恕
其小过,一俊遮百丑,成就了他二人姻缘,既遮了众人耳目,堵了
世人之口,又保全了小姐的名声、相国家谱,岂不是皆大欢喜？更
何况张生博古通今,是文章魁首;小姐国色天香,堪称仕女班头。
他们郎才女貌, 实为天生一对, 地造一双, 合当让有情人结成眷
属。对张生这个白马将军的故友,斩飞虎叛贼的恩人,咱怎能与他
反目成仇做对头？红娘说这些话可都是为了老夫人好。"

　　老夫人一边听着,一边想着,只觉又悲又急又恨:悲的是自己
千辛万苦养了这么一个女儿,实指望嫁与侄儿郑恒,亲上加亲,自
家晚年有靠,万没想到女儿竟如此不争气,八字未见一撇,就先做
出这种事来,岂不是自己前生冤孽？急的是女儿做出这等丑事,自
己孤儿寡母,如何应付才好？恨的是张生居然色胆包天,竟敢无视
俺相国尊严！红娘小贱人说得倒也在理,千不该万不该,是自己不
该养了这么个不孝之女。思量再三,狠狠心说道:"罢罢！咱家世无
犯法之男,门无再婚之女,就与了那厮吧。红娘,你唤那贱人来！"

　　红娘道声"遵命",便站立起来,揉揉发酸的膝盖,喜滋滋出了
中堂,一路急行回到后院。莺莺见红娘满脸喜气,步履轻盈,忙迎
上去拉住红娘的手,说道:"红娘,老夫人将你打疼了吧？"红娘冲

Oriole could not believe her ears. "Is it true?" she asked, grabbing Rose by both hands tightly.

"Absolutely true! Let's go to your mother now," replied Rose.

But suddenly the thought of facing her mother filled Oriole with dread. Flushed with shame, she lowered her head and twisted a handkerchief in her hands, in an agony of indecision. "Oh, Rose, how dare I stand in front of my mother face to face?"

"Young Mistress, what you did was for the sake of true love. You can hold your head high in front of the whole world, and not just in front of your mother," said Rose. With this, she half coaxed, half dragged Oriole towards the Middle Hall.

As soon as Oriole appeared in the doorway, Madame Cui started to berate her: "You wicked and unnatural daughter!" she cried. "How could you have been so deceitful?" She then dissolved into a flood of tears. Finally, she recovered sufficiently to gasp, "But there is nothing else for it; a scandal would bring intolerable disgrace on our family. Rose, go and fetch that villainous young man here!"

Zhang had been used to nightly trysts with Oriole, escorted by Rose, so when he saw Rose approach in the daytime he was filled with a sense of foreboding.

"Why are you calling on me, Rose?" asked Zhang.

"Your sneaky affair has been discovered. My mistress wants to see you right away," said Rose, with a grave look on her face.

Dumbfounded, Zhang was at a loss what to do. He appealed to the resourceful Rose: "This is terrible! How can I get out of this difficulty?"

Rose burst into laughter. "You look like a frightened schoolboy," she said. "As a matter of fact, it is probably not a bad thing that this secret liaison has come to light after all. You couldn't go on forever meeting furtively, now could you? Anyway, you don't need a go-between now."

"What do you mean?" Zhang was puzzled.

"I had no choice but to tell Madame Cui the whole truth once she got wind of what was going on. But I also told her that the only way to avoid any hint of disgrace to the family was to let you and Miss Oriole get married. And so she has agreed that you two should be wed this very day."

It took Zhang a long time to realize that he was not dreaming. When

她调皮地一眨眼道："并不曾伤了半点儿皮肉,我也怕不得许多,竹筒倒豆子,照直说了。老夫人如今着我来唤你,要与你们成合亲事。"莺莺听了,有些不相信自家的耳朵,睁大眼睛,拉住红娘的手摇晃道："当真如此?"红娘嘻嘻一笑,说道："千真万确,姐姐快随俺去堂上见老夫人去。"莺莺转忧为喜,一颗悬着的心顿时落在肚里,又一想,尽管母亲许了婚,可自己私下里做出这等事,如何见得母亲?便不由面红耳赤起来道："羞人答答的,怎么去见老夫人?"

红娘道："啊哟,这亲娘跟前有什么羞的?当日月儿才上柳梢头,你们早人约黄昏后,唧唧哝哝,说着肉麻的话儿,那其间可怎生不害半星儿羞?事到如今,反到害起羞来,快快走吧。"说着连推带搡拖着莺莺,往中堂走来。莺莺进门,低头敛衽给老夫人道了个万福。

老夫人一见女儿进来,气不打一处来,脱口道："莺莺,我怎生抬举你来,今日做下这等勾当。"说着悲从中来,珠泪滚滚。顿了顿又道："我待经官来,又怕辱没了你父亲,这等事不是俺相国人家做的。罢罢罢!谁叫俺养女不长进。红娘,你到书房里将那禽兽唤来。"

红娘忙腿脚麻利地来到西厢书院,进门便直着嗓子唤道："张生,张生。"张生今日正在书房吟诗作画,不提防红娘此时大呼大唤地进来,心中便是一惊,忙起身迎接道："姐姐唤小生做甚?"

红娘一脸秋霜道："西厢事发了,老夫人叫你去哩!"

张生顿时吓得呆若木鸡,嘴角抽搐,颤声道："这可如何是好?"

红娘见状大笑道："看你这副熊样,俺以为你是个顶天立地的大丈夫,呸,却原来是个苗而不秀的银样蜡枪头!"

张生道："小生甚是惶恐,如何见老夫人?也不知当初谁在老夫人那里说来?"

173

he did so, he made a deep bow to Rose, and said, "Thank Heaven! And thank you, Rose. The day I have looked forward to for so long has finally come!"

"Well, don't dillydally on this of all days," Rose urged. "Let's go right now."

When Zhang still hesitated, obviously too ashamed to face Madame Cui, the girl said, "You were brave enough when you climbed the tree and jumped over the wall that night. What are you afraid of today? Let's go."

Following Rose sheepishly, Zhang presented himself before Madame Cui in the Middle Hall. Bowing deeply, he said, "I, Zhang Gong, pay my most profound respects to you, Madame."

Madame Cui shot a glance full of venom at him. "A fine, upright scholar you turned out to be! It seems that I have nursed a viper in my bosom! All the time I thought that your service for our family was pure and disinterested, you were harboring shameful thoughts, it seems."

Zhang was so overcome with remorse that he could find no words with which to excuse himself.

Madame Cui continued, "If I were to hand you over to the judicial authorities — which I have every right to do — it would be the end of your career and all your fancy hopes and dreams. However, it would also bring disgrace on the late prime minister's name and the rest of his family. So I have concluded that the only way out of the mess you have got us all into is for you to marry my daughter."

Oriole, Rose and Zhang were overjoyed to hear these words, notwithstanding the fact that the preliminary part was far from flattering. Oriole was wild with joy, because she was to become the wife of a man with a brilliant career ahead of him. Rose was glad, because her efforts over the past half year to unite the lovers had not been in vain. And Zhang of course was deliriously happy to realize that his most fervent wish had come true. He threw himself on the ground at Madame Cui's feet: "Your humble son-in-law pays his heartfelt respects to his...."

But before he had chance to finish his gush of gratitude, Madame Cui cut him short: "Wait, let me finish. You must remember that for three generations our family has never had a son-in-law without an official rank. So the first thing you must do is hasten to the capital to take the civil service examination. I will take care of your future wife in the meantime. If you pass the examinations with honor, come back and marry my daughter. If not, never darken our doorstep again. Do you understand?"

　　红娘道："是俺自首去来，这做夫妻图的是天长地久，你们能偷偷摸摸一辈子不成?漏就漏了，怕甚么?有甚惶恐的?实话对你说吧，俺家老夫人已把小姐许配给你了，还不快去拜见你家岳母大人。"

　　张生一听说老夫人已许了婚姻，简直不敢相信自己的耳朵，还以为是在梦中，半晌方回过神来，对着红娘深深一揖道："谢天谢地，总算盼到这天了。"红娘掩口笑道："罢了，罢了，快走吧。"

　　张生踌躇着，尽管老夫人许了婚事，可当面去见，实在是难为情，脸红脖子粗地嗫嚅道："这……我……"红娘道："休这个那个的了，拿出当日自为媒人、攀树跳墙的勇气来，还有甚怕的?"

　　张生只得跟在红娘身后来到中堂，进门对老夫人深施一礼道："晚生张珙见过老夫人!"老夫人见了张生，狠狠剜了他两眼道："好一个读书识礼的秀才，岂不闻'非先王之德行不敢行'，竟然做出这等猪狗不如之事，真正辱没斯文。"

　　张生此时羞得无地自容，只得垂首听训。老夫人又道："我待送你到衙门里去，只恐辱没了俺清白家谱，也怕耽误了你的前程。事已至此，我也不与你再作计较，就将莺莺与你为妻。"

　　此话一出，喜坏了莺莺、红娘和张生。莺莺听了心花怒放，自家的名节终于保住，从此可与张生堂堂正正做夫妻。红娘听了十分宽慰，这事总算成了，不枉自家半年来的奔波辛苦。张生听了喜出望外，这段情缘终结正果，不禁感激涕零，双膝跪地，纳头便拜："小婿叩见岳……"不待张生"母"字出口，老夫人马上阻止道："慢慢慢，你听我把话说完。虽说俺已将莺莺许配于你，可有一条你须记着:崔家三辈儿不招白衣女婿，你明日就上京取应去，我与你养着媳妇。得官了，便拿着五花官诰来见我;倘若驳落，你就休回来了。"

Upon hearing this, Zhang was nonplussed. He now knew perfectly well that Madame Cui still did not approve of the marriage between him and Oriole, and was looking for another excuse to prevent it. If he passed the highest imperial examination, he could marry his lover. If he failed, he would lose Oriole. He thought to himself: "I am determined that I will never marry anyone but Oriole. So I am determined to be the nation's No. 1 Scholar and become a top official. Then I will come back to claim my bride." Then he said humbly, "I hear and obey your command, Madame. I will leave for the capital first thing tomorrow. I hope you will take good care of my future wife."

Oriole's eyes filled with tears when she heard her mother's harsh conditions. In her mind, she said to herself: "Mother, what you really want is to separate us." Seeing that Zhang was determined to obey Madame Cui and leave the next day, Oriole was so upset that tears ran down her cheeks.

Rose, who cursed Madame Cui in her heart, said to Zhang: "Sir, your decision is a wise one. We look forward to the day when you return, having won the highest honors in the examinations. Then you two lovebirds will be joined for ever."

"What Rose said is right," said Madame Cui. "You'd better pack your luggage and prepare for your journey right away." Then she turned to Rose: "Give orders for wine and fruit to be prepared," she said, "and invite the abbot. We will see Master Zhang off at the Pavilion of Parting tomorrow and give him a farewell feast."

"Yes, Madame," Rose said. Then Rose, Zhang and Oriole left.

Alone in the hall, Madame Cui was lost in thought: "My husband died, leaving me alone in the world. Then this unexpected scandal happened. How can I face my husband in the nether world? Nothing would have happened if Sun the Flying Tiger had not besieged the monastery. But Oriole does not understand my dilemma. My beloved daughter is too naive. What's done can't be undone. They are deeply in love. Well, it's no use trying to separate them by force, so I think my decision was for the best. If they had got married here in the monastery, we would have become a laughing stock."

Zhang left the Middle Hall and returned to the library. When his page asked why Madame Cui had called him, Zhang did not know what to say, so he remained silent, and the page was too tactful to pursue the matter.

　　张生闻言，心猛地往下一沉，清楚老夫人心中并不是真正应允了这门亲事，分明是明许暗赖。如自家高中，尚有希望；一旦名落孙山，便连同爱妻一道驳落了。心中暗自发誓："此生俺张珙非莺莺不娶，定要考个状元回来。"便对老夫人说道："晚辈遵命，明日便启程赴京。请老夫人好生待俺媳妇。"说着又深情地看了莺莺一眼。

　　莺莺听了母亲这番话，早将满心的欢喜化为乌有，泪水直在眼眶中打转，心中悲苦难言，母亲分明是想拆散我们夫妻！又见张生决意要走，深情一瞥，不免柔肠寸断，支持不住，滚下泪来。

　　红娘见状，心里直骂老夫人是个积世的恶婆婆，口中却劝张生道："张生你可要争气些呀，但愿你此去蟾宫折挂，衣锦归来，风风光光来娶俺小姐。那时候，俺便要受你的说媒红，吃你的谢亲酒哩。"

　　老夫人对张生道："红娘说得对，你这就去收拾行装，准备上路。"又对红娘道："你到厨下安排果酒，再到寺里请长老明日一同到十里长亭为张生送行。"红娘应声"是"，与张生、莺莺退出中堂。

　　老夫人等张生和莺莺出去以后，独自在堂上沉思不语。心里就像打翻了五味瓶，一时不知是什么滋味。偏偏出了这样的丑事。要不是兵围普救寺，怎能留下这祸根？莺莺怎么不懂为娘的心，这只是不得已的权宜之计，莺莺太傻了。也怪自家太大意，未将此事慎重处理，才落得今日的苦果。如今生米已做成了熟饭，看他俩的情形，特别是莺莺，自小就是刚烈性格，一时是不好将他们拆开的。只有让张珙先去赴考，暂时分开，婚姻之事，过些日子看情形再作定夺。

　　再说张生从老夫人处出来，跌跌撞撞回到书房。琴童问老夫人所唤何事，张生没法应答，沉默不语。琴童见此，知道张生与莺莺婚事难谐，也知趣地不再开口了。

CHAPTER TEN

A Tearful Farewell Feast

When Madame Cui promised her daughter's hand to Zhang, the lovers were overjoyed. But later, when she told the young man that he must first leave for the capital to take the civil service examination right away, both Oriole and Zhang were devastated.

Returning from the Middle Hall, Oriole lay listless on her bed behind the mosquito net, sighing and moaning. She did not sleep the whole night. Though Rose did her best to comfort her, Oriole could not stop weeping. At midnight, hearing leaves rustling in the wind, Rose pushed open the window, and realized that it had started to rain. "Good!" she cried. "Since it is raining, Master Zhang will certainly not start on his journey tomorrow." Oriole thought, "Heaven has had pity on us, a couple of lovers who are about to be parted, so it sheds tears for us. I can't wait to go to the Western Bower to say good-bye to my dearest. But now that our affair has been discovered, my mother will take strict precautions. On this cool autumn night, my lover has to sleep alone. He must be sad and shedding tears all night. How foolish you are, my love! You should not agree to leave for the capital tomorrow. I am already yours, so we should get married before you leave. What can I do if you fail in the civil service examination? If you pass the examination, and become an official, I hope that you will not marry the daughter of a high-ranking official in the capital, and then abandon me like an old fan...."

Before daybreak it stopped raining. When morning came, Oriole still lay on the bed and did not want to get up. It was only after Rose had urged her time and again that she arose and began her toilet. Sitting in front of her dressing table, she gazed at her disheveled hair and red-rimmed eyes in the mirror. Suddenly she heard Zhang's voice: "Miss Rose, I'm leaving. Please say good-bye to Miss Oriole for me, and tell her I shall come back as soon as possible. I hope she will take good care of herself." He spoke loudly, hoping Oriole would hear him.

第十章
长亭泣别

　　老夫人先许婚后逼试,令一对有情人一腔喜悦化作满腹愁绪。

　　莺莺从中堂回来后,长嘘短叹,粉泪不干,一夜未曾合眼。任红娘百般劝慰,也止不住珠泪滚落。夜半时分,听得窗外沙沙作响,红娘撩帘观瞧,却是雨打芭蕉,不由自言自语道:"人不留天留,这雨下得好啊!"莺莺暗忖,苍天有眼,分明是可怜俺一对有情人将别,洒下的同情之泪。有心去西厢与张生话别,怎奈事已败露,母亲肯定会严加防范。可怜张郎今夜秋霖脉脉、寒气森森、孤衾单枕,定也与自己一般愁苦难耐,涕泪难干。又想道:好个书呆子!如何就应了明日启程!你我已有夫妻之实,便当将婚事办了再走。你一旦科场失意,我能有如何下场? 想也不敢想,但愿你此番蟾宫折桂,金榜题名,咱们好洞房花烛。可一旦高中,京城名门显贵又当招婿,到那时,你可不要能不想起俺……可不要弃置如秋扇……

　　莺莺听着凄凄秋雨,一夜患得患失,眼泪不干。及至天明,雨才住了。她少气无力倚在帐中,任红娘催促再三,才勉强起床,洗手净面。独对菱花,见镜中人云鬓堆鸦,泪眼愁眉。这时,忽听得院外张生在喊红娘:"我现在就要启程了,就此和小姐告别,请转告小姐,我将及早返回,望小姐千万保重身体。"

Oriole was devastated as she listened to the sounds of the preparations for Zhang's departure.

"Why haven't you made yourself presentable yet, Miss?" asked Rose. Oriole did not answer, but she thought, "Dear Rose, how can you know the torment in my heart? How can I not feel grief and anguish? How can I rouge my cheeks and powder my face, and assume winning charms and graces?"

Finally Oriole dressed and made up her face. She and Rose then went outside, to find Madame Cui, Zhang, the abbot, the page and Fa Cong mounted on carriages ready to go to the Pavilion of Parting, where a farewell feast was to be held for Zhang.

It was late autumn; clouds floated high in the sky and the wild geese were flying south in the chilly wind. As the carriages rumbled along, Oriole gazed at the enchanting scenery, and recited a poem:

> *The cloudy sky frowns grey*
> *Over the yellow-bloom-paved way.*
> *The western breeze does bitterly blow,*
> *As north to south the wild geese go.*
> *Like a wine-flushed face are the leaves so red,*
> *Dyed in the tears that parting lovers shed."*

Wiping away her mistress' tears, Rose coaxed her: "Don't be too sad, Young Mistress. In half a year, he will come back with an official rank. Then you can be formally married."

Oriole did not answer; she was too wrapped up in her own distressful thoughts.

Madame Cui, Oriole and Rose arrived at the Pavilion of Parting just after Zhang and his page.

The young man noticed that Oriole had become wan and sallow overnight. She seemed to be wasting away. The sight reminded him of the story of Wu Zixu, an official in ancient times, who was so worried when crossing Shaoguan Pass that all his hair turned white overnight. "Worry can really be the death of a person," he thought to himself. He felt as if a knife were piercing his heart, and he felt on the verge of tears.

At Madame Cui's bidding, Rose set out the wine and dishes on the stone table in the pavilion.

虽与红娘叙话,声音却特别高,知他是让莺莺听的。又听得张生与老夫人的道别的话语,心里便不由熬熬煎煎。红娘见莺莺呆坐不动,便道:"姐姐因何还不打扮?"莺莺心中暗道:"好红娘,你哪里知道我的心事,到如今俺与张生就要伯劳分飞各西东了,还有什么心情花儿靥儿打扮得娇娇滴滴。"

稍作整理,与红娘出了绣阁,就见张生和方丈、琴童及法聪已走在前面,老夫人令丫环婆子将酒菜装盆安顿到车上,又让莺莺、红娘一同出了寺院后门,分别乘了两辆油壁车往长亭去送别。

此时天高云淡,秋风飒飒,落叶缤纷,北雁南飞。莺莺坐在车里,望着这深秋景色,不由愁容满面,想着昨日许亲,今日送别,早已是离人伤感,况值这暮秋天气,含泪吟道:"碧云天,黄花地,西风紧,北雁南飞,晓来谁染霜林醉?却总是离人泪。"

红娘抹泪劝道:"姐姐休要悲伤,不过半年六月,姐夫高中回来,你们便可堂堂正正地做夫妻了。"

莺莺不作声想着心事,她恨和张生相见太晚,怨他归去的疾,连路两旁的柳丝也绊不住马儿的腿。只盼着张生的马儿慢慢地行,自己坐的车儿快快地跑,好与心上人多一会儿相处。

不觉已来到十里长亭,只见张生和琴童早立在长亭之下等候。张生一眼看见的便是莺莺,可怜她一夜间花容憔悴,腰肢瘦损,风鬟雾鬓,朱颜顿改,方信伍子胥过韶关,一夜愁白了头是真,忧愁果能杀人啊!不由心如刀绞,险些落下泪来。

老夫人道:"红娘,安排酒宴。"红娘忙应声过来,就亭中石桌上将盘碟摆开。

老夫人对法本长老微微欠了欠身,道:"长老这厢请坐。"

Madame Cui invited the abbot to be seated first. She herself sat next to him. Oriole took the seat on the left of her mother, and sat there with her head bowed in modesty and sorrow. Zhang was the last to be seated, on the other side of the abbot.

Madame Cui looked at Oriole and Zhang while saying, "Since I have promised to marry my daughter to you, you must go to the capital and prove yourself worthy of our family by winning the top place in the examination."

Zhang was not happy to hear this. He thought: There are a great number of scholars in the country, but only one can become the No.1 Scholar. She has promised me her daughter's hand in marriage, but she is really scheming to put us asunder. She is playing the same old trick again in front of the abbot. "Thanks to your encouragement, Madame Cui," he said. "I am sure that I will have no problem gaining the highest honor in the examination."

Madame Cui thought, "This young man is talking wildly. He does not know how high the sky is or how deep the earth is. How can he face me if he fails to win the position of No.1 Scholar?"

Abbot Fa Ben, who thought that Zhang had been presumptuous, said, "Talented young men are often over-confident, Madame, but I am sure that Master Zhang will be a credit to you and your esteemed family."

Oriole detected the sharp edges to the voices of her mother and lover. She was alarmed by Zhang's boastful words, and thought, "If, after all your fine talk, you do not win the top place in the examination, I fear that you will be too ashamed to return. And then you will abandon me."

At the same time, Madame Cui was thinking, "The young man is getting carried away with his reckless ambition. That fits in neatly with my plan!" Icily calm, she ordered Rose to fill the wine cups.

Rose did so for the abbot, Madame Cui, Zhang and Oriole, one by one.

Madame Cui raised her cup and toasted Zhang, fulsomely wishing him success in the examination.

Zhang said a few words of appreciation.

"My child, you should present a cup of wine to Master Zhang," said Madame Cui to Oriole.

Rose poured the wine and gave the cup to Oriole. Oriole held the

法本长老双手合十,口诵佛号,道声:"老夫人请。"

老夫人居中坐了,法本长老坐在右边相陪。老夫人对张生道:"张生随长老坐。"又对莺莺道:"儿呀,快过来坐在为娘这里。"莺莺低着头上亭来在左边坐下。老夫人看了看莺莺,又对张生道:"俺今日将莺莺许配与你,你此番到京师可休辱没了俺孩儿,好歹挣个状元回来。"

张生觉得老夫人的话弦外有音,天下学子济济,可状元只有一个。这分明是明许暗赖,有意欺人,便故意说道:"小生托老夫人余荫,凭着胸中之才,视状元如拾芥耳。"

老夫人听得张生口出狂言,心想:年轻人不知天高地厚,看你不中之时,有何颜面见人!法本长忙在一旁为张生打圆场道:"老夫人,年轻人才高气傲,但涉世不深,不要见怪才是。不过依老僧看来,张生决非落后之人,纳为半子也是老夫人明智之举。"

莺莺刚才听出母亲话中有话,又听张生之言,心里十分着急,暗怨张生,母亲的话纵是千条不当,你怎能把话说绝!科场失意的才子何止万千,你倘未能如愿,真得就不回来了吗?

老夫人听了张生之言,也觉得他真是初生牛犊不怕虎。又一想:不怕你把话说绝,正中了我的计,便对红娘道:"红娘拿酒来,代老身斟酒。"红娘拿起酒壶,依次为法本长老、老夫人、张生、莺莺斟满酒杯。老夫人端起酒盅道:"今日张生要赴京赶考,略备水酒在此饯行,愿你鹏程万里。"说罢抿了一口。众人一看老夫人先饮,大家皆端起酒杯。

张生道:"借老夫人吉言,小生在此心领了。"

老夫人随即对莺莺道:"儿呀,你也该敬张生一杯!"

185

wine cup with trembling hands. She stood up and presented the cup of wine to Zhang: "Please...!"

Zhang glanced at Oriole and drank the wine in one gulp.

Madame Cui then told Rose to present wine to Zhang. Rose did as she was bidden, and the young man drained this cup too.

Knowing that her mother wanted to finish the farewell feast as soon as possible, Oriole felt resentful. "Oh, Mother," she said to herself, "you are so heartless. Since Zhang and I are soon to be separated, you should at least let us have a few minutes to ourselves. But since you continue to sit here we cannot have the chance of exchanging a few parting words of love." There was nothing she could do but sit motionless, gazing upon the face of her beloved.

Rose whispered in her young mistress' ear urging her to have a bite to eat. But it was all in vain; Oriole refused to touch either the food or the wine. Instead, she thought, "For fame as worthless as the horn of a snail, and for profit as trifling as the head of a fly, my mother has torn us two lovebirds apart!" At this moment both Oriole and Zhang heaved sigh after sigh.

Madame Cui was both sympathetic and annoyed. Since her daughter was unhappy, she was too. But as the daughter of later prime minister, she had no right to throw herself away on a penniless upstart like Zhang. "Well, anyway," she thought, "out of sight, out of mind. She'll forget him after a while, and if he doesn't come top of the list in the examination — which he won't — he'll be too ashamed to show his face to her again." Comforted by this thought, she ordered the carriage to be prepared for departure, and told Oriole and Rose not to be long following her. With that, she rose and left the pavilion.

Zhang took this as his cue to continue his journey to the capital. He stood up and made a bow to Fa Ben: "Thank you very much, Abbot, for coming to see me off."

Stroking his beard, Fa Ben said: "I hope you will be successful in the civil service examination, so that I can preside at your wedding ceremony. During your long journey, you must take good care of yourself."

"Thank you very much for your invaluable advice, Abbot," said Zhang.

"I will wait for the first spring thunder and expect good news from you. I will take my leave now." So saying, Fa Ben left with Fa Cong.

　　红娘斟了酒递与莺莺，莺莺双手颤抖地接过酒杯，立起身来对张生道："请……"张生抬眼看了看莺莺，接过酒杯一饮而尽。老夫人又命红娘敬酒，红娘也斟了一杯敬与张生。张生又是一饮而尽。

　　莺莺见母亲频频催着敬酒，知道她是想快些将这事应付完，催张生早走。不由心中生怨，母亲啊，你太心狠了，既是送别，也当让我们夫妻共桌而食，厮守一时半刻。莺莺情切意痴，只偷眼望着张生，一动不动。红娘见莺莺不动杯箸，附在耳旁劝道："姐姐早饭就没吃，好歹饮一口儿汤水。"

　　莺莺低头瞅着面前暖溶溶的玉酿，清澈似水，心想这哪里是酒，分明是俺夫妻的相思泪！只觉得嗓堵胸闷，没一点儿胃口，举起的筷子又放下，心想："只为了蜗角虚名，蝇头微利，俺娘便拆鸳鸯在两下里。"不由得长叹一声。张生此刻虽有万语千言，也不能对莺莺讲，只能化作声声叹息。老夫人见他二人一递一声长叹气，也是又怜又气，怜的是女儿毕竟是娘的心头肉，她不快乐，自家何乐之有？气的是，好端端一个相府千金，白白让张生这个畜牲糟蹋了。罢，罢，罢，眼不见心不烦。便对亭下车夫道："快快准备车马。"回头对众人道："老身先回去了。"说罢，起身由丫环扶着下亭登车去了。

　　张生明白老夫人是下逐客令，忙起身对长老拱手一揖道："多谢长老前来为小生送行。"

　　法本长老捻须道："此一行别无话说，贫僧就准备买《登科录》看了，想那做亲的茶饭少不得贫僧的。先生一路鞍马劳顿，可要小心在意，多加保重！"张生道："多谢长老！多谢长老！"

　　法本下亭道："从今经忏无心礼，专听春雷第一声。贫僧就等候你的好消息，就此告辞。"说罢便招呼法聪回寺。

After Madame Cui and the abbot had gone, Oriole went up to Zhang to hold his hand and say good-bye. The young man said with ardor: "I'm determined to win the highest literary honor, and then come straight back and make you my bride."

"Don't swear you won't come back unless you win the highest honor!" said Oriole. "I don't care if you become the No.1 Scholar or not; I only hope that we can be together day and night for the rest of our lives. Now it is late autumn, and the weather is growing chilly. Take care of your health on your long and arduous journey. Before your arrival at the capital, you must get used to the harsh climate. Make sure you eat properly and sensibly."

Zhang nodded, but said nothing.

Oriole continued, "I will wait for you forever. But I fear you may give up your old and faithful lover and find a new one who is more glamorous in the capital, once you have achieved success."

"My dear Miss Oriole! How could I bestow my love on anyone else but you? No one in the world can compare with you. Make yourself easy on that score. I must bid you farewell now."

Holding back his tears, Zhang mounted his horse and left. Surrounded by mountains east and west, he flicked his whip and proceeded along the sunlit road.

Seeing his form disappear at a bend in the road, Oriole recited tearfully: "To Heaven should I wail? Oh, to what avail? My tears would make the Yellow River overflow; and my grief would make the mountain peaks bend low."

The sun was sinking behind a green hill, and the birds were returning to their nests in the forest when Zhang came to a thatched-roofed inn by a bridge, over 30 miles east of Puzhou City. He dismounted and called for the innkeeper, who soon appeared and ushered him inside, promising him the best room.

Zhang straightaway lay down on the bed, saying, "I do not want anything to eat. I only want to sleep."

The innkeeper left, and the page, after stabling Zhang's horse, lay down on another bed and fell fast asleep. Tired as he was after his long ride, Zhang found that sleep would not come. He tossed and turned, all the time thinking of Miss Oriole. He heard the autumn insects buzzing all around. Reclining on his lonely pillow, he found his coverlet too cold and thin.

　　莺莺见母亲、长老都走了,忙起身过来对张生道:"郎君此行,得官不得官,疾便回来。"张生握住莺莺的手安慰道:"青霄有路终须到,金榜无名誓不归。小生这一去,白夺一个状元回来。"

　　莺莺珠泪盈盈道:"你休说金榜无名誓不归,什么状元不状元的,俺只求夫唱妇随。目下秋风飒飒,天气转凉,你鞍马途中,可要自家当心,千万珍重!"

　　张生点头道:"小生记下了,小姐还有甚言语要嘱咐小生?"

　　莺莺道:"你休忧'文齐福不齐',我则怕你'停妻再娶妻',休要'一春鱼雁无消息'。你还须记着,若见那异乡花草,休似此处栖迟。"

　　张生知莺莺放心不下,急道:"谁再似小姐你,小生又怎能再生此念?小姐放心好啦,小生就此告辞!"

　　张生强忍心酸,心肠一硬,翻身上马,一步一泣踏上驿道。此时四围山色中,一鞭残照里,莺莺看着张生远去的背影,慢慢消失在驿道的尽头,心里泛起了一种说不出的酸楚,含泪吟道:"老天不管人憔悴,泪添九曲黄河溢,恨压三峰华岳低。"

　　日隐西山,百鸟归林,烟霭凝寒,衰草凄迷,张生来到离蒲东三十里以外的草桥,见路旁有一小店,便勒缰下马。店小二从门中迎出道:"官人请进。"张生将丝缰递与琴童,自家随小二进了客房。小二点了灯问道:"官人,俺这里有上好的酒菜,您要些什么?"

　　张生往榻上歪了道:"我什么都不吃,只想好好睡上一觉。"

　　店小二道:"客官好生休息,小的就不讨扰了,有事只管唤我。"说着带了门出去。不一刻,琴童已发出鼾声。张生则对着一盏孤灯,思念着莺莺。只听秋蛩低鸣,窗纸被秋风吹得特楞楞地响,更觉衾单枕孤,凄凉难耐。

Suddenly, it seemed that in a dream he heard someone knocking at the door. Startled, he thought: "Who would come to this country inn at midnight? Maybe it's a ghost?" In a quavering voice, he called out, "Who's there?"

"It is I," replied a gentle voice. Zhang got out of bed, and peeped through a crack in the door, to find a young lady standing outside under the cool moon and stars. "If you're human, assure me of the fact. But if you're a ghost, begone this instant!" he called out, with more courage than he felt.

"Master Zhang, my dear, don't you know me?"

Zhang was overjoyed. He flung open the door, and took Oriole in his arms. "My dear, why have you pursued me like this?" he asked.

"I realized that I could no longer live without you by my side," the girl explained. "So, as soon as my mother and Rose were fast asleep, I slipped out of the Salvation Monastery to accompany you to the capital."

Oriole's clothes were in disorder, and she looked exhausted by the journey she had made. Zhang carried her into the room. "Oh, my dearest love, you have worn yourself quite out."

"I think the saddest thing for the human heart is to be torn away from the object of its love," said Oriole. "My dear, I am not afraid of this long journey. I do not want a valiant hero, nor a man rich and proud. I am willing to share with you a bed in life and a grave in death."

Zhang held Oriole tightly, crying: "My dear wife!"

At this moment, there was a commotion outside the inn. Somebody was shouting about an intruder and calling for lights. Zhang embraced Oriole tightly. "What shall we do?" he gasped.

Oriole, looking fearless, said to him: "My dear, stand behind me. Let me open the door and speak to them." So saying, she opened the door.

Outside, there was a crowd of bandits, headed by Sun the Flying Tiger, mounted on a horse. At the sight of Oriole, Sun, guffawed evilly: "You see, you cannot escape me, my girl!" he snarled.

Oriole defied the ruffian. "You had best make yourself scarce, you loathsome bandit," she cried. 'The White Horse General is coming to make mincemeat of you at this very moment."

This only made Sun roar with laughter. At a nod from him, his men

朦胧间,就听得有轻轻敲门声。张生心下便是一惊,这夜半三更,露冷星稀,荒村野店的,谁人来找?莫不是鬼魅相侵?便仗了胆子问道:"你是谁?"

"是我。"一声娇语传来,好生耳熟。张生起身下床,从门缝里向外瞧,就见冷月寒星下,一位女子立在门前,便道:"是人快说话,是鬼速湮灭!"

"张郎,是我!我是莺莺啊。"

张生一听喜出望外,忙将门扇开了,道:"小姐,娘子,你如何来的?"说着将莺莺一把拥进怀中。

莺莺泪流满面道:"张郎,妾委实是放心不下,想着你此番去了,不知何时方能相见,便趁着老夫人红娘睡了,偷偷出了普救寺,特地赶你来,和你同赴京城。"

张生将风鬟雾鬓衣衫不整的莺莺抱进屋来,心疼地说道:"我痴情的小姐,难为你夜半更深、远路风尘一双小脚儿追我而来,想是小金莲也磨出了水泡。"

莺莺道:"人生最苦是离别,妾为了张郎,也顾不得路途遥远,崎岖难行。俺想你想得废寝忘食,香消玉减,难忍那枕冷衾寒,凤只鸾孤。张郎,俺不恋豪杰,不羡骄奢,自愿与你生则同衾,死则同穴。"

张生紧拥莺莺道:"俺的好娘子!"便哭出声来。

正在此时,就听门外人喊马嘶,乱作一团,其中有一人喊道:"弟兄们,适才见一女子渡河而来,不知哪里去了?快将火把点亮仔细搜寻!"

张生吓得浑身颤抖,心想怎么小姐刚到就有人来抢,便死命搂着莺莺,道:"这可怎生了得?"

seized Oriole, and carried her off.

His own anguished cry woke Zhang from this horrible nightmare. His heart was thumping, and his whole body was drenched in sweat. Afraid of falling asleep again, he took a walk in the bright moonlight. The morning star was just rising. The wall of the inn yard was half hidden by green willow trees. Withered leaves occasionally fell from the branches in the gentle breeze. Leaning against the door of the inn, Zhang could not help giving a long sigh. It was indeed like:

> *The twittering of swallows on the branches heard*
> *Has broken the dream of union of a lonely lovebird.*

　　莺莺面无惧色，挣脱张生道："张郎，你靠后些，让我来开门对付他们。"说着把门打开。

　　火光下只见门外黑压压一片贼兵，为首的正是那孙飞虎。他坐在马上，一阵狂笑道："崔莺莺，你终究逃不出洒家的掌心。哈哈哈……"

　　莺莺娇叱道："你们这帮乱臣贼子，可知道白马将军的威名，他看一看，你们就成了肉酱；指一指，便教你化为脓血。看，他骑着白马来了……"

　　孙飞虎又是一阵狂笑道："白马将军是个鸟，他能奈我何？来呀，将这美人给我拈了来，大王我好生受用一番。"他话音未落，众贼兵蜂拥而上，将莺莺抢去。

　　张生急得大叫一声，惊醒过来，揉揉眼，原来是一场恶梦。胸口犹"咚咚"地跳个不停。他抹去头上的虚汗，透过窗棂望着月上中天，明亮如昼。眼见也睡不着了，便爬了起来，走出房门，只见一天寒露，满地霜华，晓星初上，残月犹明，绿依依墙高柳半遮，静悄悄门掩清秋夜，疏剌剌林梢落叶风，昏惨惨云际穿窗月。张生斜倚在店门上，望着眼前的景象，不由得长长叹了一口气。正是：无端燕鹊高枝上，一枕鸳鸯梦不成。

CHAPTER ELEVEN

The Wedding

After a long and weary journey, Zhang finally arrived at the capital. On the day the civil service examination began, scholars from all over the country gathered at the examination hall. Thanks to his exceptional talents, Zhang won the highest honor.

Suddenly, he was famous. The emperor himself invited him to a banquet at the imperial palace, where he was asked to write an inscription for the Goose Pagoda; high-ranking officials were eager to pay him courtesy calls, one after another; he paid a visit to his teacher; and his friends came to express their congratulations. Though the young man was eager to return to Mid-River Prefecture to be reunited with Oriole, he had to stay at the Hall for Gathering Talented People, waiting for the emperor to bestow an appointment on him. One day, when gazing at the plum blossoms in the courtyard, he thought poignantly of Oriole. "I met Oriole last spring, when the flowers were in full bloom," he thought, "and I left her when the sere leaves were tumbling from the trees. I have been parted from my dear for half a year; Oriole must be worried about me. I shall send her a letter at once." So thinking, he picked up a writing brush, and wrote a letter. As soon as he had done so, he dispatched his page to deliver it to Oriole at the Salvation Monastery.

Since Oriole had parted from Zhang at the Pavilion of Parting in the late autumn of the previous year, she had been in low spirits, showing no interest in her appearance. Her normally slender waist had grown thinner, so that all her clothes were too big for her. Whenever she went to the Embroidery Pavilion by herself, she could see only desolation all around, with trees hidden in mist, and withered grass in the distance. She waited for news from Zhang day and night, in a constant state of anxiety. Her old worries were like the undulating Zhongtiao Mountains, and her new worries, like the flowing Yellow River. Spring

第十一章
终成眷属

话说张生一路风雨进京赶考,春闱期到,与众举子文场鏖战,凭着胸中锦绣才华,一举及第,独占鳌头,中了状元,成为天子门生。一时间,金銮殿上传胪官点名,皇上赐宴曲江,杏园探花,雁塔题诗,御街夸官,接着又是拜谒宗师,同年相贺,着实忙乎了一阵子。本想高中后,就返回蒲东,只因尚未御笔钦点官职,不能擅自离京,只好耐了性子寓居招贤馆中,候旨听封。这日见馆中红梅怒放,不禁又思念起莺莺,想去年相见时,红雨纷纷点绿苔;别离际,黄叶萧萧凝暮霭。算起来与莺莺离别已倏忽半载,不知小姐在寺中如何挂念。忙提笔修书一封,令琴童星夜起程,送往普救寺。

再说那莺莺小姐,自去秋在十里长亭与张生依依惜别后,整日里神情不快,妆镜懒对,腰肢瘦损,茜裙宽褪,真个"人比黄花瘦,腰细不胜衣"。天天望,日日愁,才下眉头,又上心头,正是:旧愁似中条山隐隐,新愁似黄河水悠悠。如今又到了花染深红,柳拖青翠之时。采蕊游蜂,两两相携;弄巧黄鹂,双双作对。莺莺想着张生半载音讯皆无,不由泪遮了双眼。正在难解难分,"悔教夫婿觅封侯"之际,就见听红娘一路"咯咯"笑着进来。忙拭了泪水嗔道:"疯妮子,可有甚开心事,值得你这般疯魔痴傻?"红娘脸儿笑成了

came again, with red flowers blooming everywhere. Bees were busying collecting honey and pairs of birds sported in the sky. But for half a year, there had been no news of her lover. Oriole's eyes were misting with tears, when she heard Rose coming into the room, chuckling. "Rose," Oriole cried, "what on earth are you so happy about?"

Her face wreathed in smiles, Rose gabbled excitedly: "Good news, Young Mistress! Master Zhang has won the highest honor in the examination!"

Thinking Rose might be making fun of her, Oriole pulled a long face, and said, "That is not a joking matter. I do wish you would learn to act in a more responsible way."

Still smiling, Rose retorted, "It's true! I'm not joking, Young Mistress. It is true that Master Zhang has passed the imperial examination and is now the country's No.1 Scholar. His page has just brought a letter containing the good news. And now he is waiting to see you."

As if in a dream, Oriole said to herself: "The day I have been so looking forward to has finally come!" Then, as if waking from the dream, she said hurriedly: "Quick, let him in!"

As soon as Zhang's page entered, Oriole bombarded him with questions. When the latter had satisfied her curiosity, he handed Zhang's letter to her. With trembling fingers and eyes dimmed with tears of joy, the girl tore the letter open. The first thing she noticed was tear stains on the paper. Obviously, her lover had wept as he wrote it.

The letter read:

"I, Zhang Gong, pay my deepest regards to my dear wife-to-be. Since we parted in the late autumn of last year, half a year has elapsed. Thanks to the fortune of my ancestors, and your own matchless virtue, I have won the highest honor in the examination. I am now staying at the Hall for Gathering Talented People, awaiting an appointment. I have dispatched this letter to assure you and your esteemed mother that there is no need for you to worry about me. Though I am far away from you, my heart is always with you. I am not a man who regards academic honor as being worth more than love."

After reading the letter, Oriole fell into a reverie. She thought to herself: "Dear Zhang, I never imagined that you would win the highest honor in the imperial examination when you climbed over the wall to

一朵花,眉飞色舞地说:"难怪昨夜灯花爆,今早喜鹊噪,果真是喜事临门了。恭喜姐姐,贺喜姐姐,咱姐夫高中状元了!"

莺莺先是一愣,随即白了红娘一眼,心想定是这妮子见我心闷,生出法子哄我高兴,便冷了脸道:"红娘呵,你就不能持重些?"

红娘依旧笑道:"姐姐,俺不骗你,当真是张生他得了状元,琴童回来报喜,就在门外。"莺莺恍若梦中,喃喃道:"快唤他进来。"

红娘忙唤道:"琴童,琴童,还不快快进来,见过你家夫人、我家小姐?"琴童应声而入,纳头便拜。莺莺道:"快快起来,我且问你,你几时离的京师?""回少夫人话,小的离京已近一月,俺走时,哥哥去吃游街棍子去了。"红娘在一旁啐道:",你家哥哥又不是中得盗贼状元,吃哪门子的游街棍子? "莺莺也被他逗乐了,掩口笑道:"这孩子不懂,那是状元夸官,游街三日。"

琴童不好意思地搔搔头,从怀里掏出书信,双手递上道:"这是我家哥哥给少夫人的书信。"红娘忙过来拈了呈与莺莺。莺莺珠泪盈盈,手儿抖抖地将信接过,迫不急待地展开,就见这信纸上泪渍斑斑,便知是张生写信时洒的泪痕,信中道:"张珙百拜奉启芳卿可人妆次:自暮秋拜违,倏尔半载。上赖祖宗之荫,下托贤妻之德,举中甲第。即日于招贤馆寄迹,以伺圣旨御笔除授。惟恐岳母与贤妻忧念,特令琴童奉书驰报,庶几免虑。小生身虽遥而心常迩矣,恨不得鹣鹣比翼,邛邛并躯。重功名而薄恩爱者,诚有浅见贪饕之罪。他日面会,自当请谢不备。后成一绝,以奉清照:玉京仙府探花郎,寄语蒲东窈窕娘。指日拜恩衣昼锦,定须休作倚门妆。"

莺莺读罢书信,感慨万千:"张郎啊,谁曾想你跳东墙的脚步儿占了鳌头,谁料到你西厢惜花心能养成蟾宫折桂手。"心中一阵喜来

meet me and gave your love to me in the Western Bower. But it seems that my house is destined to become an official residence."

With mixed feelings of both happiness and sadness, Oriole ordered Rose to arrange refreshments for Zhang's page, while she wrote a reply to her true love's letter.

Together with the reply, Oriole handed to the messenger a set of fine clothes, a zither, a jade hairpin and a bamboo flute, saying, "Make sure you deliver these things safely to your master."

Rose was puzzled. She said, "Master Zhang is now a very important person, and these things are quite ordinary. I suppose they have some special meaning."

"You're right," replied Oriole. "These garments are the ones he wore when we first fell in love. Incidentally, wearing this pair of socks he will be reminded not to go to any place he should not go."

"Master Zhang already has a zither; I don't think he needs another one."

"You don't understand. This is the zither which he played when he recited a poem he had composed specially for me last year, when he first tried to attract my attention."

"What is the significance of the jade hairpin and the bamboo flute?"

"The jade hairpin will warn him not to forget me now that he has won the highest academic honor in the land. The flute is made from bamboo growing at the foot of Jiuyi Mountain. In ancient times, Consort Xiang and Emperor Shun were deeply in love. Consort Xiang wept so much when the emperor was away that her tears dropped onto the bamboo and remained as spots. Hence spotted bamboo is sign of longing for one's absent lover."

She then ordered the messenger to hasten on his way, admonishing him to be most careful with the precious letter and love tokens.

Meanwhile, soon after the page had left for the Salvation Monastery, Zhang had received an imperial edict appointing him to the post of editor of historical records at the Imperial Academy. However, despite the prestige attached to this important position, Zhang found himself unable to concentrate on his duties. He missed Oriole so much that he could neither eat nor sleep, and before long he fell ill. An imperial doctor came to see him, but Zhang, who knew well what his malady was, refused to be treated.

一阵悲,回头看见琴童风尘满面,忙问道:"琴童,你可用过饭否?"

琴童道:"启禀少夫人,小的未曾用过。"

莺莺道:"红娘快取饭来与他吃。"红娘应声去了,顷刻端了饭菜回来。莺莺关切地说:"琴童小小年纪,一路辛苦,快快趁热吃吧。"

琴童对莺莺深深一揖道:"感蒙少夫人赏赐,俺就在这里吃了。哥哥着小的索了少夫人回书,请夫人快快写吧,小的也好回命。"

莺莺道:"你放心吃饭,红娘笔砚伺候。"

红娘在书案上摆好了文房四宝,莺莺笔走龙蛇,一挥而就。信写好了,尚觉不能达意,便拿出汗衫一件,裹肚一条,锦袜一双,瑶琴一张,玉簪一枚,斑管一枝。对琴童说道:"呆会儿子你将这些东西收拾好,给你家哥哥捎去。"

红娘一旁插嘴道:"姐夫得了官,岂无这几件东西? 小姐寄与他想必是有什么缘故吧?"

莺莺道:"是啊,你不知道,这汗衫,他若是和衣而卧,便是与我一处宿,只要贴着他的皮和肉,不信他不想着我温柔。这裹肚经常的不离他前后,守着他左右,紧紧的记在心头。这袜子穿上它,则拘管他不要胡行乱走。这瑶琴嘛,想当日吟五言诗种下了情根,到后来七弦琴作成了配偶,他怎么肯冷落了诗中的深意,我恐怕他生疏了操琴的玉手。这玉簪是说他今日功成名就,不要把人抛在脑后。斑管含意更深,它用的是九嶷山下竹,当年湘妃虞舜,泪珠如秋雨,滴在竹子上,点点成斑。当时娥皇因虞舜生愁,今日莺莺为君瑞担忧。似这等泪斑宛然依旧,万古情缘一样愁。让他休忘旧。"

红娘点点头道:"噢,原来是这样。亏小姐想得如此周全。"

莺莺吩咐道:"红娘去拿十两银子来给琴童作盘缠。"然后扭

The doctor, however, being well versed in the human condition, diagnosed the problem at once. Shaking his head, the physician said, "There is only one ailment in the world which it is beyond my powers to cure, and that is lovesickness. Even if Bian Que (a famous doctor in ancient times) himself were to treat you, he could not effect a cure. I can only exhort you to take care of yourself."

Zhang wondered if he was about to die pining for Oriole, when just at that moment the page he had sent to the monastery returned. Eagerly snatching the letter from the page's hand, Zhang tore it open. It read:

"Your humble wife sends her deepest regards to you, my dear husband. In the long months since you left, my deep love for you has never waned, even for an instant. Your letter restored me to life. I am sending to you by your page some love tokens which I am sure you will understand and know how to cherish."

After reading the letter and checking everything mentioned in it, Zhang was overcome with admiration for Oriole's talent and affection for him. Examining the love tokens she had sent, Zhang suddenly felt well again. His appetite returned, and after a good night's sleep he was back to his normal self. At this moment, an imperial edict was issued, appointing him prefect of Mid-River Prefecture. Zhang immediately set off to go to his post, returning to Oriole in glory.

Now, that would have been the end of the story if it had not been for a strange coincidence. As Zhang was making his way to the Salvation Monastery, unbeknownst to him somebody he had forgotten all about had arrived before him. It was none other than Zheng Heng, Madame Cui's nephew. His father, Madame Cui's elder brother, served as the minister of rites. However, Zheng Heng was by no means a credit to his illustrious sire, being a frivolous and snobbish fop who had long abandoned himself to dissipation. At the instigation of his parents, he and his cousin Oriole had been engaged, but it happened that before the wedding ceremony could take place Prime Minister Cui had died, delaying the nuptials until the end of the lengthy mourning period. Delayed in Mid-River Prefecture by the bandit disturbance, Madame Cui had written to Zheng Heng asking for help, but the cowardly Zheng Heng had been loath to leave the comforts of the capital, especially at a time of danger. Later,

头对琴童道:"琴童,又要辛苦你了。一路上可要小心在意。"

琴童道:"小的紧记在心。"说罢向小姐叩别而去。

话说那张生打发琴童走后,便接了圣旨,被封为翰林院编修,修撰国史。可他一心只在莺莺身上,根本无意于文章之事,整日里坐卧不宁,茶不思,饭不想,单盼琴童回来。怎奈思念心切,忧愁交加,竟病倒在驿馆里。早间,太医院派了大夫前来诊治,却不料被大夫一眼看出了虚实,摇头道:"世间疑难杂症均有药可医,只有相思病无药可治。纵然是卢医、扁鹊再世,也医它不得。状元好自为之。"

张生暗忖:只要俺那莺莺知道这病为她而得,纵然是死,我也甘心情愿。正在胡思乱想之际,琴童一身征尘回来了。张生神情为之一振,急不可待地向琴童索要莺莺回信,琴童忙双手递上。只见那笺上蝇头小楷工工整整,信中道:"薄命妾崔氏拜覆,敬奉才郎君瑞文几:自音容去后,不觉许时,仰敬之心,未尝少怠。纵云日近长安远,何故鳞鸿之杳矣。莫因花柳之心,弃妾恩情之意!正念间,琴童至,得见翰墨,始知中科,使妾喜之如狂。郎之才望,亦不辱相国之家谱也。今因琴童回,无以奉贡,聊布瑶琴一张,玉簪一枚,斑管一枝,裹肚一条,汗衫一领,袜儿一双,权表妾之真诚。勿勿草字欠恭,伏乞情恕不备。谨依来韵,遂继一绝云:阑干倚遍盼才郎,莫恋宸京黄四娘。病里得书知中甲,窗前揽镜试新妆。"

读罢信,又将所寄之物一一看了,件件蕴意,心中皆已明了,不由暗叹莺莺的确堪称才女,不仅字写得绝,针线也做得好,真正心通七窍,才智过人。便吩咐琴童将这些东西好生保管。一时间精神倍增。恰巧圣旨又下,任命他为河中府尹。张生接了官诰,立刻动身赴任,衣锦还乡。

when he learned that Madame Cui had promised Oriole to Zhang in gratitude for his saving them from the bandits — and that the bandits had been driven off — he determined to hasten to the Salvation Monastery to reclaim his fiancee.

On arrival in Mid-River Prefecture, Zheng Heng decided to make no rash moves without finding out the true nature of the situation from Rose. So he put up at a local inn and sent one of his henchmen to inform Madame Cui of his presence and ask her to send Rose to meet him at the inn. It suited Madame Cui too to have Rose act as go-between until she found out what Zheng Heng's intentions were.

Zheng Heng greeted Rose warmly when she arrived at the inn escorted by his follower, and asked her about the situation with Madame Cui.

"Your aunt, sir, is somewhat put out because you did not hasten to pay your respects to her as soon as you entered the district," Rose replied.

Zheng Heng sighed. "The fact is that I'm too embarrassed to face my aunt," he said. "So I want to talk to you first. You see, when my uncle was alive, Oriole was betrothed to me. And now that the period of mourning for him has expired, I expect your mistress to choose a date for our wedding."

"Sir, please don't mention that any more. My young mistress has been betrothed to another man," Rose said.

"Nonsense!" Zheng Heng shouted, his brow as black as thunder. "A horse cannot have two saddles, and a girl cannot be betrothed to two men. When my uncle was alive, Oriole and I were engaged, but now that he is out of the way, my aunt is trying to break the promise he made. This is really outrageous!"

"Master Zheng," Rose protested, "where were you when Sun the Flying Tiger surrounded the monastery with his band of 5,000 cutthroats? If it were not for Master Zhang, Oriole would have been carried off by Sun the bandit, and the rest of us would all be dead now."

"Master Zhang is only a poverty-stricken scholar. I am a much better match for Oriole than he. I come from a rich and honored family. In addition, I and Oriole are cousins, and our marriage was approved by my late uncle," Zheng Heng yelled.

But the spirited Rose was not impressed by his boasting. "Sir, despite your claims to prestige and honor, it seems that you do not understand the rules of propriety," she retorted. "You talk about marrying my young

　　天下事无巧不成书，就在张生从京师启程奔赴普救寺的途中，已有一人先他一步到达蒲州，此人便是老夫人的娘家侄子，郑恒。此番崔老夫人领着莺莺、欢郎等扶灵回博陵，受阻寄寓普救寺，曾去信叫郑恒前来，以便回回故里。郑恒接到信后，一来怕劳累，二来也不舍京城繁华，三来也想摆架子。后来听说孙飞虎欲抢莺莺为妻，兵围普救寺，是一个叫张君瑞的书生搬来白马将军，退兵解围，姑母又将莺莺许配给了张君瑞，深感不是滋味。这才急忙来到河中府。

　　郑恒在城中客栈住下，派了个心腹家人到寺里见过老夫人，又请求老夫人派红娘出寺相见。老夫人想侄儿来到河中府，不前来问安，却要红娘前去相见，不知是什么名堂？想来多半是为了中表联姻之事，看来要有麻烦了。也好，就先让红娘摸摸底细再作定夺。

　　红娘领了老夫人之命，随郑府家人到客栈去见郑恒。红娘敛衽福了一福道："表少爷万福，老夫人问哥哥为何不到寺里来？"

　　郑恒叹道："我有甚脸面去见姑母？当日姑父在世时，曾许下中表联姻，定下这门亲事。如今姑父孝已满了，特地央求姐姐去和姑母说说，拣一个吉日成合了我和小姐莺莺的婚事。"

　　红娘道："这些话就别再提了，俺家小姐已许别人了。"

　　郑恒拧眉道："胡说！常言道：一马不备二鞍，一女不许二男。怎能姑父在世时许了我，姑父去世之后姑母倒悔亲？"

　　红娘道："表少爷，话可不能这么说。当日孙飞虎领了半万贼兵来时，少爷你在哪里？若不是张生，哪有俺一家子的性命？今日太平无事了，你却来争亲，倘若那时小姐被贼人掳了去，少爷如何去争？"

　　郑恒恨恨道："如若给了个官宦人家倒也不冤枉，却给了个穷酸饿醋。偏是我不如他？我是仁者能仁、富贵出身的根脚，又是亲

mistress as if it were a foregone conclusion. I am afraid that you overrate yourself, sir."

"I don't believe Zhang could defeat those bandits all by himself. It is just a threadbare ruse to deprive my rightful bride," sneered Zheng Heng.

"Believe it or not," said Rose. "Sun the Flying Tiger rose in rebellion, and he and his 5,000 men burned, killed and looted wherever they went. They surrounded the monastery, and Sun demanded that Oriole be handed over to him. In that desperate plight, and after seeking the abbot's advice, our mistress declared that if anyone in the monastery, priest or layman, was able to induce the bandits to withdraw, she would present her daughter to him as his wife and give him a handsome dowry. Then Master Zhang wrote a letter to his friend, the White Horse General, asking him to come to the rescue. When the general did so, Madame Cui formally betrothed her daughter to Master Zhang."

"But he's a nobody compared to me," Zheng Heng snorted. "How could my aunt throw her only daughter away like that?"

Rose retorted, raising her brows: "Master Zhang is a learned man. He constantly quotes the classics, and his poems are as good as those written by the famous poets. He speaks and acts with decorum. Madame Cui has kept her promise, and so it seems to me that there is an end to the matter."

"I am the scion of an aristocratic family," blustered Zheng Heng, "while he is only a poor scholar; such people are ten a penny. We cannot be mentioned in the same breath."

"Master Zhang relies on his teachers, friends and noble character, but you take advantage of your father's and brother's power to bully people," Rose counter-attacked. "You are so proud of your official family, but you should remember how many generals and prime ministers throughout history came from poor families!"

Zheng Heng lost patience with the waspish Rose. With a wave of his hand, he said, "I can't be bothered arguing with you any longer. It is the abbot who has caused me this trouble, I'll be bound. I'll get even with him tomorrow."

"The abbot is a kindly old monk who helps others. He never causes trouble for anyone. In my opinion, this 'trouble,' as you call it, was brought about by your own weakness of character," Rose said with scorn.

"It is my duty to carry out the behest of my late uncle," replied

上做亲,更何况还有姑父遗命!"

红娘一听心中早不耐烦,斥道:"住嘴!张生他哪点不如你?你休卖弄那仁者能仁,也别仗着富贵出身,便是你官上加官,也未必非要亲上做亲。你刚来到河中府,就要过门成亲,也太不自量了吧。"

郑恒道:"我不信贼兵来时,他一个人能退得,全是胡说八道!"

红娘不屑地道:"信不信由你,当时镇守河桥的孙飞虎反叛了朝廷,在这一带劫掠烧杀,亲自带了五千贼兵包围的寺院,要抢莺莺小姐做压寨夫人。老夫人慌了,与长老商议,拍手高叫:两廊不问僧俗,但退得贼兵者,便将莺莺许他为妻。张生立马挺身而出,亲自作书一封,请来了白马将军,退兵解围。他威而不猛,言而有信,是个至诚君子,所以俺老夫人将小姐许配于他。"

郑恒道:"一个无名小辈,有甚本领?"

红娘柳眉一扬道:"亏你是个世家子弟,说话无一点儿分寸。人家张生讲道理引经据典,填词作赋比得上韩柳诗文,他知体统为人敬人,因此上俺家讲信义知恩报恩。你哪能同他比,你值一分,他值百分;你是萤火,他是月轮;你是小人浊民,他是君子清贤。"

郑恒略一思量:"我祖代是相国之门,到不如他个白衣饿夫穷秀才!做官的到底是做官的。"

红娘道:"他凭师友君子务本,你倚父兄仗势欺人。休说什么做官的总是做官人,穷民倒老是穷民。岂不道将相出寒门?"

郑恒理屈词穷,着急道:"我不跟你个丫头计较,这桩事都是那秃驴长老弄的,这个婊子养的,我明日慢慢地和他算帐!"

红娘道:"他是个出家人,慈悲为本,方便为门。你个瞎了眼的不识好人,招祸口不知分寸。"

Zheng Heng, smiling unctuously. "I will follow the traditional procedure, and pick an auspicious day. On that benevolent and blessed morning, I will take gifts of sheep and wine to the monastery, to set in train the time-honored nuptial rites which will lead to Oriole and I being united in wedded bliss."

"Bah!" cried Rose, stamping her foot in fury. "You are not like a son of Minister Zheng, but a bandit like Sun the Flying Tiger. Your shameless ways will bring you to a disgraceful end!" Whereupon, without taking her leave, Rose turned and stormed off to report the outcome of this unsatisfactory interview to her mistress.

Watching her go, Zheng Heng allowed his face to twist in death. Suddenly he made a sinister smile, as a cunning scheme entered his head.

When Madame Cui learned from Rose what had passed between her and Zheng Heng, she was overcome with remorse. "However," she thought, "the way things turned out I had no choice but to break Oriole's engagement to my nephew. For one thing, the situation was a life-and-death one when we were besieged by the bandits. If it had not been for Zhang, Oriole would have been carried off and lost forever. Then again, when I found out that Oriole and Zhang had already become intimate, what else could I do but make sure that they were engaged to be married as soon as possible? No doubt Zheng Heng will come here tomorrow, so I must have a feast prepared, and try to reconcile him to the situation."

Late in the morning of the following day, Zheng Heng did come to the Salvation Monastery. Prostrating himself at Madame Cui's feet and weeping copious tears, he greeted his aunt: "Your unworthy nephew Zheng Heng pays his humble respects, Madame."

Madame Cui, who had always been fond of her nephew, was touched by his wretchedness. "My dear child," she said, "why didn't you come to see me as soon as you arrived?"

Zheng Heng wailed, "I was too ashamed to face you, dearest relative, now that my darling Oriole has been wrenched from me and given to another man."

Wiping her tears, Madame Cui said, "Listen to me, my child. When Sun the Flying Tiger surrounded the monastery with his army and you failed to come and rescue us, I had to promise to give Oriole to whoever could save Oriole from a fate worse than death. Zhang was the one who saved her, as well as the rest of us, and so I had to betroth Oriole to him."

"Who is this Zhang fellow?" asked Zheng Heng, with a grimace.

　　郑恒道:"这是姑夫的遗嘱,我择个吉日,牵羊担酒上门去,看姑母怎么发落我? 她若不肯,哼,我带上二三十个伙计,将莺莺抬上轿子,到了这儿脱了衣裳,待你们赶来还你一个婆娘。"

　　红娘气得牙根发痒,骂道:"呸! 你可是郑尚书的亲生子,须不是孙飞虎手下的贼兵,没一点儿脸皮,只会使粗用狠,少不得有家难奔没下场!"说罢,扭头便走。

　　郑恒见红娘去了,心想这丫头定和那酸丁张君瑞有瓜葛,这事该如何办呢? 突然他眼睛一转,计上心来,不由奸笑起来。正是:且将压善欺良意,权作尤云殢雨心。

　　却说老夫人,昨天派了红娘去见侄儿,据红娘回来说是询问亲事。这件亲事,若依自家本意是要给侄儿,况又是相国生前所定,如今是自家违背了先夫的遗愿。也是自家没有主张,以至莺莺与张生做下苟且之事。如今侄儿便是有几句怨言,也怪他不得。料他今日必来寺中问安,便吩咐下去安排酒宴。

　　日上三竿,郑恒来到普救寺,径直入梨花院到中堂来见老夫人。一见面,他跪下便拜,装模作样挤出两滴泪来道:"姑母在上,请受不孝侄儿郑恒一拜!"

　　老夫人一向疼爱侄儿,见他流泪,早就禁持不住,也滴下泪来道:"我的儿,你既来到这里,怎么不来见我?"

　　郑恒以膝代步蹭上前来,扑在老夫人膝上假哭道:"孩儿听说表妹已另许他人,还有甚脸面来见姑母?"

　　老夫人拭泪道:"孩儿你听我说,只因有孙飞虎一节,等你不来无可解危,只得许与张生。"

　　郑恒忙问:"哪个张生?"

"His full name is Zhang Gong, or Zhang Junrui. He's from Luoyang."

"Oh, him!" Zheng Heng cried in astonishment. "He won the highest honor in the imperial examination. His name was top of the list of successful candidates. I saw him parading through the streets of the capital. He is about 24 or 25 years old. So that's how it is!"

"So he did succeed in becoming the No. 1 Scholar!" Madame Cui was overjoyed at this news. But just then a crafty thought entered Zheng Heng's head.

"Oh, but I am sorry to inform you, Madame," he said, with a mournful shake of his head, "that a misfortune has overtaken that man. As he was parading through the streets in triumph, the daughter of Minister Wei threw an embroidered ball at him — that's the way the daughters of that powerful family choose their husbands, you know. Anyway, the ball hit Zhang, and he was dragged into the minister's residence, despite his protests that he was already married. It caused a sensation in the capital, I can tell you. Now Zhang and Miss Wei are already married. Moreover, Minister Wei insisted that Oriole can only be Zhang's second wife." He heaved a hypocritical sigh.

Madame Cui flew into a rage. "I knew no good would come of Oriole's infatuation with that bungling bookworm!" she stormed. "Well, no daughter of mine — and of a late prime minister, may I add — is going to play second fiddle to some little minx in the capital, with all her airs and graces. So, since Zhang is already fixed up with a wife, you, my dear nephew may pick an auspicious day to marry Oriole, in accordance with your late uncle's behest."

Zheng Heng was overjoyed to hear this, but he maintained his composure. "But aunt," he asked, "what if Zhang comes to claim Oriole for himself, claiming that you have broken your promise? He's a powerful figure now, you know."

"You just leave high-and-mighty Zhang to me," Madame Cui replied, her jaw set grimly. "Well, what are you waiting for? Off you go and pick an auspicious day for the wedding ceremony!"

Thanking his aunt profusely, and scarcely able to conceal his glee at her gullibility, Zheng Heng left to do as she had bidden him.

Now let's turn to Zhang. He arrived at Mid-River Prefecture soon after Zheng Heng's interview with Madame Cui. He met the local dignitaries, including the abbot, at the Pavilion of Parting, and then headed

"就是洛阳张珙张君瑞。"

"噢,敢情是新科状元。侄儿在京师曾经看过金榜,有洛阳张珙大名,在夸官游街三日时,我还见到过他,年纪有二十四五岁。那是夸官的第二天,到了卫尚书家门口,正碰上卫家小姐抛球选婿。张生路过彩楼之下时,有一只彩球飞来,正打中了他。当时我骑马观看,那彩球还险些打中了我呢。卫家拥出十几个仆人,上前把张生拉下马来横拖倒拽抢了进去。那时听得张生口中叫道:'我已有妻室了,我是崔相国家的女婿。'那卫尚书说道:'我女是奉圣旨结彩楼,那崔小姐是先奸后娶,充其量做个次妻也就罢了。'这事当时轰动了京师。张生早就与卫家小姐成婚了,不知我表妹是大还是小呢?"

郑恒一句话引来了老夫人雷霆之怒,吼道:"我早就知道这秀才不是什么好东西,受不得抬举,今日果然负了我家。俺相国之家,世代没有把女儿给人做小之理。也罢,既然张生已奉圣旨娶了妻,孩儿,你就拣个黄道吉日,依着你姑夫的遗言,来和莺莺拜堂成亲。"

郑恒一听心花怒放,脸上却不动声色,嗫嚅道:"姑母,倘若张生前来理论,又当如何?"

老夫人道:"他敢,放着我呢。你只管依旧做你的女婿。"

郑恒心中暗想:姑母终归是妇人,果然中我的计了,口中道:"就依姑母,我这就准备去了。"

再说张生奉旨赴任衣锦还乡,这日到达河中府。与前来接风的大小官吏以及法本长老在长亭上一一见面,而后便匆匆赶往普救寺,见了老夫人,纳头便拜道:"新科状元河中府尹小婿张珙参拜岳母大人。"

老夫人冷笑一声道:"休拜,休拜,你是奉圣旨的女婿,老身怎

directly for the Salvation Monastery. There he fell to his knees before Madame Cui, and announced, "The new No. 1 Scholar and recently appointed prefect of Mid-River Prefecture Zhang Gong pays his respects to his mother-in-law."

The other's response stunned the young man. "No more of your impudent nonsense!" snapped Madame Cui. "How dare you? The whole world knows that you've broken your promise and that you're someone else's son-in-law."

Dumbfounded, Zhang thought, "I know that the Cuis have not let a man without official rank marry into the family for three generations. But now I have won the highest honor in the imperial examination, my name is on the roll of the National Academy and I have been appointed a prefect. Madame Cui cannot say that I am not worthy of her daughter's hand. And, besides, what on earth did she mean by 'breaking my promise' and being 'someone else's son-in-law?' "

He raised his head, and pleaded, "I beg that you will explain, Madame. I don't understand your words at all. You said that if I became the No. 1 Scholar I could return and marry Oriole. Well, here I am."

"I will not allow my daughter to be the second wife of anyone, even if he is the No. 1 Scholar. And I certainly will not have her at the beck and call of the stuck-up daughter of Minister Wei!"

At this, Zhang was even more mystified. "Who told you all this?" he cried in a fit of anxiety.

At this moment, Rose came in. As a matter of fact, she had been suspicious of Zheng Heng's story right from the start, but she decided to test Zhang before committing herself to his side.

"Well, well," she chirped, "if it isn't the new No. 1 Scholar! How is your new wife? Is she more beautiful than my Young Mistress?"

Zhang was indignant. "Miss Rose," he said reproachfully, "how can you make cruel jokes when you know perfectly well how much I have suffered for love of her? Somebody has been making mischief to try to tear us apart. When I find out who that person is, he — or she — will rue the day he or she was born! You mark my words."

These bold words convinced Rose that Zhang had not proved unfaithful, and, fearing that if she hesitated to reveal the truth Madame Cui might give Oriole to Zheng Heng and so bring about calamity for the two true lovers, she hastened to explain that it was Zheng Heng who had spread the lie about Zhang marrying Minister Wei's daughter. She then turned to Madame Cui.

212

生消受得起？"

　　奉圣旨的女婿？张生十分惊诧，如同当头挨了一闷棍，半晌说不出话来。再看老夫人身边丫环，脸上也全无一点儿喜气。心想原来说相国家三代不纳白衣女婿，小生如今中了头名状元，标名翰林，官居三品，也不辱没崔家，为何老夫人反而生怨，怕是情况有变，事出有因，便道："不知老夫人此话怎讲，小生去时，老夫人亲自送行，寄与厚望。如今中选得官，老夫人反而不悦，这是为何？"

　　老夫人道："你如今哪里想着俺家？道不得个'靡不有初，鲜克有终。'俺莺莺虽然妆残貌陋，她父亲也是前朝相国。若非孙飞虎狗贼来，足下凭什么能到得俺家？今日刚中了个状元，便负了俺孩儿，攀高结贵到卫尚书家做女婿，真是天理难容！"

　　张生急道："老夫人听谁说的？若有此事，天不盖，地不载。"

　　恰在这时红娘进来，正听到张生发誓，不待老夫人开口，便上前来说道："晴天白日的，谁人红口白牙发这毒誓？啊呀，这不是新科状元么？红娘这厢有礼了。你那新夫人比俺小姐如何？"

　　张生委屈万分道："红娘姐姐，怎么连你也不相信我了？小生为小姐受过的苦，别人不知道，莫非你也不知道？小生怎能忘了待月西厢，怎能撇下吹箫伴侣！"

　　其实红娘根本不相信郑恒的鬼话，认为张生不会喜新厌旧，她正为老夫人借郑恒一面之词赖婚犯愁，听到张生回来，真正欣喜若狂，心想这下好了，定能将这事弄个水落石出。此时见了张生，故意用话激他，做给老夫人看，又见他急成这样，便道："张生你也别着急上火，这事是表少爷郑恒说的。说你游街夸官时被卫尚书家小姐的绣球儿打中，做女婿去了，为此老夫人将小姐依旧嫁与郑恒了。"

"Madame," she said, pleading with tears in her eyes, "I believe Master Zhang is a sincere person who would never abandon Oriole. Please let her come and interrogate him. Then we will find out the real situation."

"Very well, bring her here, Rose," said Madame Cui, with a decisive nod.

Oriole's pallid, gaunt features and wasted body informed Zhang as clearly as any words that the girl had been devastated by the wicked lie spread by Zheng Heng. He felt his heart ache with pity, and tears ran down his cheeks.

"Young Mistress, ask Master Zhang to his face if there is any truth to the claim that he has married the daughter of Minister Wei," Rose urged.

"My cousin Zheng Heng reported this ghastly news to my mother," said Oriole. "I have no choice but to trust the word of such a near relative."

Zhang turned to Rose: "Tell me, Rose, have you been delivering letters between your young mistress and Zheng Heng?"

"How dare you, sir?" the indignant Rose cried. "Zheng Heng is a good-for-nothing. I serve no one but the prime minister's family, an honored official family for generations. I would have nothing to do with that sinister wretch!"

Zhang wilted under this barrage, and Rose, calming down somewhat, felt a pang of remorse. "I'll tell you what," she said. "Why don't we get Zheng Heng himself to come here, and confront him with Master Zhang himself?"

At this moment Abbot Fa Ben was announced. He too had heard the rumor that Zhang had married while he was in the capital, and was consumed by curiosity to know if the story was true or not. So, on the pretext of expressing his congratulations to Madame Cui on the happiness Zhang's success must have brought the family, he came bustling in. On this occasion his curiosity got the better of his accustomed diplomacy, and after a cursory greeting he asked if it were true that Zhang had really married Minister Wei's daughter. This caused a great deal of embarrassment all round, which was changed to astonishment when the abbot announced that the White Horse General had arrived and was waiting outside the monastery.

Madame Cui was not happy to hear this, as Zhang's friend was a powerful figure who could force her to give Oriole in marriage to Zhang even if it turned out that the latter had married Minister Wei's daughter after all.

214

红娘又对老夫人道:"老夫人,不如请小姐出来亲自问他。"

老夫人道:"也好,你去把小姐请来。"

红娘应声去了,不多时扶莺莺进来。张生见莺莺花容凄惨,知是为郑恒谎言所害,心痛难忍,不禁落下泪来。

红娘道:"锣不敲不响,话不说不明。小姐,有话干脆当面说破。"

莺莺叹道:"张生,俺家何负足下?足下为何弃置妾身,到卫尚书家为婿,天理何在? "

张生道:"莺莺,你也信他的话? 我张珙之心,惟天可表! 我自到了京城一心忙于应试,生怕考场失意,辜负了小姐对我的一片真情,红娘的辛劳,哪里有个佳人与我共语! 如今你们凭空硬塞给我一个卫尚书家的千金,我若是见了她的影子便灭门绝户。"

红娘见张生垂头丧气,又生怜悯之心,长叹一声道:"罢了,罢了,你若当真没做卫家的女婿,我到老夫人跟前一力保你,等郑恒那厮来了,你和他当面对证。"于是,红娘对老夫人说道:"张生并不曾做人家女婿,都是郑少爷说谎造谣。"

老夫人道:"既然他不承认,就等郑恒来对证后再说。"

这时法本长老已从长亭回来,来到崔家别院,想看看张生婚事如何了结。进了中堂与老夫人相见,双手合十道:"阿弥陀佛! 老夫人恭喜恭喜。不知张府尹他是否入赘卫家? "

老夫人道:"据张生说未有此事,或许是误传。"

长老哈哈笑道:"老夫人,今日才相信老僧的眼力吧,我早说张生决不是那没行止的秀才,他如何敢忘了小姐,况杜将军也是媒证,他怎能把此事当儿戏,怎能悔得这门亲事?"

莺莺忙插言道:"母亲,此事必得杜将军来方可。"

"Take your young mistress back to her room," she ordered Rose.

As soon as Rose and Oriole left, Fa Cong came bustling in. "The White Horse General Du Que is impatient to greet Master Zhang," he announced excitedly. Zhang could contain himself no longer, and dashed outside in the company of the young monk and the abbot.

The two old friends were overjoyed to see each other again. General Du explained that he had come as soon as he heard of Zhang's success in the examination, and was eager to be present at his wedding with Oriole. He frowned when he heard about the dastardly trick Zheng Heng had played on his dearest friend, and said, "Don't worry about that villain. I will deal with this matter, if you will be so kind as to procure an audience for me with Madame Cui."

Thereupon, Du Que, Zhang and the abbot went to see Madame Cui.

After exchanging conventional greetings with the dowager, Du Que said, "Madame, I have learned that a minor problem concerning Brother Junrui's marriage has occurred. I think it is most regrettable. Junrui is the son of the minister of rites, and now he has won the highest honor in the imperial examination. The marriage between Junrui and Oriole is ideal in terms of social and economic status. They are a perfect match. But now I hear that you want to break off the engagement, all because of some wild rumor. Do you not think this rash?"

Madame Cui looked embarrassed. "General Du, when my late husband was alive, he betrothed my daughter to my nephew, Zheng Heng. It was only because of our desperate situation when the bandits threatened to carry her off that I promised to betroth her to any man who would save her. I kept my promise. But when I heard that Zhang had married in the capital, I was forced to break off the engagement. You see, my late husband would never have consented to Oriole's being a junior wife, even to the daughter of a minister. It is utterly impossible. She must marry her original fiance."

At this moment, they heard strains of celebratory music outside, and Zheng Heng, dressed in his holiday best, walked in, beaming all over his face.

"Zheng Heng, you have come at the right time," said Madame Cui haughtily. "Let me introduce you to the White Horse General Du Que, who is in charge of Puguan Pass. Of course, I don't need to introduce this other man to you."

"He must be...," Zheng Heng spoke evasively, his eyes glittering

216

　　老夫人不愿此时小姐插嘴,脸上露出不悦之色,对红娘说道:"扶小姐回绣阁去吧。"莺莺与红娘刚走,法聪兴冲冲来报,说杜将军已到山门外。张生听了喜出望外,忙与长老起身出外相迎。原来杜将军知张生高中,官授河中府尹,到了普救寺,便急着前来相会。一则祝贺兄弟高中,得官归来;二则想为兄弟将亲事办了。

　　张生一见杜确,拱手道:"小弟托兄长虎威,一举得中,今日回来,本待成亲,不料老夫人侄儿郑恒凭空起事,诬小弟在京城被卫尚书家招为东床,老夫人大为恼怒,又要将小姐许与郑恒。请兄长为小弟做主。"杜确道:"兄弟不要着急,此事自有哥哥为你主持公道。"说罢三人相随来见老夫人。

　　寒暄过后,杜确道:"老夫人,听说我兄弟与令嫒之事又生枝节,此事要依着我说,似有不妥。我君瑞兄弟也是礼部尚书之子,如今又得状元。可谓门当户对,郎才女貌,天生一对,地配一双,老夫人忽然悔亲,定是听了小人细言,还请老夫人三思而后行。"

　　老夫人面呈难色道:"将军有所不知,当初老相国在世时,曾将小女许嫁郑恒。不想前番遇难,情急之中,许下诺言,能退贼者招为女婿。幸得张生请将军退贼解围,使我全家得以活命。事后,老身不负前言,欲招他为婿。只是在羁旅途中,又则考期临近,便安排张生赴京入闱。不料前几日侄儿郑恒来说,张生被卫尚书家招为东床,反令我女儿做次妻。想我堂堂相国人家,怎能与人做小,这才将小姐复许郑恒。这实在也是没办法的事,请将军不要误会才是。"

　　正在这时,门口传来一阵喜乐声,郑恒一身吉服,满脸喜气,步入中堂。老夫人满脸怒气地说道:"郑恒,你来得正好,我来给你引见一下,这位是镇守蒲关的白马将军杜确,这位就不用我介绍了吧?"

with sullen hatred.

"He is Zhang Gong, alias Zhang Junrui, the new No. 1 Scholar, and newly appointed prefect of Mid-River Prefecture. You said that he had married Minister Wei's daughter. Is this true?"

Zheng Heng was taken aback at Madame Cui's change of attitude towards him. He stammered out a few words of greeting.

"Why have you come, Zheng Heng?" asked Zhang.

"Er.... I learned that the No. 1 Scholar had done the Cui family the honor of paying a courtesy call, and so I came to express my congratulations to you," said Zheng Heng, groaning inwardly.

"You're a scoundrel! Why did you cook up that story, and try to steal the girl destined to be Zhang's wife?" said Du Que sternly. "If I report this sordid matter to the emperor, he will have you executed."

"Oh sir, the fact of the matter is that I and my cousin were engaged at the express behest of my late uncle. I am the one who has been wronged."

"If you continue to babble nonsense I'll have my men arrest you," the general barked. "Take him away!"

This scared Zheng Heng almost out of his wits. "That won't be necessary!" he shrieked. "I confess that I fabricated the story about Zhang and the daughter of Minister Wei. I am willing to break off my engagement to Oriole right now."

Madame Cui stepped into the fray. "I see it all now," she declared. "He is a shameless rascal. Drive him away from here, and let us put an end to this distressing episode."

"Very well, Madame," said General Du. "Get out, and think yourself lucky to escape with your life."

Shamefaced, Zheng Heng staggered out and along the road. Coming across a flourishing apricot tree, he raised his head to look at it, and sighed deeply. "I have lost face thoroughly today," he groaned. What's the use of living any longer?" So saying, he closed his eyes, and dashed his brains out against the tree.

A passing monk witnessed this last desperate act of the wretched Zheng Heng, and lost no time reporting it to Madame Cui, who together with the others rushed to the fatal spot. Madame Cui could not help weeping sadly, but after a while she thought to herself: "He was the author of his own undoing. By trying to force himself on Oriole and slandering Zhang he embarked on a road of no return."

218

郑恒眨了眨眼,支吾着道:"他是……" 老夫人一听,便知郑恒并不认识张生,心中什么都明白了,冷笑道:"他就是新科状元,新任河中府府尹,你所说的奉旨招亲的卫尚书家女婿张珙张君瑞。"

郑恒一听是张珙,心下便是一惊,硬着头皮说道:"幸会幸会。"

张生道:"郑恒,你今日来此做甚?"

郑恒心中叫苦不迭,口中匆忙应道:"嗯……闻知状元归来,给……给给新科状元贺喜来了。"

杜确在一旁说道:"你这无赖,为何要诓骗人家妻室,行不仁不义之事,现在还有什么话说?待本官奏闻朝廷,诛了你这个贼子!"

郑恒道:"大人,你不清楚这里的根由,我与表妹的亲事是姑夫在时亲口许下,如今倒说我是诓骗人妻,真真冤枉的是我。"

杜确道:"我不想听你花言巧语,若是再要纠缠不休,将你带回我的大营给你评判。来人哪!给我将郑相公请回大营。"

郑恒闻听此言,知道去了大营是绝没有好果子吃的,早吓破了胆,急忙道:"不必了,不必了,小人自愿退亲与张生。"

老夫人急忙阻拦:"将军息怒,将他赶出去就是了。"

杜将军道:"若不是看在老夫人面上,本帅绝不饶你。快快滚了出去!"

郑恒满面羞愧,心乱如麻,踉踉跄跄地出了梨花院,漫无目的地走到花园外,一眼看到枝繁叶茂的杏树,仰天长叹道:"罢罢!今日颜面丢尽,要这性命何用,不如碰死干净!"说罢,眼一闭,心一横,往树上撞去。正是:妻子空争不到头,风流自古恋风流。三寸气在千般用,一日无常万事休!

院内的丫环和尚们见了,都吓得惊叫起来,有个和尚急急忙

She then gave permission to Abbot Fa Ben to allow Fa Cong and Hui Ming to bury the body.

Returning to her quarters, Madame Cui began to feel remorse for the way she had tried to thwart the course of true love when she had schemed to put obstacles in the way of Zhang and her daughter. "Anyway, all's well that ends well," she reminded herself. "After all, there can be no better match for Oriole than the No. 1 Scholar, and a court-appointed official to boot!" Looking around, she said out loud: "Since we have General Du and Abbot Fa Ben to act as matchmakers, let us prepare a wedding feast and celebrate the marriage of Zhang and Oriole right now!"

Everybody cheered. Zhang bowed to Du Que and the abbot, "Without Brother Du and the abbot's help, this happiness would not have been possible today. If you had not laid bare Zheng Heng's lies, I would have been separated from my true love forever."

Rose ran to the Embroidery Pavilion to report the good news to Miss Oriole.

With tears of joy coursing down her cheeks, Oriole said, "Rose, I owe everything to you! It was you who steered me right through troubled times and have remained with me until this wonderful day, on which I shall be married."

That night, the Salvation Monastery was decorated with lanterns and colored streamers, and the air was filled with the deafening sounds of gongs and drums. All the officials of Mid-River Prefecture came to express their congratulations.

Supported by Rose, Oriole, wearing a phoenix coronet and red cape, emerged. She and Zhang made a bow to thank the emperor for his kindness. Then they bowed in turn to Heaven, Earth, Madame Cui, General Du, the abbot and all the other people at the ceremony. Everyone agreed that they were a perfectly matched pair.

Rose said to Zhang in a low voice: "Brother-in-law, don't you need to bow to someone else?"

Zhang was mystified at first, but soon understood what she meant. Pulling Oriole by the hand, he tried to get both of them to bow to Rose. But Rose said, "I was only joking. Now it's time for you to go to the bridal chamber."

The bridal chamber was lit by tall red candles. The new couple recalled their first tryst, waiting for the moon in the wind, the exchange of

忙来到中堂禀与众人。众人闻听,都是一惊,急忙涌出房门,到了树前,扶起郑恒,见其脑浆崩裂,无可挽回,也不好再说什么。老夫人见状顿生伤感,老泪纵横,然事已至此,悲也无用,便叹息一声说道:"这也是命,这孩子,真是想不开,天涯何处无芳草。也罢,人死不能复生,有众位大人在,谁也没有逼他。我是他的亲姑母,此事由我作主,将他埋葬了吧。"

法本长老于是令法聪、惠明等安葬郑恒。

回到中堂,老夫人回想先前五次三番与张生为难,此刻也觉得对不起他。再者说,女儿嫁与状元,成为朝廷命妇,平生愿望已足,不如趁众人都在,将喜事办了,既了了女儿一桩心事,也领了众人情份,一举两得,皆大欢喜,何乐不为呢?于是环顾众人言道:"喜得将军光临,长老前来贺喜,二位大媒难遇,今日便做个喜庆的茶饭,让他小俩口儿拜堂成亲。"

众人听了,喜笑颜开。张生再次拜谢杜确和长老道:"当日若非兄长、长老鼎力相助,何能结此良缘?今日若非戳穿郑恒的谎言,险些又教我夫妻分离。"

红娘忙回绣阁向小姐报喜。

莺莺喜泪盈盈道:"红娘,俺夫妻能有今日,都是你的功劳。"

红娘也拭泪道:"小姐快别这么说,红娘心愿天下有情人都成了眷属。"

入夜,普救寺张灯结彩,鼓乐喧天,笙歌聒地,喜气洋洋,河中府众官员齐来贺喜。

红娘搀扶身着凤冠霞帔的莺莺出来,与张生双双拜圣恩,拜天地,拜高堂,又拜杜将军、长老与众人,再夫妻对拜。众人皆称赞

verses, expressing love through letters, and parting at the Pavilion of Parting. They had had to overcome many difficulties before they were finally united in matrimonial bliss. An old saying goes: "A brief parting is as sweet as a honeymoon." Three days later, Zhang took leave of his mother-in-law, and went to the Mid-River Prefectural office to take up his duties.

The love story of Zhang and Oriole has been handed down from generation to generation, and the pair have become symbols of perfect fidelity and affection.

他二人郎才女貌,是天作之合。

这时红娘对张生说道:"状元姐夫可少了些什么……"

张生猛然醒悟,忙拉莺莺来拜红娘,红娘含笑止住他二人道:"罢了,罢了,快入洞房吧。"

洞房里红烛高烧,张生与莺莺回想着殿上奇遇,迎风待月,联诗听琴,书笺传情,长亭送别,历经多少曲折,才成就了今宵欢爱,倍感这婚姻来之不易。常言道:久别胜似新婚,更何况今夜是久别加新婚,绸缪欢好,自不必说。三朝后,张生带着莺莺红娘,辞别老夫人,到河中府上任去了。

从此,这对有情人,如一对美满的鸳鸯,永老无离别,万古长完聚。给后人留下这一段西厢佳话。

图书在版编目(CIP)数据

西厢记:英、汉对照/(元)王实甫著;张雪静改编;刘幼生审订.
—北京:新世界出版社,2000
ISBN 7 - 80005 - 552 - 3

I. 西 … II. ①王 … ②张 … ③刘 … III. 英语 – 对照读物,文学
– 英、汉 IV. H319. 4:I

中国版本图书馆 CIP 数据核字(1999)第 65245 号

西 厢 记

原　　著: 王实甫(元)

改　　编: 张雪静

审　　订: 刘幼生

翻　　译: 匡佩华、刘军等

责任编辑: 张民捷

版式设计: 李　辉

出版发行: 新世界出版社

社　　址: 北京阜城门外百万庄路 24 号　　　邮政编码: 100037

电　　话: 0086 – 10 – 68994118(出版发行部)

传　　真: 0086 – 10 – 68326679

经　　销: 新华书店、外文书店

印　　刷: 北京外文印刷厂

开　　本: 850×1168　1/32　　字数: 168 千字

印　　张: 7.5

版　　次: 2000 年 3 月(英、汉)第 1 版第 1 次印刷

书　　号: ISBN 7 – 80005 – 552 – 3/I · 026

定　　价: 20.00 元
